JOURNAL FOR THE STUDY OF THE OLD TESTAMENT SUPPLEMENT SERIES
173

JSOT Press
Sheffield

History and Interpretation

Essays in Honour of
John H. Hayes

edited by

**M. Patrick Graham, William P. Brown
and Jeffrey K. Kuan**

Journal for the Study of the Old Testament
Supplement Series 173

Copyright © 1993 Sheffield Academic Press

Published by JSOT Press
JSOT Press is an imprint of
Sheffield Academic Press Ltd
343 Fulwood Road
Sheffield S10 3BP
England

Typeset by Sheffield Academic Press
and
Printed on acid-free paper in Great Britain by
The Charlesworth Group, Huddersfield and
Bound by Biddles Ltd, Guildford

British Library Cataloguing in Publication Data

History and Interpretation: Essays in
  Honour of John H. Hayes. - (JSOT
  Supplement Series, ISSN 0309-0787; No. 173)
  I. Graham, M.P. II. Series
  221.6

ISBN 1-85075-466-7

CONTENTS

PENTATEUCH

WILLIAM P. BROWN

JULIE GALAMBUSH

FRANK H. GORMAN, JR

HISTORICAL BOOKS

RODNEY K. DUKE

M. PATRICK GRAHAM

D.G. SCHLEY

PROPHETS

HISTORY OF ISRAEL

PREFACE

It is with sincere pleasure and pride that the students of John Haralson Hayes offer these essays. Each of us has been touched by his unassuming, gentle, and congenial character, and we take great delight in this opportunity to express appreciation to our *Doktorvater*.

As a teacher at Emory University and Candler School of Theology, John Hayes has won a reputation for his pastoral concern for students and his availability to them. His concern extends beyond the academic lives of students to their church, family, and personal concerns, and consequently he is always offering to them the most precious gift of all—his time and interest. In addition, all who have taken his courses are familiar with his lively sense of humor and energetic manner of presentation, and those who have been privileged by his careful reading of their term papers or academic theses have been impressed with his attention to detail, extensive bibliographic knowledge, and sensitivity to the nuances of expression. He takes the work of his students seriously.

In the wider scholarly community, John Hayes has established his reputation—not as one with whom all agree, but as a creative scholar who is unafraid to challenge the consensus. As his career has progressed, so has his willingness to reconsider the 'accepted results' of scholarship (including his own!) and propose new theses. Though having proved his ability to work in some of the most esoteric areas of biblical studies, he is not one to be distracted by minutiae. He never loses sight of the whole and for what is most important. His interests and knowledge are nothing short of encyclopedic, as will be demonstrated by the forthcoming publication of Abingdon's *Dictionary of Biblical Interpretation*, the most recent product of his editorial skill. This work will underscore what has been clear for years to those familiar with his publications and work as editor of the *Journal of Biblical Literature* (1977–82): he is a courageous scholar who is not discouraged from undertaking monumental projects that make exorbitant demands on his energy and time.

Therefore, it is with extreme admiration and gratitude that this volume is offered.

M. Patrick Graham
William P. Brown
Jeffrey K. Kuan

ACKNOWLEDGMENTS

The editors would like to express appreciation for the support of their respective institutions in this enterprise: Pitts Theology Library (Candler School of Theology, Emory University), Union Theological Seminary in Virginia, and Pacific School of Religion. In addition, thanks are due to David W. Santi for the photograph of the honoree and to H.G. Pattillo for financial support. Finally, we are grateful to Philip R. Davies and the Sheffield Academic Press for their continuing efforts to make the results of Old Testament scholarship widely available and for their more immediate decision to include the present volume in the JSOT Supplement Series.

ABBREVIATIONS

AASOR	Annual of the American Schools of Oriental Research
AB	Anchor Bible
ABD	D.N. Freedman (ed.), *Anchor Bible Dictionary* (6 vols.; New York: Doubleday, 1992)
ABRL	Anchor Bible Reference Library
ABS	Archaeology and Biblical Studies
ADAJ	*Annual of the Department of Antiquities of Jordan*
AfO.B	Archiv für Orientforschung. Beiheft
AJSR	*Association for Jewish Studies Review*
ANEP	J.B. Pritchard (ed.), *Ancient Near East in Pictures Relating to the Old Testament* (Princeton: Princeton University Press, 3rd edn, 1969)
ANET	J.B. Pritchard (ed.), *Ancient Near Eastern Texts Relating to the Old Testament* (Princeton: Princeton University Press, 3rd edn, 1969)
AOAT	Alter Orient und Altes Testament
ARAB	D.D. Luckenbill, *Ancient Records of Assyria and Babylonia* (2 vols.; Chicago: University of Chicago Press, 1926–27)
ARM	Archives royales de Mari
ASOR	American Schools of Oriental Research
ATAbh	Alttestamentliche Abhandlungen
ATDan	Acta theologica danica
ATR	*Anglican Theological Review*
AusBR	*Australian Biblical Review*
AzKG	Arbeiten zur Kirchengeschichte
BA	*Biblical Archaeologist*
BASOR	*Bulletin of the American Schools of Oriental Research*
BBET	Beiträge zur biblische Exegese und Theologie
BDB	F. Brown, S.R. Driver, and C.A. Briggs, *A Hebrew and English Lexicon of the Old Testament* (Oxford: Clarendon Press, 1907 [reprint 1974])
BEATJ	Beiträge zur Erforschung des Alten Testaments und des antiken Judentums
BES	Biblical Encounter Series
BethM	*Beth Mikra*
BETL	Bibliotheca ephemeridum theologicarum lovaniensium

BEvT	Beiträge zur evangelischen Theologie
BHS	K. Elliger and W. Rudolph (eds.), *Biblia hebraica stuttgartensia* (Stuttgart: Deutsche Bibelgesellschaft, 1983)
Bib	*Biblica*
BJS	Brown Judaic Studies
BKAT	Biblischer Kommentar, Altes Testament
BN	*Biblische Notizen*
BPN	Ba'al place names
BT	*Bible Translator*
BZ	*Biblische Zeitschrift*
BZAW	Beihefte zur *Zeitschrift für die alttestamentliche Wissenschaft*
CAD	I. Gelb *et al.* (eds.), *Assyrian Dictionary of the Oriental Institute of the University of Chicago* (Chicago: Oriental Institute, 1956–)
CBC	Cambridge Bible Commentary
CBQ	*Catholic Biblical Quarterly*
CBSC	Cambridge Bible for Schools and Colleges
ConBOT	Coniectanea biblica, Old Testament
EA	J.A. Knudtzon, O. Weber, and E. Ebeling (eds.), *Die el-Amarna Tafeln mit Einleitung und Erlauterungen* (Vorderasiatische Bibliothek, 2; 2 vols.; Leipzig: Hinrichs, 1915)
EncRel	M. Eliade (ed.), *Encyclopedia of Religion* (16 vols.; New York: Macmillan, 1987)
ErIsr	*Eretz Israel*
FOTL	Forms of Old Testament Literature
FRLANT	Forschungen zur Religion und Literatur des Alten und Neuen Testaments
FThSt	Freiburger theologische Studien
HAR	*Hebrew Annual Review*
HBT	*Horizons in Biblical Theology*
HDR	Harvard Dissertations in Religion
HSM	Harvard Semitic Monographs
HSS	Harvard Semitic Studies
ICC	International Critical Commentary
IDB	G.A. Buttrick (ed.), *Interpreter's Dictionary of the Bible* (4 vols.; Nashville: Abingdon, 1962)
IDBSup	K. Crim (ed.), *Supplementary volume to IDB* (Nashville: Abingdon, 1976)
IEJ	*Israel Exploration Journal*
Int	*Interpretation*
JAAR	*Journal of the American Academy of Religion*
JANESCU	*Journal of the Ancient Near Eastern Society of Columbia University*
JAOS	*Journal of the American Oriental Society*

JARCE	*Journal of the American Research Center in Egypt*
JB	A. Jones (ed.), *Jerusalem Bible* (Garden City: Doubleday, 1966)
JBL	*Journal of Biblical Literature*
JCS	*Journal of Cuneiform Studies*
JJS	*Journal for Jewish Studies*
JNES	*Journal of Near Eastern Studies*
JPSV	Jewish Publication Society Version (*Tanakh, A New Translation of the Holy Scriptures*)
JR	*Journal of Religion*
JSNTSup	Journal for the Study of the New Testament Supplement Series
JSOT	*Journal for the Study of the Old Testament*
JSOTSup	Journal for the Study of the Old Testament Supplement Series
JSPSup	Journal for the Study of the Pseudepigrapha Supplement Series
JSS	*Journal of Semitic Studies*
JSSEA	*Journal of the Society for the Study of Egyptian Antiquities*
KAI	H. Donner and W. Röllig (eds.), *Kanaanäische und aramäische Inschriften* (3 vols.; Wiesbaden: Otto Harrassowitz, 1962)
KAT	Kommentar zum Alten Testament
KB	L. Koehler and W. Baumgartner, *Lexicon in Veteris Testamenti libros* (Leiden: Brill, 1958)
KEHAT	Kurzgefasstes exegetisches Handbuch zum Alten Testament
KHCAT	Kurzer Hand-Commentar zum Alten Testament
KJV	King James Version
KRI	K. Kitchen, *Ramesside Inscriptions, Historical and Biographical* (7 vols.; Oxford: Blackwell, 1968–)
KS	A. Alt, *Kleine Schriften zur Geschichte des Volkes Israel* (3 vols.; München: Beck, 1953–59)
LAPO	Littératures anciennes du Proche-Orient
LCL	Loeb Classical Library
LTQ	*Lexington Theological Quarterly*
MBA	Middle Bronze Age
NCB	New Century Bible
NEB	New English Bible
NICOT	New International Commentary on the Old Testament
NIV	New International Version
OBO	Orbis biblicus et orientalis
ÖBS	Österreichische biblische Studien
OBT	Overtures to Biblical Theology
OIP	Oriental Institute Publications
OTL	Old Testament Library
OTS	*Oudtestamentische Studiën*
PÄ	Probleme der Ägyptologie
PEQ	*Palestine Exploration Quarterly*
PJ	*Palästina-Jahrbuch*

RAS	Rassegna degli archivi di stato
RE	A. Hauck (ed.), *Realencyklopädie für protestantische Theologie und Kirche* (3rd edn; Leipzig: Hinrichs, 1897–1913)
RSV	Revised Standard Version
SAM	Sheffield Archaeological Monographs
SB	Sources bibliques
SBLDS	Society for Biblical Literature Dissertation Series
SBLSP	*Society for Biblical Literature Seminar Papers*
SBT	Studies in Biblical Theology
ScrHier	*Scripta hierosolymitana*
SJLA	Studies in Judaism in Late Antiquity
SJOT	*Scandinavian Journal of the Old Testament*
StP	Studia Pohl
TA	*Tel Aviv*
TD	*Theology Digest*
TDOT	G.J. Botterweck and H. Ringgren (eds.), *Theological Dictionary of the Old Testament* (Grand Rapids: Eerdmans, rev. edn, 1977–)
TEV	Today's English Version
TTod	*Theology Today*
ThWAT	G.J. Botterweck, H. Ringgren, and H.J. Fabry (eds.), *Theologisches Wörterbuch zum Alten Testament* (Stuttgart: Kohlhammer, 1970–)
VT	*Vetus Testamentum*
VTSup	Vetus Testamentum, Supplements
UF	*Ugarit-Forschungen*
WBC	Word Biblical Commentary
WMANT	Wissenschaftliche Monographien zum Alten und Neuen Testament
WO	*Die Welt des Orients*
WTJ	*Westminster Theological Journal*
ZA	*Zeitschrift für Assyriologie*
ZAW	*Zeitschrift für die alttestamentliche Wissenschaft*
ZDPV	*Zeitschrift des deutschen Palästina-Vereins*

LIST OF CONTRIBUTORS

Ehud Ben Zvi
University of Alberta

George R. Boudreau, O.P.
Providence College

William P. Brown
Union Theological Seminary in Virginia

Phillip R. Callaway
Chapel Hill Jr High School, Lithonia, Georgia

J. Andrew Dearman
Austin Presbyterian Theological Seminary

Rodney K. Duke
Appalachian State University

Julie Galambush
St Olaf College

Yehoshua Gitay
University of Cape Town

Frank H. Gorman, Jr
Bethany College

M. Patrick Graham
Pitts Theology Library, Emory University

Paul K. Hooker
Emory University

Kenneth D. Hutchens
Emory University

Stewart A. Irvine
Louisiana State University

Brian C. Jones
Emory University

Jeffrey K. Kuan
Pacific School of Religion

Janet L.R. Melnyk
Emory University

D.G. Schley
The University of Colorado, Colorado Springs

DIVINE ACT AND THE ART OF PERSUASION IN GENESIS 1

William P. Brown

Introduction

At least since Philo of Alexandria (20 BCE–50 CE) early Jewish and Christian interpreters of Genesis 1 have noted, if not exploited, certain similarities between Plato's *Timaeus* and the Priestly account of creation.[1] The *Timaeus* was frequently employed in early Jewish and Christian biblical interpretation as a hermeneutical entry point through which the meaning behind the Priestly account of creation could best be grasped. In contrast, however, one finds among *modern* commentaries on Genesis little reference to the *Timaeus* or even to Platonic doctrine in general, and understandably so.[2] Despite the fact that the Priestly author of Genesis 1 and Plato were products of two

---

1. See, e.g., *Opficio Mundi* 10 and 29-34. For Philo's as well as early Christian dependence on the *Timaeus*, see F.E. Robbins, *The Hexaemeral Literature: A Study of the Greek and Latin Commentaries on Genesis* (Chicago: University of Chicago Press, 1912), pp. 1-13. The notion, for example, of an ideal pattern, as espoused by Plato and modified by Philo, runs throughout much of the Christian hexaemeral literature from Theophilus of Antioch to Augustine up to the Middle Ages. Rabbinical use of Philo's work includes R. Osha'aya's allusion to *Timaeus* 29 ('The artificer looked for a pattern to that which is eternal') in *Gen. R.* 1.1 ('God looked to the Torah and created the world') and Wis. 11.18, which echoes *Timaeus* 50d. See A. Altmann, 'A Note on the Rabbinic Doctrine of Creation', *JJS* 7 (1956), pp. 195-96. In addition, the 'philosopher' who converses with R. Gamaliel in *Gen. R.* 1.9 is evidently steeped in Platonic doctrine.

2. In his massive commentary, C. Westermann cites Plato only twice in connection with Gen. 1.1–2.4a: the possible 'Platonic tendency' or 'rationalizing tendency' behind the Septuagint's translation of *tōhû wābōhû* and Plato's description of the primeval human being's developing taste for meat (*Genesis 1–11: A Commentary* [Continental Commentaries; Minneapolis: Augsburg, 1984], p. 104). Robbins suggests a direct connection between Gen. 1.20 and *The Sophist* 220b (*The Hexaemeral Literature*, p. 32 n. 3).

distinct cultures and separated by at least a century, I hope to demonstrate that the *Timaeus*[3] still provides a helpful point of departure for
discerning in Genesis 1 the complex coherence between divine word
and creative act and, more broadly, the very relationship between God
and creation.

The Timaeus and Creation

In Plato's work, Timaeus of Locri, a distinguished mathematician and
astronomer, attempts to describe systematically the work of God in
fashioning the cosmos. Timaeus likens God to an artisan (*demiourgos*)
who utilizes primordial matter to shape and order the universe into a
harmonious whole in accordance with an incorporeal, eternal model
(*Timaeus* 28a; 29a). Plato describes the initial phase in the following
manner:

> When [God] took over all that was visible, seeing that it was not in a state
> of rest but in a state of discordant and disorderly motion, he brought it
> into order out of disorder (*ataxis*), deeming that the former state is in all
> ways better than the latter (30a).[4]

3. The philosophical status of the *Timaeus* is still a matter of intense debate. The
discussion is about whether the creation portrayed in the *Timaeus* is to be considered
fictional (or mythological), given the logical tensions within the work, or literal, viz.,
philosophical. See, for example, the debate between G. Vlastos, 'Creation in the
Timaeus: Is it a Fiction?', in R.E. Allen (ed.), *Studies in Plato's Metaphysics*
(London: Routledge and Kegan Paul, 1965), pp. 401-19; and L. Taran, 'The
Creation Myth in Plato's *Timaeus*', in J.P. Anton and G.L. Kustas (eds.), *Essays in
Ancient Greek Philosophy* (Albany: State University of New York, 1971), pp. 372-
407. See also R.D. Mohr, 'Plato's Theology Reconsidered: What the Demiurge
Does', in J.P. Anton and A.A. Preuss (eds.), *Essays in Ancient Greek Philosophy:
Plato* (New York: State University of New York, 1989), pp. 293-95. Undeniably, a
generally rational tenor pervades the *Timaeus*, given the systematic, though not
entirely logical, manner in which cosmogony is depicted. Timaeus himself admits
that all inquiries into cosmogony will by nature be inconsistent and inexact, to which
Socrates enthusiastically agrees (*Timaeus* 29c-d). In short, Timaeus' account of
creation is more a treatise than a mythological narrative.
4. This and the following translations are based on that of R.G. Bury, *Plato
with an English Translation. VII. Timaeus, Critias, Cleitophon, Menexenus, Epistles*
(LCL, Greek Authors; Cambridge, MA: Harvard University; London: William
Heinemann, 1929), p. 55.

More specifically, the Demiurge acts as follows:

> All these things were in a state of disorder when God implanted in them
> symmetry both in relation to themselves and in their relations to one
> another, to the extent that it was possible for them to be in harmony and in
> proportion (69c).

In short, the Demiurge implants symmetry, harmony, and order
(69b-c), viz., God 'geometrizes'.[5] Such cosmic qualities find their
intersection in the aesthetic notion of *kalon* or *agathos*, that is, the
good, beautiful, or desirable (e.g., 29a; 30a).[6] The universe is invested
with the fullest possible measure of goodness and rationality in accordance with the Forms, which provide the ideal model (*paradeigma*) of
the universe.

How God brings about creation is found in the curious section of
Timaeus 48a:

> While controlling necessity (*anankē*), intelligence persuaded it (*tō peithein
> autēn*)..., and in this way this universe was constructed from the
> beginning, through necessity yielding by means of intelligent persuasion
> (*hypo peithous emphronos* [48a]).[7]

The key concepts in the passage are 'necessity' (*anankē*) and
'persuasion' (*peithō*). Necessity or the 'wandering cause' (*h ē
planōmene aitia*, 48a) characterizes the pre-creative state, described
earlier as disorder (30a). Elsewhere, Plato regards God and necessity
as two types of causes. Necessity, on the one hand, designates causes
that 'without intelligence always produce accidental and chance
effects' (46e). The 'works of necessity' or 'auxiliary causes' (*synaitia*)
constitute the materials from which God fashions the universe. On the
other hand, the primary causes or the works of the Demiurge promote
the good and the beautiful (46e). As Morrow points out, the raw
materials and powers out of which God fashions the universe must
exhibit dependable structures and behavior if they are to be usable for
the creator's ends.[8] Far from being a chaos of hostile powers, without
divine intervention this realm of materials was, nevertheless,

---

5. *Plato with an English Introduction*, p. 13.
6. Similar to the use of the Hebrew *ṭôb* in the approbation formula in Gen. 1.
7. See also *Timaeus* 56c and 75b.
8. G.R. Morrow, 'Necessity and Persuasion in Plato's *Timaeus*', in Allen
(ed.), *Studies in Plato's Metaphysics*, p. 428.

disorderly, a world of continuous instability, capable of producing nothing more than chance effects (*tychē*).

Creation and Persuasion

'Persuasion' is what characterizes the work of the Demiurge on necessity. Given the root metaphor of God as artisan, this metaphor seems in context mixed and thus inappropriate. Plato, however, borrows the metaphor from rhetoric in order to contrast the cosmogony of Timaeus with the sort of creation that is effected by compulsion or force.[9] In the *Phaedrus* 260a and 271d-272b, Plato stresses the importance of discriminating knowledge for the orator who seeks to persuade. Such knowledge includes a cognitive grasp of the good and of the souls of his or her audience in order that the orator can appeal effectively. Rhetoric, in short, is the art of leading souls towards the good. Analogously, the skilled artisan must know his or her materials in order to select the ones best suited for creative ends. Thus, persuasion, in its broadest sense, denotes the effective, yet non-compulsive, technique of intelligence to bring about methodically the desired end, viz., the good. In the *Timaeus*, Plato describes the process of creation as a result of God's working with the powers inherent in the primordial materials. Nowhere within the series of creative events does divine intelligence subvert the natural sequence or replace the natural powers. Stress is laid rather on the order and intelligible structure of the cosmos that results from a methodical unfolding of sequential acts rather than in the divine origin of the cosmos.[10] The result is an approximation of the best or highest good (*aristos*, 68e).

Plato acknowledges that there are conflicts within the system of nature, but nowhere are there conflicts between nature and God or Intelligence. Persuasion is the art of eliciting the creative powers inherent in the materials involved rather than the forceful imposition of order from without. Consequently, persuasion is a surer, albeit

9. Morrow, 'Necessity and Persuasion', p. 429.
10. D. Furley, 'The Cosmological Crisis in Classical Antiquity', in J.J. Cleary (ed.), *Proceedings of the Boston Area Colloquium in Ancient Philosophy* (Lanham: University Press of America, 1987), II, p. 7.

much slower, process than the way of compulsion.[11] In his analysis of persuasion and necessity in the *Timaeus*, Morrow suggests:

> Persuasion is a process of eliciting cooperation among powers and forces that were previously indifferent, if not hostile, to one another. The creator makes them 'friends' (32c, 88e) and thus produces, not merely a more stable foundation for higher ends, but also an intrinsic good, the kind of good that is essential to any community.[12]

For Plato, the resulting goodness or beauty of creation is no doubt inextricably tied to the peaceful method by which creation comes about. The product reflects the process.

The Rhetoric of Creation in Genesis 1

It is not suggested that the Platonic theory of creation is directly transferable to the kind of cosmogony described by the Priestly author of Genesis 1. Indeed, there are marked differences both in form and content that keep these two accounts far apart theologically. God (*'ĕlōhîm*) is more than simply an artisan who works with ready materials, even if one takes Gen. 1.1 as a dependent clause, which indeed seems best.[13] God is far more a creator than the Demiurge, given the simple observation that anything resembling the Platonic Forms is entirely absent in the Priestly creation account, despite the philosophical reflections of Philo on Genesis as well as the rabbinic dialogues preserved in early midrash.[14] Plato's Demiurge is more a copier than a creator.

Furthermore, it is nowhere clear in Genesis 1 that God was limited to a base of 'raw materials' out of which the universe was fashioned, despite the anonymous philosopher's claim in his argument with Rabban Gamaliel in *Gen. R.* 1.9. In Genesis, the preexistence of the earth, the waters, wind, and darkness in no way limits God to creating

11. Morrow, 'Necessity and Persuasion', p. 436.
12. Morrow, 'Necessity and Persuasion', p. 436.
13. The literature regarding the debate over whether the first verse of Genesis is to be considered grammatically independent or dependent is immense. However, the latter position has strong precedent in the HB, as well as in ancient Near Eastern literature in general. See W.P. Brown, *Structure, Role, and Ideology in the Hebrew and Greek Texts of Genesis 1:1–2:3* (SBLDS, 132; Atlanta: Scholars Press, 1993), pp. 62-72.
14. See n. 1.

things only out of such preexistent material. Light, for example, is neither a primordial element nor a derivative of anything primordial. It is simply created *ex voce* and then contrasted with darkness. Similarly, the *rāqîa'* ('firmament') of Gen. 1.6 is not created out of any preexisting element. In short, God's creative power is far more prodigious than that of the Platonic diety, in light of the uniquely creative role that the divine word plays in the Priestly account. Yet it is precisely in the repeated use of the *Wortbericht* that Plato's concept of persuasion finds striking resonance in Genesis 1.

Whereas Plato employed this rhetorical term for the purposes of *analogy* in describing the non-compulsive actions of the Demiurge, the Priestly account of the divine word provides concrete instances of God's creative rhetoric in Genesis 1. Three commands in particular stand out in rhetorical artistry: vv. 11, 15, and 20. Linguistically, the commands are expressed utilizing the *figura etymologica* constructions that link the verbal command with the object or subject, specifically by correlating the jussive verb with its object.

v. 11   *wayyō'mer 'ĕlōhîm tadšē' hā'āreṣ deše'* . . .

v. 15   *wĕhāyû li-m'ôrōt birqîa' haššāmayim lĕhā'îr* . . .

v. 20   *wayyō'mer 'ĕlōhîm yišrĕṣû hammayim šereṣ* . . .

Such constructions in which the predicate is related etymologically to its object or subject constitute the language of production in P's account: the earth 'produces' (*tadšē'*) vegetation (*deše'*) in 1.11; the waters 'produce' (*yišrĕṣû*) sea creatures (*šereṣ*) in 1.20;[15] and celestial bodies (*mĕ'ôrōt*) 'produce' light (*lĕhā'îr*) in 1.15. In each case, the means of production is verbally related to the product.

In addition, it is not fortuitous that the language of verbal correspondence is reserved *only* for the divine commands. On the aesthetic level, the fact that such verbal correspondence does not occur in the parallel fulfillment reports (*Tatberichte*) heightens the rhetorical artistry of the divine speech. On the rhetorical level, the commands

15. Many modern English translations understand the verb *šrṣ* in Gen. 1.20-21 to have the meaning 'to teem or swarm with', viz., with an intransitive meaning. However, in comparison with such parallel texts as Exod. 7.28 and Ps. 105.30, in which the verb clearly has an object in the qal as in Gen. 1.20-21, coupled with the evidence from textual versions, which uniformly translate the verb causatively, the overall evidence suggests a transitive, causative rendering of the verb in Gen. 1.20 (see Brown, *Structure, Role, and Ideology*, pp. 105-106 n. 25).

exhibit a verbal precision by which the earth and the waters are enlisted to exercise the means appropriate for producing their respective products.

This rhetorical feature, typical of the divine commands, has been noted in varying degrees by commentators but without serious consideration. Westermann, for example, sees the etymological correspondence solely as a result of stylistic considerations on the part of P:

> This etymological formation (as also in v. 20) serves the steady *monotonous* style that characterizes this chapter [italics added].[16]

However, there seem to be more than just stylistic concerns at stake. Schmidt notes with respect to v. 11 that

> God's word...now abdicates its creative power, i.e., the word now allows what has just been created to be the origin of something new.[17]

Indeed, such is the case at every instance in which this etymological feature is present.

That this rhetorical feature is typical of divine speech is underlined by the variations in terminology in the *Tatberichte*. Note, for example, that the fulfillment in v. 12 of the command in v. 11 begins with *tôṣē' hā'āreṣ deše'*, in contrast to the command *tadšē' hā'āreṣ deše'*. The choice of the more generic verb *yṣ'* over and against *dš'* is revealing. There is a certain rhetorical distinction in God's command to the earth that is lacking in the report of the earth's fulfillment of the divine injunction. Indeed, the hiphil form of *dš'* employed in the divine command is a *terminus technicus* in the Priestly account, attested only here in the HB.[18]

Similarly, in v. 20 the object and the verb are etymologically related in the command to the waters (*yišrĕṣû* and *šereṣ*), whereas the fulfillment report in v. 21 is quite different:

> v. 20: *yišrĕṣû hammayim šereṣ nepeš ḥayyâ wĕ'ôp yĕ'ôpēp*. . .
> Let the waters bring forth swarms of living creatures
> and let winged creatures fly. . .
> v. 21: *wayyibrā' 'ĕlōhîm 'et-hattannînim haggĕdōlîm wĕ'ēt kol-nepeš haḥayyâ hārōmešet 'ăšer šārĕṣû hammayim*. . . *wĕ'ēt kol-'ôp*
> So God created the great sea monsters and every living

16. Westermann, *Genesis 1–11*, p. 124.

17. W.H. Schmidt, *Die Schöpfungsgeschichte der Priesterschrift* (WMANT, 17; Neukirchen–Vluyn: Neukirchener Verlag, 1964), p. 106.

18. The qal is attested only in Joel 2.22.

> creature that moves, which the waters brought forth. . .
> and every winged creature.

Along with the change in the creating subject (from *hammayim* to
'ĕlōhîm), the verbal mode of production is altered (*šrṣ* is replaced by
br' in 21a), although the original verb is retained in the relative clause
in 21b, but without its etymologically related object, *šereṣ*. The
phrase, *šereṣ nepeš ḥayyâ* ('swarms of living creatures'), is replaced
by the two classes of sea creatures: *hattannînim* and *kol-nepeš haḥayyâ*
hārōmeśet. The object of creation in the fulfillment report essentially
represents an additional class of sea creatures, the *tannînim*, but
neither class is described as *šereṣ*, as in the command. The terminological shift from command to fulfillment is intentional: a move is
made from the verbal elegance and simplicity of the command, which
highlights the waters' productive capacity, to the concrete, 'hands-on'
mechanics of the creative act, in which God's action comes to the
foreground, while the waters recede into the background without
altogether losing their productive capacity.

Text-critically, there is reason to believe that the command in v. 20
originally assigned to the waters the task of producing not only the
swarming sea creatures but also the winged creatures, reading *wĕ'ôp*
yĕ'ôpĕpû (cf. the LXX).[19] Thus, we have possibly another instance in
which a command is directed to a particular cosmic element, namely
the waters, in *figura etymologica* style.

In sum, the verbal puns in the commands of vv. 11 and 20 set in
relief the rhetorical quality of divine speech in contrast to the respective fulfillment reports. Consequently, the role of God as *creative*

---

19. The Greek (LXX) reads:

> *kai eipen ho theos, exagagetō ta hudata herpeta psuchōn zōsōn, kai peteina petomena*
> *epi tēs gēs . . .*
> And God said, 'Let the waters bring forth sea creatures of living souls and winged
> creatures that fly upon the earth. . . '

If, indeed, the Greek translation is based on a Hebrew *Vorlage* that is at variance
with the MT, the Hebrew would most probably read:

> *wayyō'mer 'ĕlōhîm yišrĕṣû hammayim šereṣ nepeš ḥayyâ wĕ'ôp yĕ'ôpĕpû 'al*
> *hā'āreṣ . . .*

The MT text evidently suffered the loss of only one consonant, namely the *waw* at
the end of the verb *'wp*. See Brown, *Structure, Role, and Ideology*, pp. 139-40
n. 29.

speaker is highlighted not simply by the overall structural repetition of divine speech throughout the account, but also by the verbal identification between the product and its mode of production in the commands. This verbal correspondence underlines God as creative speaker in both senses of the term: God utters speech that exhibits creative force and is itself rhetorically artistic.

In addition, the verbal similarity highlights the nature of the indirect addressees in the command. In the commands of vv. 11 and 20 the verbal correspondence between the mode of production and product specifies precisely the creative powers or means inherent in the earth and the waters. The means of production and the product are inextricably united by the etymological construction of the verb with its object. This verbal coherence thus stresses the active nature of the earth and the waters in the creation process, the two most active 'agents' in creation other than God.[20] When employed within an indirect command, this divine eloquence becomes imbued with rhetorical nuance aimed at enlisting the earth and the waters, the two ancillary actors in the creation account, to exercise their respective powers of production, namely, in producing such things as vegetation, swarming sea creatures, and in the case of the Hebrew *Vorlage* of the LXX, the flying winged creatures.[21] The rhetorical force of the divine commands, in effect, highlights the active roles of the earth and the waters and incorporates them into the cosmogonic process.

It may be overstating the case to claim that this rhetorical dimension of the divine command in Genesis points to a clear 'persuasive' intent in the divine commands. However, like Plato, the concept of persuasion is a helpful heuristic analogy for describing God's relationship to the created *and creating* order, perhaps even more applicable to the Priestly account of creation than Platonic cosmogony, since Timaeus reports only one instance of divine speech.[22] The Demiurge's behavior is described consistently on the level of artistic act, in which the notion of persuasion constitutes a root, albeit mixed, metaphor. The analogy of persuasion highlights the cooperative, interdependent relationship between the elements and God in a manner that excludes

20. In addition to Gen. 1.11, 20, 21, the earth is commanded in v. 24 to 'bring forth living creatures'.

21. See n. 19.

22. The only exception is in 41a-d, in which the Demiurge addresses the gods concerning his plan to have them create mortals.

any implication of coercive force or compulsion in the process of creation. As mentioned above, the metaphor of persuasion also sets in relief the active, independent nature of the elements (earth and water), similar to the notion of *hylozoism* among the pre-Socratic philosophers, namely, the assumption that the basic cosmological elements are capable of movement and, therefore, exhibit qualities of life.[23] In biblical literature, one need only look to Pss. 19.1-6 and 114, Isaiah 35 and much of Isaiah 40–55 to find nature described as exhibiting living qualities. Even more suggestive, however, is the very nature of divine act in relation to creation itself. God is not set *over and against* creation but rather *with* creation, exhorting certain elements to yield their appropriate products (vegetation, sea creatures, etc.). Such a creative process does not thereby imply a God who simply imposes order on unruly matter or creates everything *ex nihilo*. Rather, the commands to the earth and the waters are invitations to enter into the grand creative sweep of God's designs. Such a perspective is entirely at odds with Y. Kaufmann's view that although God 'fashions some of his creatures out of matter already at hand, this matter is not alive, charged with divine forces; it neither opposes nor participates in creation'.[24] To the contrary, the earth and the waters are far from being inert matter; their role in creation is one of positive participation.

The Good

The positive participation or cooperation of the elements, as well as the absence of compulsion throughout in the Priestly account, nuances the repeated approbation formula in a particular way. The granting of divine approbation upon the *successive* stages of creation reflects approval of both the end-product and the process by which it was achieved. From a structural standpoint, the very fact that creation is perceived as good at successive stages of the process (Gen. 1.4, 10, 12, 18, 21, 25, 31), and not simply at its completion (Gen. 1.30), suggests

23. See the discussions in W.K.C. Guthrie, *A History of Greek Philosophy* (Cambridge: Cambridge University Press, 1962), I, pp. 62-63; and Furley, 'The Cosmological Crisis', p. 15. Also of note is Plato's insistence that the cosmos was created as a 'living creature' (*Timaeus* 32b).

24. Y. Kaufmann, *The Religion of Israel: From its Beginnings to the Babylonian Exile* (New York: Schocken Books, 1972), p. 68.

an overriding concern regarding the *manner* by which creation was achieved. Indeed, the verb *ṭwb* frequently refers to a quality of action or conduct (1 Sam. 16.17; Ps. 33.3; Isa. 23.16; Jer. 1.2). Moreover, the consistent pairing of the word with the verb *rā'â* ('to perceive') in Genesis 1 suggests that more than just the utilitarian value of the finished product is meant by *ṭôb*.[25] Clearly, an aesthetic dimension is to be included in the notion of the good as employed in divine speech. Like the *Timaeus*, the goal of the good cannot be separated from the means.[26]

Creation and Tabernacle

The concern for process in creation is well illustrated in another Priestly text, namely, Exodus 35–40, which bears certain structural similarities to Genesis 1.[27] As Levenson has pointed out, the sanctuary in its completed form is itself a micro-*cosmos*.[28] In addition to the material correlation between temple and cosmos, however, there is also striking coherence with regard to their respective manners of construction as described in these Priestly texts. Kearney has noted correlations between the Priestly instructions given to Moses concerning the construction of the sanctuary in Exodus 25–31, which occurs in seven speeches, and each day of creation in Gen. 1.1–2.3.[29]

In addition, the roles that the active characters assume in these texts correlate in terms of function and contribution to the process of construction. In Exodus 35–40, for example, Bezalel and Moses, as artisan and speech-giver respectively, comprise a composite role similar to that of *'ĕlōhîm* in Genesis 1. Bezalel is filled with the *rûaḥ 'ĕlōhîm* and leads the construction of the tabernacle, which involves the enlistment and cooperative participation of all Israelites who are of a 'willing heart' (*nĕdîb libbô*, Exod. 35.5). Indeed, the theme of

25. Contra I. Höver-Johag, '*ṭôb, ṭûb, yṭb*', *TDOT*, V (1986), p. 304.
26. See above.
27. See J. Blenkinsopp, 'The Structure of P', *CBQ* 38 (1976), pp. 276-78; Brown, *Structure, Role, and Ideology*, pp. 209-14.
28. J.D. Levenson, *Creation and the Persistence of Evil: The Jewish Drama of Divine Omnipotence* (San Francisco: Harper & Row, 1988), p. 86.
29. P.J. Kearney, 'Creation and Liturgy: The P Redaction of Ex 25–30', *ZAW* 89 (1977), p. 375. The fact that some of Kearney's alleged parallels are a bit forced does not entirely undermine his argument.

'cooperation' in Exodus 35–36 takes on an idealistic dimension when Moses feels compelled to limit the abundance of freewill offerings given by the over-eager Israelites for the construction of the tabernacle (Exod. 36.2-7)! In addition, the process of construction is spelled out with painstaking precision (Exod. 36.8–39.42) and ends with Moses' own approbation (39.43), which is similar to Genesis 1. In short, given the methodical nature of both Priestly narratives, the process of construction, viz., the concern with who does it and how it is done, is of equal importance to the finished product. Tabernacle and cosmos are the result of total cooperation and control.

Conflict and Creation

Set within the wider biblical and ancient Near Eastern context, in which the role of conflict and force is typical of stories of creation, God in Genesis acts to *incorporate* the natural powers, rather than 'divide and conquer' them.[30] This is particularly the case with respect to the cosmogonic role of water. Frequently, water is regarded in biblical literature as a negative force that has to be rebuked (Ps. 104.6-7; Isa. 50.2b), struck down in the figure of a mythological beast (Job 26.12; Ezek. 32.2-6; Ps. 74.13-14; Isa. 27.1), or contained (Jer. 5.22; Prov. 8.29; Ps. 33.7).[31] In light of this, the emphasis in the Priestly account on harmonious cooperation in the created order finds little precedent elsewhere in the HB, much less in ancient Near Eastern traditions. Indeed, any attempt to read into Genesis 1 some motif of conflict or conquest is entirely mistaken.[32]

From a modern theological perspective, Welker has suggested jettisoning the 'production and dependence model' that has so characterized theological reflection on Genesis 1 in favor of a model that

30. E.g., the Babylonian myth *Enuma Elish* and the Ugaritic Baal cycle (*ANET*, pp. 60-72, 129-31).

31. For a fuller treatment of the inimical role of the 'many waters' (*mayim rabbîm*) in biblical literature, see H.G. May, 'Some Cosmic Connotations of Mayim Rabbim, "Many Waters". . . ', *JBL* 74 (1955), pp. 9-21.

32. See, for example, W. Brueggemann's observation that in P 'creation comes to be expressed in conquest language' ('The Kerygma of the Priestly Writers', in W. Brueggemann and H.W. Wolff, *The Vitality of Old Testament Traditions* [Atlanta: John Knox, 1975], p. 108).

stresses cooperation and interdependence.[33] This is surely a move in the right direction. Ossified abstractions must be discarded for more descriptive ways that seek to convey this more subtle, interactive side of divine act in creation. Yet one must add a caveat that is grounded in a simple observation. By discarding certain abstract terms that stress the otherness of God, God and creation are not then to be set on the same plane. Only God is given the facility of speech and, thus, has the ability to create (*bārā'*) in the technical sense. The complex picture that results from a close reading of the Priestly creation text alongside the *Timaeus* is one that affirms the positive participation and interdependence of the natural elements of creation with the creator. The elevation of the elements from the level of inert matter or hostile forces, however, in no way diminishes the deity's incomparable status vis-à-vis creation in Genesis 1.

The Beginning and the End

Much of the argument regarding the syntactical status of the first verse of Genesis has revolved around the theological issue of the absolute or contingent nature of God. Indeed, the vigor with which both modern (and ancient) commentators have argued opposing positions betrays the fact that more than simply syntactical precision is at stake; there are also deep-seated theological conflicts over the way in which God is to be viewed in relation to the cosmos. Does a circumstantial rendering of Gen. 1.1 imply an elevation of 'chaos' at the expense of God's transcendent character?[34] It may be significant to note that such a label as the 'autonomy of chaos' in the context of creation is arrived at only by presupposing its logical opposite, *creatio ex nihilo*, which Gen. 1.1-3 neither rejects nor endorses, and thus does not address.[35]

33. M. Welker, 'What is Creation? Rereading Genesis 1 and 2', *TTod* 48 (1991), pp. 63-71.

34. So, for example, W. Eichrodt, 'In the Beginning. A Contribution to the Interpretation of the First Word of the Bible', in B.W. Anderson and W.J. Harrelson (eds.), *Israel's Prophetic Heritage: Essays in Honor of J. Muilenburg* (New York: Harper & Row, 1962), p. 10.

35. The notion of *creatio ex nihilo* did not clearly emerge as a doctrine until the second century BCE (G. May, *Schöpfung aus dem Nichts* [AzKG, 48; Berlin: de Grutyer, 1978], p. 78). Related texts that point toward such a doctrine include *Gen. R.* 1.9 and 2 Macc. 7.22-29.

As has been suggested, what is described in Gen. 1.2 is not malevolent, autonomous chaos, but the earth and the waters as living 'elements' that are enlisted by divine command to participate positively in the creative process. As illustrated in the dynamics of rhetorically nuanced speech, God chooses and implements noncoercive ways of creating, thereby allowing the elements to share positively in cosmogony. In short, divine act in creation is not depicted as an inbreaking but as an unfolding. For the Priestly writer, like Plato's character Timaeus, only by the 'friendly' convergence of divine power and earthly powers can a stable foundation for living creation be established.

'ĀDĀM FROM 'ĂDĀMÂ, 'IŠŠÂ FROM 'ÎŠ
Derivation and Subordination in Genesis 2.4b–3.24

Julie Galambush

The story about the woman and the man in Gen. 2.4b–3.24 has been analysed according to a variety of methods and understood to have various purposes: the story describes the origin of human beings; it describes the origin of sin;[1] it is a story justifying patriarchal structures;[2] it is a story criticizing patriarchal structures;[3] it is a story extolling the era and court of David (or of Solomon); or it is a story criticizing the era and the court of David (or of Solomon).[4] A story

---

1. Virtually all commentators recognize the story as an etiology of human existence, especially our alienation from God; see, e.g., G.M. Tucker, 'The Creation and the Fall: A Reconsideration', *LTQ* 13 (1978), pp. 113-24; C. Westermann, *Genesis 1–11: A Commentary* (Continental Commentaries; Minneapolis: Augsburg, 1984), p. 193.

2. The story has been understood to support patriarchal hierarchy by both supporters and opponents of that hierarchy. Among supporters who use the text as evidence that woman was created to be subordinate, see J.T. Walsh, 'Genesis 2:4b–3:24: A Synchronic Approach', *JBL* 96 (1977), pp. 161-77, esp. p. 174. Among those who criticize the text's perceived patriarchal agenda, see E.C. Stanton's introduction to E.C. Stanton, L.D. Blake, *et al.*, *The Woman's Bible* (New York: European Publishing, 1895), esp. p. 25; and M. Bal, *Lethal Love: Feminist Literary Readings of Biblical Love Stories* (Indiana Studies in Biblical Literature; Bloomington: Indiana University Press, 1987), pp. 110, 128.

3. See P. Trible, *God and the Rhetoric of Sexuality* (OBT; Philadelphia: Fortress, 1978), pp. 72-143; and Tucker, 'Creation and Fall', p. 120.

4. J. Rosenberg, *King and Kin: Political Allegory in the Hebrew Bible* (Indiana Studies in Biblical Literature; Bloomington: Indiana University Press, 1986), pp. 189-210; W.H. Schmidt, 'A Theologian of the Solomonic Era? A Plea for the Yahwist', in T. Ishida (ed.), *Studies in the Period of David and Solomon and Other Essays* (Winona Lake, IN: Eisenbrauns, 1982), pp. 55-73.

that has borne many readings through the ages, the Genesis account literally bears rereading.

The purpose of this essay is to read Genesis 2–3 once again in order to expose yet another of its facets, one that has not found its way into our common understanding of the narrative. I should like to propose that in Gen. 2.4b–3.24 the different physical origins of the man and woman give rise to the differences, initially between the words *'iššâ* and *'ādām*, but later, to differences between male and female biology, work, and social roles. Even the different type of suffering that each is assigned in ch. 3 derives from the difference in the substances from which the first couple was formed.[5] The creation of *'ādām* ('human being/man') from *'ădāmâ* ('earth') and *'iššâ* ('woman') from *'îš* ('man') is the critical moment on which the rest of the plot turns.

When in Gen. 2.23 the first woman is first seen by the first man, the *'ādām* quips, 'This is *'iššâ*, because this is taken from *'îš*—roughly, wo-man, because from-man.[6] The man's designation for his partner emphasizes the near identity of the two beings. From the man's point of view, the woman is bone from his bone and flesh from his flesh, and the only being truly related to him. The man perceives that the woman was created in response to his lack, and he thus defines her in

5.   Various scholars have noted the poignancy of *'ādām*'s return to *'ădāmâ* (see, e.g., P.D. Miller, *Genesis 1–11: Studies in Structure and Theme* [JSOTSup, 8; Sheffield: JSOT Press, 1978], pp. 37-42). The return and subjection of *'ādām* to the *'ădāmâ*, however, is only half of the story, or perhaps less than half. It is precisely the analogy between *'ādām*'s and *'iššâ*'s experiences that establishes a theme of painful return to one's source (cf. A. Tosato, 'On Genesis 2:24', *CBQ* 52 [1990], pp. 389-409, esp. p. 392). The failure to notice that the *'ādām*'s and *'iššâ*'s experiences are symmetrical—*'ādām* is to *'ădāmâ* as *'iššâ* is to *'îš*—may devolve from the assumption that the *'ādām*'s (man's) experiences are generic. The *'ādām*'s return to *'ădāmâ* is thus interpreted as 'universal', while the *'iššâ*'s experience, particularly her subjugation, is understood as pertaining exclusively to women. While it is true that both men and women undergo death and decay, in the terms of the narrative only the *'ādām*'s transformation to dust can strictly be called a 'return'. The *'iššâ*'s fateful (and potentially fatal) return is to *'îš*.

6.   In addition to the pun created by the assonance between *'îš* and *'iššâ*, a further pun may be intended, based on the final *h* of *'iššâ*. If the final *h* of *'iššâ* is read as an *h* directive, then the *'ādām*'s statement becomes a double pun: this one will be called ''*'îš*-ward', because 'from-*'îš*' this one was taken. It is impossible to know how the intended audience would have heard the wordplay, but the movement of *'îš* towards *'iššâ* (v. 24) and the return of *'iššâ* to the *'îš* (3.16) take on an ironic twist if *'iššâ* is punningly rendered ''*'îš*-ward' in 2.23.

terms of himself. In this respect the *'ādām*'s point of view is also the narrator's. The *'iššâ* is fashioned to correspond to the *'ādām* and is brought to him for approval. Given *'iššâ*'s functional correspondence to the man, it is reasonable for him to assume that her name also corresponds to his.[7] What the man's joyful proclamation—*'iššâ* from *'îš*—ignores, however, is the substantial difference between man and woman, a difference established within the narrative every bit as firmly as the celebrated correspondence between *'iššâ* and *'îš*.

The man, after all, was not created as *'îš* but as *'ādām*, the being formed from *'ădāmâ*. While no one at *'ādām*'s creation exclaimed, 'This is *'ādām* because he was taken out of *'ădāmâ*!', the pun is obvious.[8] The *'ādām* stresses the unity of substance between himself and the woman, but thereby belies the substantial difference—literally the difference in substance—between woman and man.[9] Scholars have, like the first man, tended to note only the initial equality and complementarity between the first couple, while disregarding the radical difference between the two. Even those who claim women's inferiority based on Gen. 3.16 often construe this debasement as woman's punishment rather than her created state.[10] Trible, arguing from a feminist perspective, claims that the shift in terminology from *'ādām* to *'îš* signals the complementarity between *'îš* and *'iššâ*. Prior to the creation of *'iššâ* the human creature was generic, an androgynous *'ādām*. Only with the creation of the woman is the man recognized by the narrator and by himself as *'îš*, the male counterpart of *'iššâ*.[11] Trible's emphasis on the substantial unity of the man and woman

---

7. As Westermann has pointed out, 'one could not say in 2.18 that man is created as a helper for the woman' (*Genesis 1–11*, p. 262). On this point, see also S.S. Lanser, '(Feminist) Criticism in the Garden: Inferring Genesis 2–3', *Semeia* 41 (1988), pp. 67-84, 73-74. This evident male perspective conflicts with H. Bloom's thesis that 'J' was a woman (H. Bloom and D. Rosenberg, *The Book of J* [New York: Grove Weidenfeld, 1990]).

8. Cf. *m. Ber.* 17.4, in which the *'ādām* names himself *'ādām*, saying, 'because I was taken from the *'ădāmâ*'.

9. It could be argued that it is the animals, not the woman, who are of one substance with the *'ādām*, having been formed, like him, from the *'ădāmâ*.

10. Luther notes that the woman was initially 'in no respect inferior' to her mate (*Lectures on Genesis, Chapters 1–5* in J. Pelikan [ed.], *Luther's Works* [St Louis: Concordia, 1958], p. 115), though elsewhere he expresses the apparently opposite opinion (p. 69).

11. *God and Rhetoric*, pp. 97-99.

reflects the mutuality implied both by the creation of *'iššâ* from the flesh of *'ādām* and by the *'ādām*'s playful etymology of the word-pair *'îš*/*'iššâ*. Mutuality is clearly within the scope of the narrative, but this bone-deep intimacy between man and woman is only half the story.

The first couple is not, after all, *'îš* and *'iššâ*, but *'ādām* and *'iššâ*. With the creation of *'iššâ* both the narrator and the *'ādām* recognize the man as *'îš*. This recognition does not, however, change the *'ādām* into an *'îš*. Rather, his 'manli-ness' becomes apparent—or relevant— only in contrast with the feminine *'iššâ*. The character introduced as *'ādām* in 2.7 and (further) recognized as *'îš* in 2.23-24 continues to be designated in the narrative as *'ādām*. Only in phrases describing his relationship to *'iššâ* is the *'ādām* designated *'îš*.[12] *'îš* functions in the narrative roughly to mean 'husband', while the male character proper is designated *hā'ādām*.[13]

This persistent verbal distinction between *'iššâ* and *'ādām* is not incidental but reflects the couple's underlying ontologies. The *'ādām* retains his identity as the one taken from *'ădāmâ*, while the *'iššâ* is 'the one taken from *'îš*'. This indelible reference to the man's and woman's physical sources also reflects the differing reasons for which the two were created. *'ādām* is the worker needed by the *'ădāmâ*, and *'iššâ* the cohort needed by the *'îš*. Despite the mutuality of male and female, the terms *'ādām* and *'iššâ* reflect abiding differences between the two. Male and female turn out to be, now one flesh, and now two. The tension between woman and man's correspondence and their difference is crucial to the plot of Gen. 2.4b–3.24. While the 'flesh and bone' unity between male and female accounts for the urge to reunite as 'one flesh' (2.24), the difference reflected in the characters' designation as *'iššâ* and *'ādām* will surface over the course of the narrative.

For the purposes of this discussion, Gen. 2.4b–3.24 may be divided into four parts: (1) the creation of the *'ādām* (2.4b-17), (2) the creation of the *'iššâ* (2.18-25), (3) the disobedience of the man and

---

12. In 3.6 the *'iššâ* gives fruit to 'her *'îš*', and in 3.16 she is told that she will desire her *'îš*.

13. On this point, see B.S. Childs, *Old Testament Theology in a Canonical Context* (Philadelphia: Fortress Press, 1985), pp. 189-91, and also the criticism of Lanser, '(Feminist) Criticism', and Rosenberg, *King and Kin*, p. 59. On the narrative development of the characters of *'ādām* and *'iššâ*, see Bal, *Lethal Love*, pp. 104-30.

woman (3.1-7), and (4) God's discovery of and response to that disobedience (3.8-24).[14] Part One, the creation of the *'ādām*, begins with the report of a lack, a lacuna in the cosmos. On the day that Yahweh God made heaven and earth, there was no vegetation, since no rain had fallen and no *'ādām* existed to work (*'bd*) the *'ădāmâ*. Beginning with the desired result, God first plants a garden and then goes about creating the conditions necessary to sustain it: rivers and an *'ādām*, a worker made of *'ădāmâ* and placed in the garden to tend it. Creation's initial lack is supplied, and the plot comes to rest with the positioning of the *'ādām* in the garden in 2.15.[15] A potential problem is raised, however, in the conclusion of this first episode. God forbids the *'ādām* (2.16) to eat from the tree in the middle of the garden. This prohibition, while not disruptive in itself, raises the troubling possibility of transgression. The prospect of the *'ādām*'s disobedience plus God's threatened punishment (death) undermines the initial closure the creation of *'ādām* provided. The solution is no sooner introduced than it is threatened, since the *'ādām*'s death would again leave the *'ădāmâ* without a servant and infertile. The 'conclusion' to Part One is marked with uneasiness.[16]

Part Two opens with a new lack; not the *'ādām*'s disobedience, but his unhappiness. God sees that it is not good (*lō' ṭôb*) for the *'ādām* to be alone. The question of *'ādām*'s obedience (and mortality) is put aside as God sets about to provide what *'ādām* is lacking. God's initial solution is the same as that in Part One: God makes more creatures from the *'ădāmâ*, this time the animals. The *'ādām* finds names for each, but in these fellow *'ădāmâ*-creatures he does not find his match. Changing tactics, God puts the *'ādām* to sleep, removes his side, and builds from it an *'iššâ*. This new being, already recognized as *'iššâ* (2.22) by the narrator, is, like the animals, brought to the *'ādām*. The *'ādām* enthusiastically affirms that this is indeed *'iššâ*, the one taken out of *'îš*. The *'ādām*'s lack, like the *'ădāmâ*'s, is thereby supplied, and the problem posed in Part Two resolved. Like the destabilizing

14. W. Brueggemann (*Genesis* [Interpretation; Atlanta: John Knox, 1982]) sees the same divisions. For an alternate view, see Walsh, 'Synchronic Approach'.

15. On lack and supply as defining the narrative structure of Gen. 2–3, see T. Boomershine, 'The Structure of Narrative Rhetoric in Genesis 2–3', *Semeia* 18 (1980), pp. 113-29; esp. p. 115.

16. Boomershine ('Narrative Rhetoric') similarly notes this pattern of incomplete or unstable conclusions.

conclusion of Part One ('Do not eat. . . lest'), however, the ending of
Part Two is ambiguous: 'They were naked, the two of them, the *'ādām*
and his *'iššâ*, and were not ashamed'. The message, while superficially
positive (they were not ashamed), raises a troubling specter. If the
man and woman are entirely at ease with their nakedness, why does
the narrator even mention shame? Shame's absence is noteworthy only
in a world characterized by its presence. By drawing attention to the
man and woman's lack of shame, the narrator invites the implied
reader to supply the appropriate conclusion: This shamelessness is
temporary. For a second time, notice of a 'solution' is accompanied by
the suggestion of the solution's fragility. Each conclusion foreshadows
future difficulties.

   If Part Three were to follow the pattern of Parts One and Two, it
should open with the announcement of a lack in God's creation. The
'iššâ, created in Part Two to supply the lack of the *'ādām*, who in
turn supplied the lack of *'ădāmâ*, seems the most likely candidate to
exhibit a lack and so set the plot in motion. The straightforward
pattern established by Parts One and Two is, however, complicated in
Part Three. The concluding observation in 2.25 that the *'ādām* and his
'iššâ were naked (*'ărûmmîm*) and without shame is followed immediately in 3.1 by the announcement that the snake was more *'ārûm*—
either 'tricky' or 'naked'[17]—than any other wild creature God had
made. The snake is *'ārûm*, but in a sense nearly opposite that applied
to the human couple. The snake is as shameless of his trickery as the
humans are innocent of their nakedness. The snake and the woman,
both created in response to the *'ādām*'s lack, together will raise the
problem of Part Three, in which the foreboding conclusions to Parts
One and Two will play themselves out.

   Unlike the unworked *'ădāmâ* of Part One or the lonely *'ādām* of
Part Two, the snake and the *'iššâ* do not present any apparent lack to
be supplied. The snake, however, creates a lack, or at least the appearance of a lack. The snake approaches the *'iššâ* and misrepresents God,
claiming, 'God said, "You really may not eat from all of the trees of

---

17. While *'ārûm* is certainly intended to denote 'tricky' or 'subtle', the unpointed
text could be read as the homomorphic *'ārôm*, 'naked'. The proximity of *'ārûm* to the
observation in 2.25 that the man and woman were *'ărûmmîm* ensures that some
comparison between the condition of the humans and the character of the snake is
intended (cf. H. Niehr, " *'āram*', *ThWAT* 6 [1989], cols. 387-92).

the garden.'"[18] The *'iššâ* corrects the snake's statement by placing it in context: 'We may eat the fruit of all the trees—except one.' The *'iššâ*'s solution does not suffice, however, and the snake goes on directly to contradict God: 'You will not die'. Professing to know what God knows, the snake claims that God has in effect withheld the good from the *'iššâ*: God knows that you will become like God, knowing good and evil. The *'iššâ* settles the dispute through action. Seeing that the tree is 'good' (thus mirroring Yahweh, who in Part One made every tree that was 'good' [2.9] and in Part Two saw that it was 'not good' [2.18] for the *'ādām* to be alone), she acts to fulfil her perceived lack of wisdom. The *'iššâ* and 'her *'îš*' eat, and the two suddenly 'know' both nakedness and shame.

For the first time in the story, it is not Yahweh who sees and supplies the needs of creation, but the creatures themselves who define their needs and attempt solutions. The *'iššâ*'s solution, urged by the snake and shared by the *'ādām*, is at best only partially effective. The human couple gain knowledge, but only knowledge of their nakedness and hence their shame. A foreboding conclusion to Part Three, the couple's transgression and shame serve to resolve the unstable conclusions to Parts One and Two. Both God's prohibition against eating from the tree in Part One and the narrator's comment in Part Two— that though naked the couple felt no shame—raised the potential for narrative development. The prospect of both disobedience and shame was introduced. In attempting in Part Three to fulfil their own lack, the *'ādām* and the *'iššâ* fulfil instead the potential for failure introduced in the earlier sections: the man has disobeyed and the couple are ashamed. Part Three closes with the notice that, seeing their nakedness, the *'ādām* and *'iššâ* make loincloths for themselves of leaves. Instead of supplying their lack the couple has succeeded only in perceiving a new lack—clothing—and they now act again to supply this additional need. The conclusion to Part Three is charged with anxiety. The man and woman's solution is pitifully insubstantial. Moreover, whereas the threat of shame, merely implicit in Part Two,

18. For the argument in favor of translating the snake's words as a statement rather than a question, see Walsh, 'Synchronic Approach', p. 164; and cf. E.A. Speiser, *Genesis* (AB, 1; Garden City, NY: Doubleday, 1964), who translates, 'Even though God told you not to eat of any tree in the garden. . . ', at which point the woman interrupts (p. 21).

has been realized, God's explicit threat of death, made in Part One, awaits fulfilment.

Part Four of the narrative (3.8-24) describes Yahweh's discovery of the couple's wrongdoing and his pronouncement of their fates. The initial harmony of creation breaks down as Yahweh challenges the *'ādām*, the *'ādām* accuses the *'iššâ* (and implicitly, Yahweh), and the *'iššâ* blames the snake. Disobedience results in disunity and the introduction of suffering into creation. Yahweh, who previously acted to supply the needs of the created world, now announces that anguish will not only appear but will remain a permanent feature of creation.

It is in Part Four that the difference built into the *'iššâ* and *'ādām* makes a difference: *'iššâ* and *'ādām* receive separate punishments from Yahweh. While the separation of the woman from the man reflects their new alienation, their differing punishments stem directly from their primordial differences in function and in substance. The *'ādām* and *'iššâ* are assigned fates reflecting their different beginnings. *'iššâ* and *'ādām* will both suffer, each in relation to the substance of origin: *'iššâ* in subordination to the *'îš*, and *'ādām* in servitude to *'ădāmâ*. The happy complementarity between the *'ādām* and his mate is eclipsed by their harsh subordination to their respective elementary substances.

The *'iššâ* is destined to suffer in childbirth (3.16), a misfortune directly related to her creation. Built from the flesh of *'îš* to remedy his lack of others corresponding to him, *'iššâ* will continue her original function: she will create other humans. Now, however, she finds that she will undergo suffering, returning in humiliation to a domineering *'îš*. Initially taken from *'îš* in joy, *'iššâ* will be bound to him in anguish (*'iṣṣābôn*).

The *'iššâ*'s punishment is stated in terms of her *'îš*, her namesake. The man is punished in terms of *'ădāmâ*, and is accordingly addressed in 3.17-19 as *'ādām*.[19] The *'ādām* will work (literally, 'serving' [*'bd*]) the *'ădāmâ*, the task for which he was created. The *'ădāmâ*, however, will no longer bring forth only food that is good to eat (2.9), but briars and thorns. The *'ādām* will be painfully bound to the *'ădāmâ* all the days of his life. Ultimately, his anguish (*'iṣṣābôn*) will culminate in return to that dust from which he was formed.

---

19. The English translation, 'man and woman', masks the rather striking fact that the two are *not* addressed as a matched pair, *'îš* and *'iššâ*. Rather, the two are described using titles reflecting their different origins.

The '*iššâ*, once taken from '*îš* in response to his need for her, will now need him but be subjected to his domination. The '*ādām*, formed to fulfil the needs of '*ădāmâ*, must now struggle with the '*ădāmâ* to satisfy his own needs. The '*ădāmâ* he once aided now resists him. '*ādām* and '*iššâ*, each born through differentiation from their primordial substances, learn that the substances that constituted them will ultimately oppress them.

The connection drawn in Gen. 3.8-24 between the '*iššâ*'s and '*ādām*'s origins and their fates is confirmed by the fate accorded the snake. While the man and woman, once described as 'one flesh', suffer very different ends, the punishments of the '*ādām* and the snake are closely related. God's addresses to the snake and the '*ādām* share the following elements: (1) a reason ('Because you have done x. . . '); (2) a curse (against the snake directly and against the '*ădāmâ* because of the ' *ādām*—or perhaps in place of him? [*ba 'ăbûrekā*]); (3) unpleasantness associated with eating (the snake will eat dust and the man will suffer to eat from the '*ădāmâ*); (4) an announcement that this way of eating will continue 'all the days of your life'; and (5) references to both the ground and to dust ('*āpār*)—the snake will travel on its belly and will eat dust; the '*ādām* will eat from '*ădāmâ* and, because he is dust, will ultimately return to '*ădāmâ*.

Note that all the elements common to the pronouncements against the '*ādām* and the snake are absent from the account of the woman's fate. The woman will suffer in her own body and in her relationship to the '*îš*. No curse is pronounced over her, no mention of the '*ădāmâ* or of dust, no sentence lasting 'all the days' of her life, and perhaps most surprisingly (considering who took the first bite), no mention of eating. This fraternity between the '*ādām* and the snake is puzzling, given the lack of any direct interaction between the two. Interaction, however, is secondary; the creatures' ends are governed by their physical beginnings. The '*ādām* and the snake share an original substance. Whereas '*ādām* and '*iššâ* were formed from '*ădāmâ* and '*îš* respectively, the snake is, like the '*ādām*, a creature formed from '*ădāmâ*. The snake and the '*ādām* will therefore suffer corresponding returns to the dust, while the '*iššâ* will cling—despite suffering—to the '*îš*. All three creatures return in humiliation to their origins.

Formed as they were by differentiation from '*ădāmâ* and '*îš*, the reassimilation of '*ādām* and '*iššâ* represents their symbolic annihilation. In fact, the suggestion of death appears in the pronouncements against both *'iššâ* and *'ādām*. The *'iššâ*'s longing for her husband has consequences that are not only painful but life-threatening. Childbirth was a leading cause of female mortality in the ancient world,[20] and the mention of extremely painful birthing overshadows the *'iššâ*'s sexual desire with the possibility of her death. The *'ādām* is explicitly told that his painful service to the *'ădāmâ* will end in death. Suffering, he will live off the land until he is literally reabsorbed—dust to dust. For both woman and man, return is colored not only by suffering but by overtones of death.

This harsh subjection, the movement deathward back to the source, is also, however, a movement into life. The work that threatens the lives of *'iššâ* and *'ādām* also symbolically re-enacts each one's creation. The *'iššâ*, taken from human flesh, learns that though she will suffer, her flesh will itself produce human life. The *'îš*-derived *'iššâ* will bring forth more of her own kind—human flesh from human flesh. The *'ādām* likewise undergoes pain specifically as he continues the fertility of his originative substance. The creature formed from the dust will work the dust, and his goal will be to produce more life out of the earth. Risking their lives to produce new life, *'iššâ* and *'ādām* renew the fertility of their respective sources.

Each character's lot is mixed. Each finds him-/herself at once circumscribed by his/her origins and empowered to perpetuate the life that each was originally given. Reproduction, the literal re-production of their origins, is connected for woman and man alike with suffering and with death. The *'ādām* brings life from the dust until he becomes dust, the woman bears flesh from her flesh despite anguish and mortal danger. *'ādām* and *'iššâ*, the namesakes of their originative substances, return to their sources under an ambiguous sentence encompassing birth and death, fulfilment and failure.

The author of Gen. 2.4b–3.24 proposes a creation in which the physical origins of man and woman, he from the ground and she from the body of man, determine not only the names *'ādām* and *'iššâ*, but ultimately, the relationship between man and woman, their relative place in society, and their modes of productive labor. This narrative connection between origin and destiny is, of course, illusory. The author (or earlier members of the culture) began with the words

20. See C.L. Meyers, *Discovering Eve: Ancient Israelite Women in Context* (New York: Oxford University Press, 1988) for data on childbirth as a 'gender-specific life-threat' (p. 113) in ancient Israel.

'ādām, 'ădāmâ , 'iššâ, and *'îš,* and with the range of biological and sociological differences (and similarities) between men and women. These observed and linguistic and cultural phenomena were then 'accounted for' in an etiological story. The etiology integrates a number of paradoxical similarities and differences. The narrative explains how it is that women and men can be so deeply connected and yet so alienated: they are simultaneously 'of one flesh' and of different substances. A reason is provided for the fact that only women can give birth: the one who produces flesh does so because she herself was originally made from flesh.[21] Social roles are similarly accounted for: each party is subordinated to the substance from which she or he was taken, and each is bound to sustain the fertility of his/her originative element.

Finally, a linguistic anomaly is explained: the unbalanced pair, *'îš* (m.)/*'iššâ* (f.) and *'ādām* (m.)/*'ădāmâ* (f.).[22] Why do both grammatically masculine nouns refer to men, while one feminine noun refers to woman and the other means 'earth'? Why should 'earth' (*'ădāmâ*) be the grammatical counterpart of 'man/human' (*'ādām*)? The author solves the linguistic puzzle by contradicting the grammatical correspondence between *'îš*/*'iššâ* and *'ādām*/*'ădāmâ*. Rather than asserting that *'ādām* is to *'ădāmâ,* as *'îš* is to *'iššâ* (setting up two male/female pairs for comparison), the author inverts the gender correspondence between the noun pairs, claiming that *'ādām* is to *'ădāmâ* as *'iššâ* is to *'îš* (male is to female as female is to male). Instead of associating *'iššâ* with the earth (*'ădāmâ*), her symbolic alter-ego and the 'other' Mother of All Living, the author asserts that *'ādām* is most closely akin to *'ădāmâ,* as is *'iššâ* to *'îš.* The masculine *'ādām* was derived from the feminine *'ădāmâ,* and the feminine *'iššâ* derived from the masculine *'îš.*

In this wordplay, both male and female are 'derivative', each derived from its (grammatically) opposite-sexed original. This

21. The story of the first man giving birth to woman may serve as some compensation for the male's actual inability to give birth. On this reversal of biological fact, see J. Milgrom, 'Some Second Thoughts about Adam's First Wife', in G.A. Robbins (ed.), *Genesis 1–3 in the History of Exegesis* (Studies in Women and Religion, 27; Lewiston, NY: Edwin Mellen, 1988), pp. 225-53, esp. pp. 240-41.

22. On the relationship between 'folk-grammar' and genuine etymology in Gen. 2–3, see Rosenberg, *King and Kin,* pp. 58-59, 232, and the excursus on *'ādām* in Westermann, *Genesis 1–11,* pp. 201-208.

surprising linguistic turn supplies the rationale for the entire etiology. The grammatical conundrum becomes the paradigm for the paradoxical relation between man and woman. Man recognizes in woman one entirely his equal, who yet remains a very different type of creature. The *'ādām*'s recognition of *'iššâ* as his flesh and blood, the one with whom he would (re)unite, is only half the story, belying the radical difference between man and woman. Ultimately, neither gender complementarity nor difference is the subject of the etiology, but the tension and ambiguity of human relationships.[23]

The relationships between *'ādām* and *'ădāmâ* and between *'iššâ* and *'îš*, distorted by disobedience, bear fruit in the next generation in the person of Cain. In Gen. 4.1 the *'iššâ*-from-*'îš* paradigm is reversed as *'iššâ* brings forth from her body an *'îš*. Mirroring the *'ādām*'s announcement, 'This one was taken out of *'îš*', the new mother exclaims, 'I made an *'îš*!'[24] Cain is the fulfilment of his mother's life-producing labor, but he also fulfils his father's task: he works (*'bd*; 4.2; cf. 2.15; 3.23) the earth. The first product of *'iššâ* and *'ādām*, Cain inherits the fates of both parents. As a worker of the now-cursed *'ădāmâ*, Cain's labor is frustrated when earth's produce finds no favor with Yahweh. This failure becomes the more galling when Cain finds himself in competition with the one corresponding to him, his brother Abel. As Abel's offering is accepted and Cain's refused, a *de facto* hierarchy emerges. Unsatisfied in serving the *'ădāmâ* and diminished in relation to his fellow-human, Cain suffers the punishments assigned both his parents.

Like his parents, Cain also faces the possibility of disobedience. Yahweh warns that sin's desire is for him, but Cain must be master over it (4.7). Desire (*tĕšûqâ*) in 3.16 was described as *'iššâ*'s fate, and mastery (*mšl*) the role of *'ādām*. Cain, summoned to master sin, chooses mastery over another rather than self-mastery, and so

23. The story is also an etiology about humanity's relationship with God, but that etiology hinges on the claim that humans, male and female, were created by God, rather than on the substance of which they were made or the words used to describe them.

24. Eve's exclamation, *qānîtî 'îš'et-yhwh*, is notoriously difficult to translate. The translation of D. Rosenberg, 'I have created a man as Yahweh has' (*Book of J*, p. 65; cf. p. 187) captures the *'iššâ*'s recapitulation through Cain's birth of her own creation. As Yahweh once brought *'iššâ* forth from the body of the *'îš*, now *'iššâ* brings forth an *'îš*. Note that the offspring of *'iššâ* is not called a *yeled* or an *'ādām*. To all appearances, she has made an *'îš*, as Yahweh did.

murders his brother. The curse that '*ădāmâ* bore because of '*ādām* (3.17) is returned upon '*ādām*'s fruit: 'Cursed are you from the ground' (4.11).[25] Alienation between human and human and between human being and the earth, the respective fates of the '*iššâ* and the '*ādām*, are compounded in the couple's first child.

Conclusion

In Gen. 2.4b–3.24 the physical origins of male and female—he from the earth and she from his flesh—are first posited and then shown to account for differences in the terminology, the biology, and the social roles assigned men and women. Although both the story of '*iššâ*'s derivation from '*îš* and the word-pair, '*iššâ*/'*îš*, bespeak the characters' complementarity, this complementarity always stands in tension with the substantial difference between the woman and man. The narrative simultaneously renders, reflects, and accounts for a world in which women and men have the potential for mutuality but instead live in antagonistic relationships of domination and subordination.

As has been widely noted, this story is not a prescription for the world but a description of the world in which the author lived.[26] Subordinate status is not mandated for women any more than are crop failure or careers in agriculture for men. Rather, the current state of affairs is a sad one, reflecting human failure to live out the mutuality for which we were created. The world of Gen. 3.8-24 is not the world as God intended it.

If the story of Gen. 2.4b–3.24 depicts the subordinate status of women as a distortion of God's plan, however, it does not thereby become a call to change women's status. While the narrator deplores the '*iššâ*'s fate, it is not clear that the author of Gen. 2.4b–3.24 imagined, much less called for, change. As we have demonstrated, within the terms of the narrative, the disobedience of '*ādām* and '*iššâ* leads inexorably to their subjugation to their elementary substances. If

---

25. The phrase *min-hā'ădāmâ* could also be translated 'more than the earth', in which case a parallel would obtain between Cain, cursed more than the earth, and the snake, more cursed than all animals (3.8).

26. See, e.g., Trible, *God and Rhetoric*, p. 128; Brueggemann, *Genesis*, p. 51; Westermann, *Genesis 1–11*, p. 262; and L.D. Blake (*The Woman's Bible*, p. 27), who observes that women's subordination 'has been called the curse', but asks, 'Is it not rather a prediction?'

anything, the etiology contains a mechanistic strain: man's and woman's essence—their literal substance—determines their experience. The author constructs an etiology to explain rather than to remedy the hard facts of life. Regardless of the opinions held by the author of Genesis 2–3, the text, by explaining rather than challenging the subordination of women, functions in a conservative manner. The subordination of women, like the hardships of agriculture or the experience of shame, is perceived as a given, however unpleasant.

Even an author who foresaw no change, however, could imagine a world and a time in which male and female were complementary and their differences implied no oppression. The author of Genesis 2–3 did not inhabit that God-intended world. How female and male difference might develop in the context of obedience rather than rebellion remains to be explored.

PRIESTLY RITUALS OF FOUNDING: TIME, SPACE, AND STATUS

Frank H. Gorman, Jr

Introduction

Priestly rituals have received a great deal of critical and scholarly examination in recent years with illuminating and insightful results. The emphasis, however, has focused on the details of distinct ritual acts. Two issues need additional attention. First, there needs to be critical examination of the world-view within which Priestly ritual is enacted. This larger context is the Priestly theology of creation. Secondly, attention must be given to the way in which Priestly ritual functions to construct a world of meaning. The discussion of Priestly rituals must be broadened to include both the world-view in which they are meaningful and the world-view which they help to create.

This paper will suggest a general typology for locating three types of Priestly rituals: (1) rituals of founding, (2) rituals of maintenance, and (3) rituals of restoration. It will then examine three texts in more detail and argue that they narrate, describe, or depict rituals of founding: Gen. 1.1–2.4a; Exod. 40.16-33; and Leviticus 8–9. More specifically, it will demonstrate that each of these texts reflects the founding, creation, or establishment of a particular category of the sacred that is of crucial importance in Priestly rituals and in the Priestly view of the world: sacred time (Gen. 1.1–2.4a), sacred space (Exod. 40.16-33), and sacred persons (Lev. 8–9). In addition, it will be argued that rituals of founding provide important clues for understanding the Priestly view of history and human existence. These texts indicate that Priestly rituals are interwoven conceptually with Priestly views of creation, history, and human existence.[1]

---

1. I want to thank John Hayes for helping me to see some of the relationships that exist between creation, history, and ritual and for encouraging me to pursue the study of these relationships.

A Typology of Priestly Rituals

The structure and function of Priestly rituals should provide access, at least in part, to significant aspects of the Priestly view of the world.[2] A general typology of Priestly rituals in terms of their function would be helpful,[3] and van Gennep's work on rites of passage provides a useful starting point.[4] He argued that rites and rituals associated with transitions reflect a fairly basic and consistent structure: separation from one status, transition, and aggregation into a new status. Such rites function in society to move an individual or group from one status to another. Rituals of transition are prevalent in the Priestly ritual system. Rituals of purification, for example, are concerned with the transition from an unclean to a clean state. In light of the fact that such rituals are undertaken specifically because a person or group has contracted uncleanness, it is clear that the state of cleanness or purity is considered the normative or, at least, preferable status.[5] Thus,

2. The way that Priestly ritual functions to enact world needs critical examination and evaluation. The intimate connection between ritual and world-view is widely recognized and discussed. See, e.g., R.A. Rappaport, *Ecology, Meaning, and Religion* (Richmond, CA: North Atlantic Books, 1979), pp. 93-97; B. Kapferer, 'Performance and the Structuring of Meaning and Experience', in V.W. Turner and E.M. Bruner (eds.), *The Anthropology of Experience* (Urbana/Chicago: University of Illinois Press, 1986), pp. 188-203; and T.F. Driver, *The Magic of Ritual* (San Francisco: Harper Collins, 1991), p. 136. Important critical issues relating to this relationship are discussed in C. Bell, *Ritual Theory, Ritual Practice* (Oxford: Oxford University Press, 1992), pp. 69-93.

3. The typology presented here is not intended to be all-inclusive for the Priestly ritual system. It is designed to organize a series of rituals concerned with world order. See P. Smith, 'Aspects of the Organization of Rites', in M. Izard and P. Smith (eds.), *Between Belief and Transgression* (Chicago: University of Chicago Press, 1982), pp. 103-28. For discussions of the Priestly ritual system, see M. Haran, 'The Complex of Ritual Acts Performed Inside the Tabernacle', *ScrHier* 8 (1961), pp. 272-302 and A.F. Rainey, 'The Order of Sacrifices in Old Testament Ritual Texts', *Bib* 51 (1970), pp. 485-98.

4. A. van Gennep, *The Rites of Passage* (Chicago: University of Chicago Press, 1960). The work of V. Turner is important for further refinements. See his *Dramas, Fields, and Metaphors* (Ithaca, NY: Cornell University Press, 1974), pp. 231-99; and *From Ritual to Theatre* (New York: Performing Arts Journal Publications, 1982), pp. 20-87.

5. See G.J. Wenham, *The Book of Leviticus* (NICOT, 3; Grand Rapids: Eerdmans, 1979), pp. 18-25; J. Milgrom, *Leviticus 1–16* (AB, 3; New York:

rituals of purification may be regarded as *rituals of restoration* that restore a person who has contracted impurity to a state of purity. Two aspects of this must be recognized and taken seriously. First, rituals of restoration reflect a process or movement[6] that moves a person or group from one status to another through the process of a ritual.[7] The structure of the ritual itself reflects a linear movement, but it is a movement that effects the restoration of and return to a previous state.[8] Secondly, these rituals take place within the context of a world understood, envisioned, and inhabited as a world in process. It is a world in which humans experience life as movement between purity and defilement. Ritual states that structure and nuance everyday life reflect process and movement. The Priestly ritual system does not reflect a static view of either life or history. Life and history are both viewed as *processes* characterized by continuous movement between purity and defilement, life and death, hope and despair.[9]

Doubleday, 1991), pp. 42-51, 976-1004. For a comparative perspective, see E.M. Zuesse, 'Taboo and the Divine Order', *JAAR* 42 (1974), pp. 482-504.

6. V. Turner has emphasized the processual nature of ritual. See his 'The Anthropology of Performance', in *Process, Performance, and Pilgrimage: A Study in Comparative Symbology* (RAS, 1; New Delhi: Concept, 1979), pp. 60-93.

7. The ritual processes of the Priestly traditions and the liturgical processes of the Psalms need to be examined together. Without entering into the discussion of whether the Priestly cult was 'silent' or not, the processes by which Israel approached its God—ritual and liturgical—should have important connections. On the liturgical presentation of God's alternative future, see W. Brueggemann, 'The Rhetoric of Hurt and Hope: Ethics Odd and Crucial', in P.D. Miller (ed.), *Old Testament Theology* (Minneapolis: Fortress Press, 1992), pp. 50-58.

8. On the relation of linear and cyclical processes in Priestly theology, see my *The Ideology of Ritual* (JSOTSup, 91; Sheffield: JSOT Press, 1990), pp. 215-27.

9. These sets of categories, to which may be added that of order/chaos, are operative throughout the Priestly ritual system (in addition to n. 5 above, see J.E. Hartley, *Leviticus* [WBC, 4; Dallas: Word Books, 1992], pp. 141-46). The same categories operative in Priestly rituals will be used in the Priestly interpretation of history. In terms of purity/impurity as organizing categories for history, see T. Frymer-Kensky, 'Pollution, Purification, and Purgation in Biblical Israel', in C.L. Meyers and M. O'Connor (eds.), *The Word of the Lord Shall Go Forth* (Winona Lake, IN: Eisenbrauns, 1983), pp. 399-414. R. Rendtorff ('"Covenant" as a Structuring Concept in Genesis and Exodus', *JBL* 108 [1989], pp. 385-93) has demonstrated that 'covenant' is used as a structuring category in Genesis and Exodus, while R.H. Moye ('In the Beginning: Myth and History in Genesis and Exodus', *JBL* 109 [1990], pp. 577-98) has argued that in Genesis, for example, one can see the movement from 'historicized myth' toward 'mythicized history'.

It is clear, however, that not all Priestly rituals function in this way. The ritual calendar in Numbers 28–29, for example, prescribes specific sacrifices for specific moments of the year without regard to the issues of contracted impurity or defilement. Such regularly prescribed ritual occasions are best understood as *rituals of maintenance* that delimit and maintain a pre-existing order. In Numbers 28–29, an annual ritual order is established that both delimits sacred moments and maintains the normative order of Israel's national and cultic existence.[10]

Clearly, both rituals of restoration *and* rituals of maintenance assume that there is a normative order that exists and must be (1) maintained by regularly prescribed rituals (rituals of maintenance) and (2) restored after disruption caused by sin and impurity (rituals of restoration). If this normative state is one that can be manipulated through rituals of maintenance and rituals of restoration, then it is likely that it will have a ritual base. If an order exists that is subject to ritual manipulation, indeed, if it is dependent upon it, then it is not surprising to find that it is generated by and grounded in ritual. Thus, *rituals of founding* bring the normative state into being and so reflect to some extent transition, but in such a way that the transition creates a state that did not exist before the enactment of the ritual. Rituals of founding are creative in that they effect a state, a thing, or a category that did not previously exist.

Genesis 1.1–2.4a: The Founding of Sacred Time

Genesis 1.1–2.4a describes God's construction and founding of the cosmos,[11] tracing the movement from primordial chaos to ordered cosmos. The divine creator founds cosmos—cosmos understood as and characterized by order based on separation—through acts of speech,

---

10. See Rappaport, *Ecology*, pp. 187-92; Smith, 'Aspects of the Organization of Rites', pp. 108-10; Gorman, *Ideology*, pp. 215-27.

11. M. Fishbane's *Text and Texture* (New York: Schocken Books, 1979), pp. 3-16, remains one of the best discussions of this text. In addition, see G. von Rad, *Genesis* (OTL; Philadelphia: Westminster, 1972), pp. 45-67; W. Brueggemann, *Genesis* (Interpretation; Atlanta: John Knox, 1982), pp. 22-39; C. Westermann, *Genesis 1–11: A Commentary* (Continental Commentaries; Minneapolis: Augsburg, 1984), pp. 78-177.

acts of separation, and acts of making.[12] Creation comes into being and is characterized by transition and process.

This text resonates with ritual elements that suggest it should be read as a divine ritual of founding.[13] First, the text belongs to the Priestly traditions, which not only contain prescriptions for and descriptions of rituals, but also reflect a ritual way of thinking about world, history, and human existence. As the passage deals with creation, it does so in ritual categories. History itself is viewed in ritual categories—rituals of founding, rituals of maintenance, and rituals of restoration. Secondly, the very style of the text suggests a ritual context. The formal, systematic, and repetitive use of language and action reflects the Priestly mode of ritualized discourse and thought. Thirdly, the seven-day process of creation points to a ritual context. In the Priestly traditions, seven days is a temporal unit that reflects ritual categories. In particular, rituals of major transition require a seven-day process (e.g., Num. 19 [corpse-contamination]; Lev. 13–14 [leprosy]). The movement from chaos to cosmos clearly reflects a major transition and, thus, points to a ritual process.[14] Fourthly, the fact that the process of creation ends with the setting apart of the sabbath demonstrates a clear concern for ritual and ritual time. Thus, Gen. 1.1–2.4a may be read as a ritual of founding enacted by the divine creator. Two primary acts of founding are narrated and enacted: (1) the founding of cosmos and (2) the founding of sabbath and time.

The basic structure of Gen. 1.1–2.4a has often been discussed.[15] Beginning with the primordial chaos, God constructs the cosmos in seven days. While the text distinguishes between God's creative activity on six days and God's rest on the seventh day, it is clear from the larger structure and movement of the text that the consecration of the seventh day is part of the larger creative process.[16] The sabbath,

---

12. Gorman, *Ideology*, pp. 39-45.

13. Brueggemann (*Genesis*, pp. 29-39) discusses this text as a creation liturgy.

14. It has not been uncommon to read ritual texts with an eye on Gen. 1.1–2.4a. It should be recognized, however, that it is also appropriate to read Gen. 1.1–2.4a with an eye on ritual texts.

15. See, e.g., U. Cassuto, *A Commentary on the Book of Genesis* (Jerusalem: Magnes, 1961), I, pp. 16-17; Fishbane, *Text and Texture*, pp. 3-16; C. Hyers, *The Meaning of Creation* (Atlanta: John Knox, 1984), pp. 67-71.

16. Westermann, *Genesis*, pp. 89-90, 170-72.

even though it is a day set apart from the other days of the week, is still one of the days of creation and part of the larger order of creation. Thus, time is part of the created order.[17]

Indeed, creative acts reflecting temporal concerns are suggestively placed in this text. The first creative act of God is the creation of 'the day'. God creates the light, separates it from the darkness, calls them 'day' and 'night' respectively, and thereby brings into being 'the day'. Thus, the establishing of the day is the original act of creation and a basic structural element of the created order.[18] On day four, the midpoint of the week of creation, God creates the sun, moon, planets, and stars and places them in the sky 'for signs and for seasons and for days and for years' (v. 14). The final creative act of God is the founding of the sabbath as a holy day. The sabbath comes as the culminating act of the original process of creation and functions to mark its end. The setting apart of the sabbath (i.e., making it holy) gives closure to the larger process of creation and marks the end of this divine ritual of founding. Thus, the concern for temporal categories is evident at the beginning, midpoint, and end of the original process of creation.

That these 'times' are of crucial importance for the Priestly traditions is further demonstrated by the fact that each of these three moments in 'the creation of time' is marked by specifically prescribed rituals. The creation of the day, the regular cycle of day and night, is marked by the morning and evening sacrifices (Exod. 29.38-46),[19] which in turn are linked with (1) the promise of God's presence in the midst of Israel in the tabernacle and (2) God's redemptive activity in bringing Israel out of Egypt (vv. 45-46). This demonstrates that creation, ritual, and historical events are significantly interrelated in the Priestly traditions. The creation of the celestial lights is related to the regularly prescribed rituals for the cycle of the year in Numbers 28–29. These rituals of maintenance are required at specific times that are identified, in part, through their relationship to 'the seasons' marked by the celestial bodies created in Gen. 1.14.[20] Finally, the

17. S. Herrmann, *Time and History* (BES; Nashville: Abingdon, 1981), pp. 122-23.

18. The importance of this in Israel is seen in Job's speech in Job 3, in which he calls for the overthrow of the day as a symbol of world order. See L.G. Perdue, 'Job's Assault on Creation', *HAR* 10 (1986), pp. 295-315.

19. Gorman, *Ideology*, pp. 219-20.

20. On the relation of the 'seasons' of Gen. 1.14 and the 'festivals' of Numbers

founding of the sabbath is marked by the weekly observance, through imitation of the divine rest, of this day as a day set apart from the other days. Each of these prescribed ritual activities, related as they are to a specific moment of temporal creativity and establishment, must be understood in terms of ritual maintenance. In observing these rituals, human beings become participants in the maintenance of the order of creation.

It is important to note that the 'ordered cosmos' of the Priestly creation reflects an interweaving of order *and* chaos. The original elements of chaos, *těhôm* and *ḥōšek*, are not eliminated but become part of the created cosmos.[21] Thus, if chaos is woven into the fabric of cosmos, and temporal processes are a central aspect of cosmos, it follows that chaos is also woven into the fabric of history. History itself, like cosmos, reflects the dynamic tension and interplay of order and chaos.[22] History moves between the possibilities of order and chaos. Furthermore, inasmuch as ritual is intimately related to the Priestly temporal categories and the Priestly understanding of the created order, it also will reflect this interplay of chaos and order. Ritual for the Priestly traditions becomes a means for the Israelite community to move creatively and ritually between the possibilities of chaos and order. Ritual takes place, then, not in the context of a perfectly ordered cosmos that is free of chaos, but within the context of the inevitable movement between order and chaos. Cosmos, history, and ritual thus intersect and interweave precisely in the

28-29, see W.H. Schmidt, *Die Schöpfungsgeschichte der Priesterschrift* (WMANT, 17; Neukirchen–Vluyn: Neukirchener Verlag, 1964), p. 114; Westermann, *Genesis*, pp. 129-31.

21. Hyers, *The Meaning of Creation*, pp. 67-71; J.D. Levenson, *Creation and the Persistence of Evil* (San Francisco: Harper & Row, 1988), pp. 122-23.

22. The founding of cosmos and the founding of time are understood as the beginning of history. The Priestly traditions do not recognize the dichotomy between the time of founding and the beginning of history. Indeed, the founding of cosmos provides a primal date for the enactment of several significant moments in Israel's history and national story (see J. Blenkinsopp, 'The Structure of P', *CBQ* 38 [1976], pp. 275-92). Creation and history are connected in such a way that creation cannot be said to be the stage for history. Creation begins history and history begins with creation. Thus, creation theology is theology of history. See T.E. Fretheim, *Exodus* (Interpretation; Louisville: John Knox, 1991), pp. 12-14, 268-71.

movement between order and chaos, purity and impurity, hope and
despair, life and death.[23]

The conjunction of divine creative activity, historical process, and
ritual enactment demonstrates that the Priestly traditions take seriously the intersection of the activity of God and that of the Israelite
community in the construction and movement of history. In the
Priestly creation tradition, human beings are created in the image and
likeness of God, blessed with fertility, commanded to be (co-)creators,
and given the directive to watch over the order of creation.[24] Human
beings, male and female, are imaged as the representatives of God
within the created order and are called upon to (1) found specific
elements of the order of creation, (2) maintain the order of creation,
and (3) when necessary, restore the order of creation. Rituals of
founding, maintenance, and restoration are prescribed as ways in
which humans may participate with God in the continuing processes of
creation and history.[25] The altar, the focal point of ritual activity,
becomes a symbol of the intersection and interaction of God and
humans in the processes of cosmos and history.

Exodus 40.16-33: The Founding of Sacred Space

Exod. 40.16-38 narrates two significantly related events. First, Moses,
acting in accordance with the instructions given by YHWH (Exodus
25–31), constructs the tabernacle (vv. 16-33). Secondly, when Moses
finishes the work of construction, the divine glory fills the tabernacle
and comes to rest on the tent (vv. 34-38). Just as Gen. 1.1–2.4a
narrates the construction of the cosmos and the founding of sacred
time, so Exod. 40.16-38 narrates the construction of the tabernacle
and begins to detail the process by which sacred space is established.

---

23. The relations between these various sets of categories must be kept in mind if
the depth and complexity of Priestly ritual is to be appreciated. I have tried to
demonstrate the interrelationship of these categories in various Priestly rituals in
Ideology, esp. pp. 229-34.

24. See O.H. Steck, *World and Environment* (BES; Nashville: Abingdon, 1980),
pp. 102-108; P. Trible, *God and the Rhetoric of Sexuality* (OBT; Philadelphia:
Fortress Press, 1978), pp. 12-23; Brueggemann, *Genesis*, pp. 31-36.

25. Ritual must be given its voice in biblical theology. The narrative construction
and construal of the world and the liturgical construction and construal of the world
have both been explored theologically. The ritual construal and construction needs
more attention. See Fretheim, *Exodus*, pp. 133-36.

The narration of the founding of sacred space,[26] however, is more complex because it (1) reflects a tension within Priestly theology itself and (2) requires the dual activity of God and humans. The tension within the Priestly thinking is reflected in the following question: what is required for the founding of sacred space? Priestly theology gives two answers. On the one hand, it is clearly God's presence that makes the place holy. God says, 'I will meet with the Israelites there [at the entrance of the tent of meeting], and it shall be sanctified [*wĕniqdaš*] by my glory; I will consecrate [*wĕqiddaštî*] the tent of meeting and the altar; Aaron also and his sons I will consecrate ['*ăqaddēš*], to serve me as priests' (Exod. 29.43-44). On the other hand, it is also ritual that makes a place holy: 'Then Moses took the anointing oil and anointed the tabernacle and all that was in it, and consecrated [*wayqaddēš*] them' (Lev. 8.10). Sacred space is founded through the dual process of the manifestation of the divine presence and the enactment of the appropriate ritual. In terms of the founding of the sacred space of the tabernacle, this dual requirement reflects the Priestly view that the entrance of the tent of meeting and the altar serve as the primary places where the divine–human encounter occurs. Since sacred space provides the 'common ground' for this meeting, it can only be effected through the dual activity of the two parties. The directive to observe the sabbath as a day set apart is based on the Priestly call to imitate God in observing a day of rest (Exod. 31.12-17).[27] Sacred time is founded by God.[28] With the construction of the tabernacle, however, creation is understood as a continuing process *within history*, i.e., as being contextualized in part by the temporal categories established 'in the beginning', which require the cooperative activity of God and humans. Thus, the founding of sacred space, especially because of the significance of sacred space as divine dwelling place within the context of Israel's history, requires both God's presence and human enactment of appropriate ritual.[29]

Further, it must be recognized that the Priestly traditions place the

26. On space as a ritual category in biblical religions, see J.Z. Smith, *To Take Place* (Chicago: University of Chicago Press, 1987), pp. 96-117.

27. See the brief comment of Levenson, *Creation*, p. 82.

28. Westermann, *Genesis*, pp. 170-72.

29. For a theological discussion of the issue of divine presence, see W. Brueggemann, 'The Crisis and Promise of Presence in Israel', in P.D. Miller (ed.), *Old Testament Theology* (Minneapolis: Fortress Press, 1992), pp. 150-82.

founding of sacred space in the larger context of the founding of cosmos.[30] There are parallel features found in the instructions for the construction of the tabernacle in Exodus 25–31 and the creation in Gen. 1.1–2.4a.[31] First, the process of creation in Gen. 1.1–2.4a takes place in seven days and the text emphasizes God's speech. Similarly, the divine instructions for constructing the tabernacle are given to Moses in seven speeches introduced with the phrase, 'and YHWH said to Moses' (Exod. 25.1; 30.11, 17, 22, 34; 31.1, 12). Secondly, as noted above, the final speech (31.12-17) instructs the Israelites to observe the sabbath as a holy day and then relates the Israelite observance of sabbath to the divine act of sabbath-founding in creation.

Exod. 40.16-38 itself gives clear evidence that the construction of the tabernacle is significantly related to the construction of the cosmos. First, Moses undertakes the construction of the tabernacle on the first day of the first month (v. 17).[32] The construction of the tabernacle thus occurs on the anniversary of the beginning of God's construction of the cosmos. Secondly, the structure of Exod. 40.16-33 breaks Moses' activity into seven parts, as indicated by the statement that Moses did things 'just as YHWH commanded him' (vv. 19, 21, 23, 25, 27, 29, 32). This phrase also connects the construction of the tabernacle to the instructions for it. Thirdly, the text concludes with the statement, 'so Moses finished the work'. This phrase closely parallels Gen. 2.2 ('and God finished the work that God had done') and draws attention to the 'connectedness' of cosmos and tabernacle.[33]

A discussion of the Priestly understanding of the role of the tabernacle as found in four interrelated texts will provide a larger framework for understanding the significance of the founding of sacred space. The first text, Exod. 25.1-9, stands at the beginning of the texts providing instructions for the construction of the tabernacle and

30. Fretheim, *Exodus*, pp. 270-71.

31. See the discussions of P.J. Kearney, 'Creation and Liturgy: The P Redaction of Ex 25-40', *ZAW* 89 (1977), pp. 375-87; V. Hurowitz, 'The Priestly Account of Building the Tabernacle', *JAOS* 105 (1985), pp. 21-30; Levenson, *Creation*, pp. 80-86; Fretheim, *Exodus*, pp. 268-72.

32. Blenkinsopp ('The Structure of P', pp. 283-84) discusses the importance of this date for Priestly theology.

33. Blenkinsopp, 'The Structure of P', pp. 280-83; N. Lohfink, 'Creation and Salvation in Priestly Theology', *TD* 30 (1982), pp. 3-6.

consists of (1) a call for contributions from the people, (2) specifications for materials that are needed, and (3) a statement concerning the purpose of the tabernacle. It reads in part:

> YHWH said to Moses: 'Tell the Israelites to take for me an offering; from all whose hearts prompt them to give you shall receive the offering for me... And have them make me a sanctuary, so that I may dwell among them. In accordance with all that I show you concerning the pattern of the tabernacle and of all its furniture, so you shall make it' (Exod. 25.1-2, 8-9).

Two comments are in order for the present argument. First, this text supports the view that the construction of the tabernacle and the founding of sacred space require the dual activity of YHWH (instructions) and Israel (materials). Second, the tabernacle will be the dwelling place of YHWH *in the midst* of Israel. This is the place at which the divine presence will be manifested to Israel.

The second text, Exod. 29.44-46, also understands the tent to be the dwelling place of God and relates the divine presence in the midst of Israel to the exodus from Egypt.

> I will consecrate [*wĕqiddaštî*] the tent of meeting and the altar; Aaron also and his sons I will consecrate ['*ăqaddēš*], to serve me as priests. And I will dwell among the people of Israel, and will be their God. And they shall know that I am YHWH their God, who brought them forth out of Egypt in order that I might dwell in their midst. I am YHWH their God.

This statement is of crucial theological significance for the Priestly traditions and provides important clues for understanding the larger Priestly story. The reason for the exodus from Egypt is clearly stated—in order that YHWH might dwell in the midst of the people. A crucial aspect of what it means for Israel to know that YHWH is Israel's God is for Israel to experience the divine presence in its midst. This understanding of the exodus as a basis for Israel's knowledge of God is already indicated in the Priestly account of the commissioning of Moses in Exod. 6.2-8. YHWH states, 'I will take you as my people, and I will be your God. You shall know that I am YHWH your God, who has freed you from the burdens of the Egyptians' (v. 7). Thus, the tabernacle as divine dwelling place forms a significant part of the future that God anticipates and acts to create for Israel in freeing the nation from Egyptian oppression. At the same time, the tabernacle realizes, in part, the promise made to the ancestors. In Gen. 17.4-8, God promises to establish an everlasting covenant with Abraham's descendants and to give them the land of Canaan. In that context God declares, 'and I will be their God' (v. 8). This promise means that the story of God and the story of the descendants of Abraham and Sarah will become one story. The promise, reiterated in God's commissioning of Moses, is realized in the construction of the tabernacle. Thus, for the Priestly traditions, both the promise of God to the ancestors and the redemptive activity of God in the exodus anticipate a future in which the divine presence dwells in the midst of Israel in the tabernacle.

Exod. 25.10-22, the third text, details the instructions for the construction of the ark of the covenant and concludes with the following statement, 'There I will meet with you, and from above the *kappōret*, from between the two cherubim that are on the ark of the covenant, I will deliver to you all my instructions for the Israelites' (v. 22). While this text does not focus specifically on the tabernacle, it is important in the present discussion in that the ark is placed inside the tabernacle and is associated with the divine presence. The tabernacle is not only the dwelling place of Israel's God; it also serves as the meeting place for God and Moses and will be the place from which God will give commandments to Israel. This text clearly recognizes the continuous presence and activity of God in the life and history of Israel through God's manifestation above and communication from the ark of the covenant, which is inside the tabernacle.

Finally, Exod. 40.1-15 summarizes the instructions for erecting the tabernacle, including a statement that anticipates the ordination of the priesthood (cf. Exod. 29.44-46 above) and so the tabernacle as cultic center. Moses is told to bring Aaron and his sons to the entrance of the tent and anoint them to be priests. The need for a priesthood clearly reflects the Priestly view of the tabernacle as cultic site and, as will be seen below, the final ritual founding of sacred space will occur in conjunction with the founding and ordination of the priesthood. Thus, in the Priestly traditions the tabernacle is understood as divine dwelling place, the place of divine–human encounter, the place for continuing divine instruction, and the place of ritual activity.

The construction and founding of sacred space must be seen in the convergence of three distinct yet ultimately inseparable contexts—the continuing dynamics of cosmos, the history of Israel, and the ritual life of Israel. Linked as it is to the founding of cosmos, the erection of the tabernacle must be viewed as a continuation of the founding of cosmos.[34] The construction of sacred space—conceived as divine dwelling place, the place of meeting, the place of instruction, and the place of ritual—is understood as part of the construction of cosmos. Thus, the larger context of cosmos includes the founding of sacred time, the sabbath, as well as the founding of sacred space, the tabernacle. In addition, the Priestly traditions place the founding of Israel as the people of God in the larger context of the founding of cosmos.[35] Cosmogony and history converge and refuse to be separated. The founding of cosmos is not only an event in the past; it is also the present and continuing context for the unfolding of the history of God and Israel.

The actual erection of the tabernacle by Moses is narrated in concise language. The emphasis throughout Exod. 40.16-33 is that Moses did everything just as YHWH had commanded him. The conclusion of this scene is crucial for an adequate appreciation of the larger Priestly theology. When Moses had finished the work, the cloud covered the tent and the glory of YHWH filled the tabernacle. While the tabernacle will be anointed and consecrated in a later ritual (see Leviticus 8), it is now set apart by the presence of God as manifested by the glory. This not only suggests divine approval but also serves as graphic and dramatic realization of the divine promise to be Israel's God and to dwell in the midst of the people of Israel. This is further supported by the image of the cloud and fire leading the people in the wilderness. In a reversal of Gen. 1.1–2.4a, in which humans are called to participate in the continuing maintenance of the divine order, this text narrates YHWH's participation in the maintenance of the continuing life of Israel. YHWH has entered dramatically into the life of Israel. The founding of cosmos and the history of a people are inseparably bound together in images of the divine creator dwelling in the midst of a people and leading them through the wilderness. There is a radical convergence of stories.

Leviticus 8–9: The Founding of Sacred Status

Four primary events take place in Leviticus 8–9: (1) the tabernacle and altar are anointed and made holy; (2) Aaron is anointed and made

34. Levenson, *Creation*, pp. 82-87; Fretheim, *Exodus*, pp. 268-77.
35. See R. Knierim, 'Cosmos and History in Israel's Theology', *HBT* 3 (1981), pp. 59-123.

holy; (3) Aaron's sons are ordained; and (4) the newly ordained and initiated Aaronide priesthood offers sacrifices and offerings for the first time. Two reasons argue for the location of these rituals in the larger context of the on-going founding of cosmos that has already been seen in the establishment of sacred time and space. First, these rituals continue the process begun in Exod. 40.16-38.[36] The tabernacle has been constructed and the glory of YHWH has entered it. Now, it will be ritually anointed and made holy. It is clear that the founding of sacred space is not complete until the anointing ritual is enacted. Sacred space must be ritually founded. Secondly, Leviticus 8 is partitioned into seven units by the repeated statement that Moses did 'just as YHWH commanded him' (vv. 4, 9, 13, 17, 21, 29, 36).[37] This parallels a structural feature seen in Gen. 1.1–2.4a and Exod. 40.16-33.

The discussion will focus on Leviticus 8 in terms of (1) the completion of the founding of sacred space and (2) the founding of sacred status in the ordination of the priesthood. The ritual has the following basic structure:

I.   Preparations (vv. 1-5)
II. Ritual washing of Aaron, his sons, and his clothing (vv. 6-9)
III. Anointing of the tabernacle, altar, and Aaron (vv. 10-12)
IV. Ritual clothing of Aaron's sons (v. 13)
V.   Sacrifices offered (vv. 14-29)
     A. The bull of purgation (vv. 14-17)
     B. The ram of the whole-burnt offering (vv. 18-21)
     C. The ram of ordination (vv. 22-29)
VI. Anointing of Aaron *and* his sons (v. 30)
VII. Final instructions (vv. 31-36)

36. It has long been argued that Leviticus 1–7 interrupts the *narrative* flow of Exod. 40.16-38 and Leviticus 8–9. This literary-critical evaluation is based in no small measure on the belief that Priestly narratives must be seen as distinct from Priestly ritual texts. Such a strong disjunction between these two types of texts must be critically reexamined. While the instructions for the sacrifices and offerings in Leviticus 1–7 may disrupt the narrative, they do not disrupt the logic of the larger story. The divine glory designates the place that is to be consecrated. At the same time, however, it indicates the place where the ritual of founding must be enacted in order to complete the process of founding. Before the ritual can be completed, instructions for the ritual must be given. Thus, theological and dramatic considerations may need to be given more attention than strictly literary-critical, if the redaction is to be understood.

37. On the structure of this text, see Milgrom, *Leviticus*, pp. 542-44.

The introduction states that the ritual is to take place at the door of the tent of meeting in the presence of the whole congregation (vv. 1-5). Three comments are in order. First, it must be recognized that the consecration of the tabernacle and the ordination of the priesthood are dual elements of a community ritual and must take place in the presence and context of the community. Secondly, the ritual takes place at the door of the tent, the place where the sacred intersects the life of the people in ritual.[38] The door of the tent is the place where the people will bring their ritual sacrifices and offerings to the priesthood for presentation to the God who dwells within the tent and in the midst of the people. Thirdly, Leviticus 8 combines and interweaves the ritual consecration of sacred space and the priesthood. The ritual for making the tabernacle holy is enacted in conjunction with the ritual for making those persons holy who will serve in the holy place. Sacred space and sacred status are mutually founded and bound together.

The ritual consecration and founding of sacred space has two distinct aspects. The first has to do with the anointing oil that Moses places on the tabernacle and sprinkles on the altar (vv. 10-11).[39] The text specifically states the purpose of this oil: to consecrate (*qdš*) the objects on which it is placed. The second aspect of the ritual process, as it relates to sacred space, involves the sacrifice of the bull of purgation, the whole-burnt ram, and the ram of ordination. While the anointing oil functions to sanctify the tabernacle area as holy space, the presentation of these sacrifices serves to establish this area as the appropriate space for the performance of ritual. This offering of the sacrifices provides the basic pattern for their future presentation. Thus, sacred space *and* ritual space are simultaneously founded in this ritual.

At the same time and in parallel fashion, the priesthood is consecrated for its role in the cult. The structure of this part of the ritual demonstrates the interconnectedness of sacred space and the priesthood.

38. See Milgrom, *Leviticus*, pp. 147-49, for a discussion of 'the door of the tent'.

39. See Milgrom, *Leviticus*, pp. 545-49, for an extensive discussion of the literary-critical problems associated with Leviticus 8 and Exodus 29 and the anointing of the tabernacle.

I.   Ritual washing of Aaron and his sons (v. 6)
II.   Ritual clothing of Aaron as high priest (vv. 7-9)
III.   Ritual anointing of the tabernacle and altar with the anointing oil (vv. 10-11)
IV.   Ritual anointing of Aaron with the anointing oil (v. 12)
V.   Ritual clothing of Aaron's sons (v. 13)

Three points need to be made concerning this part of the ritual. First, it must be noted that Moses is the one who presides over the ritual. This is necessary because the priesthood does not yet exist. Thus, Moses might best be viewed in these texts as the inaugurator of the tabernacle cult.[40] Secondly, the ritual clothing of Aaron and his sons functions as an indicator of the new status into which they are now moving.[41] Thirdly, Aaron alone, presumably as high priest, is initially anointed with the anointing oil. This special anointing of Aaron in conjunction with the tabernacle and the altar serves to consecrate sacred and ritual space and, at the same time, to sanctify the person who presides over this sacred and ritual space.

The presentation of the sacrifices and offerings in relation to the ordination of the priests may be viewed in at least two ways. First, it may be said that these sacrifices and offerings are presented on behalf of the priesthood and carry their normal ritual functions. Secondly, the presentation of the sacrifices and offerings may be said to be instructional. Moses, as the inaugurator of the tabernacle cult, demonstrates for the priests the proper ritual procedures. In rites of passage, the initiates are often given instructions regarding their new status.[42] It is likely that both these views are represented in the text.

An exception to the normal ritual structure is the sacrifice of the ram of ordination. It is generally recognized that it is similar to the 'well-being offering' (*zebaḥ šĕlāmîm*) and falls in the place normally occupied by these sacrifices. Levine has argued that the *šĕlāmîm* were often concerned with acts of dedication and beginnings.[43] This makes sense in the context of the founding of the priesthood. The ritual

40. Gorman, *Ideology*, pp. 141-49. For a discussion of Moses as priest, see T.B. Dozeman, *God on the Mountain* (SBLMS, 37; Atlanta: Scholars Press, 1989), pp. 136-41.

41. Gorman, *Ideology*, pp. 117-18.

42. Turner, *Dramas*, pp. 239-40.

43. B.A. Levine, *In the Presence of the Lord* (SJLA, 5; Leiden: Brill, 1974), pp. 27-33.

undertaken with the ram of ordination differs, however, from the well-being offering in a significant way. The blood of the ram of ordination is placed on the extremities of Aaron and his sons (vv. 22-24), an act that appears elsewhere only in the ritual for the recovered leper (Lev. 14.14). Both cases are concerned with major transitions of persons from one state to another and reflect a dangerous transition—the leper from a state like death to renewed life and the priests from a common status to the holy status of priesthood. Passage into the holy is dangerous. Indeed, the priesthood, in its cultic and mediatorial role, functions at the intersection of the sacred and the profane, purity and impurity, hope and despair, life and death. The blood of the ram of ordination moves Aaron and his sons safely into their official status as priests, i.e., those who traffic in the sacred realm.[44]

A final anointing of Aaron and his vestments and of Aaron's sons and their vestments is described in v. 30. In this case, the mixture used is a combination of the anointing oil and the blood taken from the altar. As the text clearly states, this act serves to consecrate the persons and objects on which the mixture is placed.[45] This is more than just another act of consecration, however, within the larger ritual. It is specifically designed to bind together the priesthood and the altar in a common moment of consecration. Sacred space and sacred status are merged through their common anointing.

The concluding instructions in Lev. 8.31-36 emphasize that the priests are to remain at the door of the tent for seven days, the time necessary to complete their ordination. This period reflects the seven days of creation, as well as the seven days of rites of major transition. On the eighth day, Aaron and his sons offer the first sacrifices as the newly founded priesthood (Leviticus 9). These sacrifices are to be presented by the priests in the presence of *the whole congregation* so that the glory of YHWH will appear to the people (v. 6).[46] The

44. See Gorman (*Ideology*, pp. 124-35) for a discussion of this ritual in terms of the movement of the priests from death to life.

45. See Milgrom, *Leviticus*, pp. 532-34.

46. The statement that the fire was seen by 'all the people' (Lev. 9.24) recalls the report that the descent of the glory in the cloud onto the tabernacle was visible 'before the eyes of all the house of Israel' (Exod. 40.16-38) and the note that the glory on Mt Sinai was seen by the people (Exod. 24.15-18). This emphasizes the presence of the people in relation to the cultic presence of God. The tabernacling presence has now become the cultic presence of fire. An excellent discussion of the Priestly view of presence is found in Dozeman, *God on the Mountain*, pp. 87-143.

sacrifices are offered as prescribed and Aaron blesses the people.

> And the glory of YHWH appeared to all the people. Fire came forth from
> YHWH and consumed the burnt offerings and the fat on the altar. And
> when all the people saw it, they shouted and fell on their faces (vv. 23b-
> 24).

The sacrifices and the priesthood have been accepted. The tabernacle
cult is now founded—sacred space, sacred activity, and sacred
persons.

Conclusion

This paper has demonstrated that Gen. 1.1–2.4a; Exod. 40.16-33; and
Leviticus 8–9 may be read as rituals of founding that create sacred
time, space, and status. For the Priestly traditions, the world is
founded in and through ritual. At the same time, these ritual acts of
founding are related to the Priestly understanding of history. Cosmos,
history, and ritual converge in Priestly theology. Both cosmos and
history are viewed as in-process and are understood to be constituted
through the ritual activity of God and human beings. In the Priestly
traditions, both (1) cosmos and history and (2) the divine and human
stories are radically and dramatically merged in, through, and by
ritual.

A MODEL FOR A THEOLOGY OF BIBLICAL HISTORICAL NARRATIVES
Proposed and Demonstrated with the Books of Chronicles

Rodney K. Duke

Introduction

In the section, 'History, Tradition, and Story', of the closing chapter of the history of Old Testament theology by Hayes and Prussner, Hayes notes that there has been a shift by some theologians to explore the biblical historical narratives as story.[1] He closes the section by raising the following issues:

> Exactly how such an approach to the Old Testament as story will work itself out has yet to be demonstrated in Old Testament theology. Does it mean that theology will consist of merely retelling the story or merely reading the story? If theology deals in some fashion with truth claims, how does this factor impact upon reading the narrative as if it were fiction or no more than history-like? Can the modern person, or could the ancient person, listen to and learn from a history-like story without becoming engaged in the question of the facticity of its episodes? Is the resort to story as a description merely a means to avoid the issues over which the debates about history, salvation-history, God's acts in history, and other matters have so long raged?[2]

In response to some of the above questions, I wish to identify the working assumptions that support a model for the theological exegesis of biblical historical narrative,[3] to present the model itself, and to

---

1. J.H. Hayes and F. Prussner, *Old Testament Theology: Its History and Development* (Atlanta: John Knox, 1985), pp. 260-64.

2. Hayes and Prussner, *Theology*, p. 264.

3. By 'historical narrative' I am referring broadly to narrative texts written from the authorial stance of recording the past. I am not imposing modern presuppositional and stylistic criteria that might label such texts as 'history-like' or 'fictionalized history'. The primary criterion that distinguishes historical narrative from fictional narrative is not form (they share the same form) or subject matter or aesthetic appeal

demonstrate how this model would work by applying it briefly to the books of Chronicles. I am advocating a type of theological exegesis that attempts to be sensitive to how the genre of historical narrative communicates meaning in accord with one of its rhetorical functions.[4] By the phrase 'rhetorical functions' I am referring to primary functions that I would identify as operative behind the Old Testament genre of historical narrative, such as the following: (1) to preserve the traditions, and consequently the identity, of Israel; (2) to respond to the needs and questions of the intended audience of the author/editor; and (3) to present and inculcate a world-view, a description of how the world operates.[5] My primary focus, however, will be on the last

or the citation of sources or even the credibility of the events to a given reader. It is the authorial stance which claims that the text refers to the actual past. For further discussion of this position, see P. Hernadi, 'Clio's Cousins: Historiography as Translation, Fiction, and Criticism', *New Literary History* 7 (1976), pp. 245-57; P. Ricoeur, 'The Narrative Function', *Semeia* 13 (1978), pp. 177-202; R. Scholes, 'Afterthoughts on Narrative II: Language, Narrative, and Anti-Narrative', *Critical Inquiry* 7 (1980), pp. 204-12; C. Walhout, 'Texts and Actions', in R. Lundin, A.C. Thiselton, and C. Walhout (eds.), *The Responsibility of Hermeneutics* (Grand Rapids: Eerdmans, 1985), pp. 69-77; and within biblical studies, M. Sternberg, *The Poetics of Biblical Narrative: Ideological Literature and the Drama of Reading* (Indiana Studies in Biblical Literature; Bloomington: Indiana University Press, 1985), pp. 23-35.

In the history of biblical scholarship regarding the 'emergence' of Israelite history writing and regarding the classification of biblical narrative into genres, one finds that the above distinction between fiction and history writing was generally overlooked. For a survey of this history of research, see J. Van Seters, *In Search of History: Historiography in the Ancient World and the Origins of Biblical History* (New Haven: Yale University Press, 1983), pp. 209-48.

Also, I am not making a distinction among such proposed sub-genres of historical narrative in the Bible as 'report', 'historical story', etc. For a sensitive description of biblical historical literature, see B.O. Long, *1 Kings: With an Introduction to Historical Literature* (FOTL, 9; Grand Rapids: Eerdmans, 1984), pp. 2-8.

4.   Jesper Høgenhaven proposes that one's theological exposition be organized by genre (*Problems and Prospects of Old Testament Theology* [Biblical Seminar; Sheffield: JSOT Press, 1987], pp. 95-98).

5.   In regard to the third function, the mimetic quality of narrative has been recognized in literary criticism at least since Aristotle's *Poetics*, although the nature of narrative referentiality is a debated topic in contemporary literary criticism. Until recently, literary critics, having drawn a false dichotomy between history and fiction, have focused on the mimetic quality of fictional narrative. However, historical narrative shares the same formative elements of narrative as fictional narrative. In

function, because it holds the greatest import for theological exegesis.

In summary, the model that I propose for the analysis of biblical historical narratives rests on four observations. First, the creative selection of subject matter by the 'historian' from the historical field of the past, as found in the historical narrative, reveals and communicates that person's values. Secondly, the relationships that the historian perceives among past events in the historical field communicate the laws of reality operating within the world-view of that person. Thirdly, the weaving of the events into the plot of a narrative story-line communicates a teleology or direction to history. Finally, the elements sketched above (values, laws of reality, and direction of history) combine to communicate implicitly a general ideology that prescribes the proper course of human action within the world.[6]

Working Assumptions

Before developing the model outlined above, a few issues involving presuppositions and methodology need to be identified and clarified.

other words, history, conceived of and communicated in the form of narrative, participates in the mimetic function of all stories. See Hernadi, 'Clio's Cousins', pp. 245-57; L.O. Mink, 'History and Fiction as Modes of Comprehending', *New Literary Inquiry* 1 (1969–70), pp. 541-58; Ricoeur, 'The Narrative Function', pp. 177-202; R. Scholes and R. Kellogg, *The Nature of Narrative* (Oxford: Oxford University Press, 1966); H. White, *Metahistory* (Baltimore: Johns Hopkins University, 1973); *idem*, 'The Value of Narrativity in the Representation of Reality', *Critical Inquiry* 7 (1980), pp. 5-27.

6. The last three categories, as well as much of my understanding of the nature of how one constructs historical narrative, come from White, *Metahistory*, pp. 1-42. My system of analysis differs from White's in some major respects. First, our goals are quite different. White seeks to identify and classify the surface structures of historical narratives in order to work back to the deeper structure which characterizes the historical imagination. I part company with this philosophical goal of finding a structure at the deeper level. I find that the so-called 'surface structures' are those which are most important in communicating meaning, particularly of a theological nature, to the audience of the narrative. Secondly, for each of his categories of analysis, White works with only four possible typological options. For instance, according to White, the plot one perceives in history will either be comedic, tragic, romantic, or satirical. Although such categories are helpful, I find them too limiting. Further, I am less interested in labeling each 'structure' of the historical narrative than I am in understanding what the historian communicates. Finally, I have simplified, modified, and supplemented White's original method of analysis so much that I would not want him to be blamed for my results.

First, there are various descriptions of the scope and goal of biblical theology. I am in agreement with the view that a distinction should be drawn between histories of biblical religion on the one hand and biblical theology on the other. A history of Israelite religion, for example, turns to the HB as one source among many in the search for data. Such an effort operates within the field of historical reconstruction and primarily serves the interests of academicians. On the other hand, a theology of the HB turns to the texts of the HB as the scripture or canon of a community of faith in search for meaning.[7] This enterprise operates within the field of hermeneutics and serves the interests of a community of faith. Such a distinction identifies biblical theology as a hermeneutical inquiry.

Secondly, the model of theological exegesis that I am proposing assumes that one can recover something of what the text was intended to communicate to the original audience, despite all the pitfalls of such an effort.[8] This goal may be achieved in part by exploring the rhetorical function of the genre employed and its literary features. That is to say, one should first ask: What is the purpose of this genre? What kind of impact on its audience was intended? How is this impact achieved? If we understand how the genre functions to communicate an impact, then we will come closer to ascertaining the meaning intended by the author or editor.[9]

A significant backdrop against which I am working is the continuing debate over the method to be used in a final synthesis of the biblical material at the level of canon. Questions have been raised about which method best synthesizes the whole of the biblical material, or if such a

---

7. So, too, B.S. Childs, *Old Testament Theology in a Canonical Context* (Philadelphia: Fortress Press, 1985), pp. 6-12.

8. In defense of seeking the 'authorial intention', an admittedly difficult enterprise, see Walhout's discussion of the limits of the literature-as-language model and the principles of the literature-as-action model ('Texts', pp. 34-49); Sternberg, *Poetics*, pp. 8-11; and nn. 9 and 14 below.

9. An author's intention and a genre's function are not to be equated, but they are related. The communication process is deliberate. An author starts with a rhetorical intention that she/he hopes will equal the impact the reader receives when encountering the text. In the composition of the text, the author then employs various formal elements and literary devices because of the way they generally function to create an impact on the reader. Therefore, an exploration of the genre and its particular literary features, as well as the effort to place the text in its total historical and literary context, should lead back to some insight into the intention of the text.

task should even be attempted in light of the variety of material found in the Bible.[10] Although the model that I propose does not function at the level of canon, it has implications for the questions addressed at that level. Specifically, I am advocating that theological exegesis be more genre-sensitive than it generally has been, before one seeks a final synthesis of theological meaning. At a sociological level, biblical exegesis has been very genre sensitive, but not so often at the theological level. Prior to the 'Biblical Theology Movement' of the mid-twentieth century, one tended to do a theology of any text of the HB, regardless of its genre, by looking for propositional statements, or by identifying and examining key themes, or by doing theological word studies, or by asking how the subject matter related to a perceived central focus of the scriptures. The Biblical Theology Movement placed an emphasis on historical narratives, and the proponents of the movement tended to see the historical narratives as testimonies to the revelation located in the mighty acts of God.[11] Wright, for example, found the locus of meaning for historical narratives to be in their role of pointing back to the events of revelation.[12] Von Rad stressed the function of narratives in the actualization and re-actualization of the community's understanding of their identity and place in Yahweh's economy of promise and fulfillment.[13] Still, this emphasis on historical narratives did not lead to a new method of analysis and synthesis founded upon the rhetorical functions of this genre.[14]

10. Hayes and Prussner, *Theology*, pp. 257-60.

11. Hayes and Prussner, *Theology*, pp. 209-20, 239-45.

12. G.E. Wright, *God Who Acts* (SBT, 8; London: SCM, 1952).

13. G. von Rad, *Old Testament Theology* (2 vols.; Edinburgh/London: Oliver & Boyd, 1962, 1965), I, pp. 105-28; II, pp. 410-25.

14. In connection with the last mentioned point, I recognize that a plethora of approaches to reading the biblical narratives has arisen since the period of the Biblical Theology Movement. To cite just a few: Sternberg, *Poetics*; D.M. Gunn, *The Fate of King Saul: An Interpretation of a Biblical Story* (JSOTSup, 14; Sheffield: JSOT Press, 1980); D.J.A. Clines, D.M. Gunn, and A.J. Hauser, *Art and Meaning: Rhetoric in Biblical Literature* (JSOTSup, 19; Sheffield: JSOT Press, 1982); A. Berlin, *Poetics and Interpretation of Biblical Narrative* (Sheffield: Almond Press, 1983); and other works in this publisher's 'Bible and Literature Series'.

Such works have generally identified and illustrated specific literary devices and have discussed theoretically the power of narrative for expressing theology. However, I know of none that has focused on the rhetorical function of the genre and sought to present an overarching model for theological synthesis—although I am

Thirdly, my proposal is based on the conviction that one of the most significant rhetorical functions of historical narrative is to present a world-view. In modern Western culture, when one asks how we

sure such a work must be out there.

Further, I also particularly wish to distinguish my approach from those that are derived from the so-called 'post-modern' hermeneutics. This hermeneutical trend emphasizes the multiplicity of meanings a text may generate and often maintains that there is no such thing as the intention of an author or editor to be recovered. Such claims place it outside the enterprise of biblical theology as described above. Since the claims of this trend stand in strong opposition to the model I present, I offer the following brief critique of it in defense of my proposal.

Current biblical literary criticism, as defined by post-modern hermeneutics, appears to be the product of some questionable shifts in literary theory. First, in Western thought, beginning in the seventeenth century, a distinction was made between aesthetics and ethics that carried over to literary theory. One now conceived a category of literature, 'imaginative literature' or *belles-lettres*, which had solely and purely a poetic or aesthetic function. (For this historical shift, see R. Lundin, 'Our Hermeneutical Inheritance', in R. Lundin, A.C. Thiselton, and C. Walhout, *The Responsibility of Hermeneutics* [Grand Rapids: Eerdmans, 1985], pp. 1-29, 115-20, esp. p. 9.) Secondly, biblical scholars have been applying the theories of current literary criticism to biblical historical narrative and other genres of biblical texts, as if such texts belonged to the artificial category of *belles-lettres*. Thirdly, in the twentieth century, 'literary criticism' has shifted to 'philosophy of language', as if a literary text were just a piece of language and that an analysis of language would sufficiently explain how literature functions. (See Walhout, 'Texts', pp. 31-34.)

All three shifts are reductionistic. In the case of the first, literary theorists ignored that any text has several functions (e.g., emotive, conative, poetic, 'referential', etc.) that are present in every communication, although the degree of emphasis on any function varies as the type of communication varies. In the case of the second shift, even if there were such a category of literature that had solely a poetic function, the biblical texts were not produced and preserved within the mindset of this relatively recent literary theory.

In the third case, the identification of literature and language is also reductionistic. Literary theorists who make this identification tend to ignore: (1) that texts, unlike some word in the abstract, are products of deliberate actions and themselves are agents of action, so that texts have intended functions; and (2) that texts, like language in real life, belong to the realm of communication, a domain of 'common' agreement (cf. Walhout, 'Texts', pp. 34-49). The metaphysical—or better yet, ametaphysical—assumptions of some current philosophers of language may lead one to conclude that words have no pure ontic referentiality, so that one cannot validly speak of the meaning or intention of a text ('a piece of language'). Nevertheless, one must not ignore that societal conventions regarding a language and its genres actually do produce effective communication. For example, certainly the language event of

should evaluate historical narratives, the general reply is that one must determine whether the 'facts' of who, what, when, and where are correct. Yet when one asks why we 'do history', the answer is often on a different level: for the purpose of learning from it, how we got here, where we are headed, what mistakes should not be repeated, etc. In other words, a primary reason we do history is for the 'why' questions that it answers, viz., what it says about the way the world works. Indeed, this function was acknowledged by ancient historians such as Livy and Thucydides.[15] The who, what, when, and where are not the locus of the meaning that we generally seek. They are the warp through which one weaves the narrative. They are just the bones. The 'why' is the flesh and blood of doing history. A primary rhetorical function of historical narrative, then, is to convey meaning, meaning about how the world works and the implicit concomitant response that one should make. Despite the way we modern people cloak history-telling in a rhetorical style of 'objectivity', we have first conceived a view of the world and how it works, a view which we then communicate through the historical narratives that we construct. If historical narratives do, in fact, have the rhetorical function of conveying meaning about how the world works, then it follows that one should employ a model of theological exegesis that is sensitive to just how the genre of historical narratives conveys that meaning.

Finally, before proceeding to the model itself, it is useful to note

---

encountering the word 'dog' creates a different conception for each person. 'Dog' has no pure ontic referent pointing to some Platonic, archetypal dog. However, if someone with functional control of English is going to a pet store to bring me back a pet of my choice, and I say, 'Bring me a dog, not a cat', communication will take place and the intention of the communication will be fulfilled. In the above example of communication, 'dog' does have some referentiality, because there is sufficient agreement between the addresser and addressee about what constitutes 'dogness', although their individual connotations vary. It seems reasonable to me, therefore, to ask about the function of a literary genre, to ask about the social and historical setting of a text, and to expect to recover something of what the text was intended to communicate.

15. Livy discusses how one may learn moral lessons through history in the 'Preface' of his *The History of Rome* (trans. D. Spillan and C. Edmonds; Harper's Classical Library; 2 vols.; New York: Harper & Brothers, 1875–81). Thucydides sees his work as having abiding value, since, human nature being what it is, events of the past will be repeated in the future (*History of the Peloponnesian War* [trans. R. Warner; Penguin Classics, 139; Baltimore: Penguin Books, 1954], bk.1, ch. 1).

that the above understanding of the rhetorical function of historical narrative addresses one of the opening questions raised by Hayes: 'If theology deals in some fashion with truth claims, how does this factor impact upon reading the narrative as if it were fiction or no more than history-like?'[16] I would maintain that reading the biblical historical narratives as 'story', viz., in accord with a function inherent in the form used for conveying history, explores their claims about the nature of reality. To read them as 'story' is not the same as reading them as fiction.[17] What I have referred to as the 'pegs' of history are not unimportant. For the sake of preserving one's tradition and identity, they certainly are important. Moreover, if none of the 'facts' of the narrative could come from the historical field of the past, then there is obviously no support for the world that the narrative presents. On the other hand, the confusion or misplacement of some of the pegs, or even the loss of incidental ones, would not necessarily invalidate the world presented by the narrative.

16. Hayes and Prussner, *Theology*, p. 264.

17. As Sternberg notes, biblical narratives have been shaped by three sets of regulating principles: ideological, historiographic, and aesthetic (*Poetics*, pp. 41-57). However, in the practice of biblical studies the co-working of these functions has usually been overlooked. When biblical scholars who are focused on historical reconstruction have identified an ideological or aesthetic function to a text, they have tended, at best, to regard the text as poor historiography, and at worst, to relabel the genre as history-like fiction. (For examples regarding the books of Chronicles, see R.K. Duke, *The Persuasive Appeal of the Chronicler: A Rhetorical Analysis* [Bible and Literature Series, 25; Sheffield: Almond Press, 1990], pp. 13-18.) Now that the trend is to focus on the aesthetics of biblical narrative, and sometimes its ideology, once again the historiographic function is usually overlooked. (Note how the methodological discussions in Gunn ['Biblical Story and the Literary Critic', *Fate*, pp. 11-19] and in Clines, Gunn, and Hauser [Martin Kessler, 'A Methodological Setting for Rhetorical Criticism', *Art*, pp. 1-19] omit recognition of this function.) It is often believed that reading such texts as 'story' is to read them as fiction. (For such a misrepresentation, see D. Robertson, *The Old Testament and the Literary Critic* [Guides to Biblical Scholarship, Old Testament Series; Philadelphia: Fortress Press, 1977], pp. 1-10.) I am contending that all historical narratives, not just biblical ones, hold forth an ideology and share in the creative nature of story, although admittedly some are not as aesthetically pleasing as others.

Theoretical Model

My model of theological exegesis is based on the conviction that how one configures the field of the past in order to comprehend it is analogous to how one formulates any narrative. There are three explicit components of narrative, as well as a fourth implicit one.

There is first of all the selection of, or one might say the creation of, the subject matter: the key characters and events. When one 'does history', one perceives within the historical field a subject matter that corresponds to one's system of values. Therefore, when one offers such a narrative to an audience, the narrative communicates what is to be regarded as significant.

Secondly, relationships are perceived to exist among the events of the historical field. For example, on one extreme, events may be perceived and presented as mechanistically related so that event B had to follow from event A. On the other extreme, they may be perceived as random and without direct connection to each other. At this level, narratives create a world that operates according to certain perceived laws of reality. Therefore, narratives communicate meaning at a second level as they present a view of how the world operates.

Thirdly, although the field of the past has no beginning, middle, or ending, one still configures the past in terms of a story-line with a beginning, middle, and end. As a result, when one does history, one presents it teleologically, viz., history takes on movement and purpose. Therefore, historical narratives communicate meaning on a third level as they weave the events of the historical field into a story. They present the direction in which reality moves.

Finally, there is a fourth component to narratives, historical or fictional, which is drawn from the first three components. If one knows what values are significant (from the first component), and if one knows the laws of reality operative in the world and the direction things are moving as a result (from the second and third components), then implicitly an ideology is presented to guide human action within that world. Therefore, narratives also communicate meaning on the level of ideology and attempt to influence the audience's behavior.

Application of the Method to the Books of Chronicles[18]

I would like to demonstrate in brief form how this model of theological exegesis might be employed by applying it to the books of Chronicles. The first level of analysis focuses on the Chronicler's values. The subject matter for the Chronicler's history has as its primary characters Yahweh, the Davidic monarch, the cult and the Levitical priesthood, prophetic figures, and 'all Israel', a phrase that varies in the scope of its constituency in Chronicles.[19] The primary events of the Chronicler's narrative are events that have bearing on the establishment of the Davidic monarchy, the establishment of the cultic institutions of the worship of Yahweh, the continued proper worship of Yahweh, and the status of Israel, viz., Israel's level of prosperity and success or its level of decline vis-à-vis its faithfulness to Yahweh. These elements are presented in stereotypical terms: people are good or bad, and events follow certain patterns (e.g., good actions result in success and evil actions result in calamity).[20] These are the elements which are of greatest value.

The second level of analysis identifies the Chronicler's laws of

---

18. It is not my claim that the following observations are unique to me, but rather that the model I present offers a new perspective for synthesizing the theology of Chronicles. For a fuller discussion of the nature of Chronicles, see Duke, *Persuasive*, esp. pp. 47-79. For some representative works on the theology of Chronicles, see: G. von Rad, *Das Geschichtsbild des Chronistischen Werkes* (BWANT, 54; Stuttgart: W. Kohlhammer, 1930); A.C. Welch, *The Work of the Chronicler: Its Purpose and Date* (London: Oxford University Press, 1939); R. North, 'Theology of the Chronicler', *JBL* 82 (1963), pp. 369-81; J.M. Myers, 'The Kerygma of the Chronicler: History and Theology in the Service of Religion', *Int* 20 (1966), pp. 259-73; R. Mosis, *Untersuchungen zur Theologie des chronistischen Geschichtswerkes* (FThSt, 92; Freiburg: Herder, 1973); P.R. Ackroyd, 'The Theology of the Chronicler', *LTQ* 8 (1973), pp. 101-16; H.G.M. Williamson, *Israel in the Books of Chronicles* (Cambridge: Cambridge University Press, 1977); R.L. Braun, 'Chronicles, Ezra and Nehemiah: Theology and Literary History', in J.A. Emerton (ed.), *Studies in the Historical Books of the Old Testament* (VTSup, 30; Leiden: Brill, 1979), pp. 52-64; R.B. Dillard, 'Reward and Punishment in Chronicles: The Theology of Immediate Retribution', *WTJ* 46 (1984), pp. 164-72; and S. Japhet, *The Ideology of the Book of Chronicles and its Place in Biblical Thought* (BEATAJ, 9; Frankfurt am Main: Peter Lang, 1989).

19. See particularly Williamson, *Israel*.

20. See particularly Dillard, 'Reward'.

reality. The Chronicler depicts a world in which Yahweh is the primary agent of history. The existence of Yahweh and Yahweh's ability to intervene in history are assumed from the outset. In the Chronicler's world God is sovereign, but God does not dictate the course that the chosen people take. All Israel, the kings, and the Levitical priesthood are held accountable for their actions, since they are responsible for maintaining a right relationship with God. They choose to seek or forsake Yahweh. Indeed, it is the action of seeking (or forsaking) Yahweh that sets into motion the primary laws of reality perceived by the Chronicler.[21] 'Seeking' and 'forsaking', as defined distinctively by the Chronicler in cultic terms, result in divine blessing or cursing, respectively. Furthermore, these laws of divine reaction are short-lived in comparison, for example, to those operative in the narrative of Samuel–Kings. In the Chronicler's presentation of reality, reversals of blessing or cursing could take place within a given reign or generation—even more than once. The potential for a change of fate always existed.

The third level of analysis seeks the Chronicler's teleology of history. Much of the biblical narrative consists of individual stories within a greater story. This is true as well for Chronicles, within whose larger plot Israel is birthed, receives the Davidic king, finds its identity in the worship of Yahweh, has its life threatened, and is promised restoration. The greater story-line of Chronicles, however, has little movement and generates little attention. It has been noted by von Rad and others that the Chronicler presents a vignette or picture of each Davidic king as a self-contained slice of history with little or no movement from king to king.[22] Developments of tensions and resolutions within each slice simply demonstrate further the divine laws of reward and retribution operating in the world.

When one compares the emplotment of the historical narrative of Samuel–Kings to Chronicles, one notes that the Chronicler's emplotment is more positive in two respects.[23] First, in terms of the overall story-lines, Samuel–Kings plots a somewhat fatalistic and pessimistic course. At least from Manasseh onwards the fate of Israel appears to

21. See particularly G.E. Schaefer, 'The Significance of Seeking God in the Purpose of the Chronicler' (ThD dissertation, Southern Baptist Theological Seminary, 1972).
22. Von Rad, *Theology*, I, p. 350.
23. Duke, *Persuasive*, pp. 70-72.

be sealed; the nation is headed toward disaster (2 Kgs 21.10-15). In contrast, the story-line of Chronicles ends with the promise of restoration. Secondly, because the plots within each slice of history receive emphasis in Chronicles, and because in these separate episodes several reversals of one's status occur (being blessed or cursed), the Chronicler communicates a hopeful course of history. It is not as deterministic as the course plotted in Samuel–Kings, but is dependent on the actions of each generation and is always capable of ending well.

The fourth level of analysis uncovers the Chronicler's ideology and prescription for action. The Chronicler's presentation of the past implicitly calls for a response by his intended audience in the present. Through his stereotypical presentation of the subject matter, his portrayal of relationships among events, and his mode of emplotment, he invites his audience to evaluate each of his portraits of the genera-tions of their past and to understand why things happened as they did. In addition, the audience is implicitly invited to evaluate its current status as blessed or cursed, and to respond appropriately. Faithfulness to Yahweh is still of utmost importance, and the laws of reality that governed the past are still operative in the present. The audience now knows that seeking God brings blessing, but forsaking God brings ruin, and that the situation may be reversed for good or ill. Therefore, through his re-presentation of his audience's past, the Chronicler calls his community to a proper relationship with Yahweh and offers them the hope of blessing.

Conclusion: Contribution and Implication

In conclusion, what contribution might this model of theological exegesis make? It does not offer anything radically new and certainly overlaps with other approaches in some categories of analysis and in some of the results obtained. What it offers, however, is a different theoretical perspective about how historical narratives convey mean-ing and, therefore, a different model for analyzing and synthesizing the biblical genre of historical narrative.

Further, and by implication, the working assumptions of this model have bearing on an issue that has confronted theologians over much of this century. Those theologians, who see their task as grounded in the biblical texts as the canon of their community of faith, are faced with the question of how one may move from what the biblical texts meant in their original contexts to what they mean for communities of faith today. Nineteenth-century liberal theology openly dispensed with the biblical world-view as unenlightened. Partly in reaction against liberal theology, the Biblical Theology Movement sought to return to a biblical foundation.[24] However, one of the observations that gave pause to the Biblical Theology Movement was the recognition of equivocation on the part of its proponents. The latter tended to employ the biblical language of God acting in history, which presupposed one world-view, while in reality they operated out of a contrasting world-view.[25] Consequently, theologians were faced with the clear imperative of explaining just how a text shaped by one world-view could have its meaning translated for a people with a different world-view. I would suggest that the issue should be more sharply defined. An important function of the genre of biblical historical narratives was to communicate a world-view, to convince its audience that this view is the proper view of how the world works, and to elicit from them a consequent behavior. If this is a function of the biblical historical narratives, then seeking to translate such texts into a foreign world-view would be a contradictory—or even illegitimate—enterprise. The genre of historical narrative confronts biblical theologians with the decision to accept or reject its world-view.

24. Hayes and Prussner, *Theology*, p. 212.
25. L. Gilkey exposed the equivocation among theologians regarding this point in 'Cosmology, Ontology, and the Travail of the Biblical Language', *JR* 41 (1961), pp. 194-205.

Aspects of the Structure and Rhetoric of 2 Chronicles 25[*]

M. Patrick Graham

Introduction

During the last two decades there has been a resurgence of scholarly interest in the books of Chronicles. Several studies have been devoted to the Chronicler's usefulness for the historical reconstruction of the pre-exilic period,[1] and even more have dealt with the Chronicler's theology.[2] Considerably less attention, however, has been given to the literary and rhetorical techniques of the Chronicler.[3] The present

---

[*] Thanks go to Robert Detweiler, Raymond B. Dillard, Phillip McMillion, and members of the Chronicles–Ezra–Nehemiah Section of the SBL for their criticisms of earlier versions of this paper. Responsibility for the deficiencies that remain, however, is accepted by the author.

1. P. Welten, *Geschichte und Geschichtsdarstellung* (WMANT, 42; Neukirchen–Vluyn: Neukirchener Verlag, 1973); S. Japhet, 'The Historical Reliability of Chronicles', *JSOT* 33 (1985), pp. 83-107; and M.P. Graham, *The Utilization of 1 and 2 Chronicles in the Reconstruction of Israelite History of the Nineteenth Century* (SBLDS, 116; Atlanta: Scholars Press, 1990).

2. T. Willi, *Die Chronik als Auslegung* (FRLANT, 106; Göttingen: Vandenhoeck & Ruprecht, 1972); R. Mosis, *Untersuchungen zur Theologie des chronistischen Geschichtswerkes* (FThSt, 92; Freiburg: Herder, 1973); H.G.M. Williamson, *Israel in the Books of Chronicles* (Cambridge: Cambridge University Press, 1977); G.J. Petter, 'A Study of the Theology of the Books of Chronicles' (PhD dissertation, Vanderbilt University, 1985); S. Japhet, *The Ideology of the Book of Chronicles and Its Place in Biblical Thought* (BEATJ, 9; Frankfurt am Main: Peter Lang, 1989); and K. Strübind, *Tradition als Interpretation in der Chronik: König Josaphat als Paradigma chronistischer Hermeneutik und Theologie* (BZAW, 201; Berlin: de Gruyter, 1991).

3. The following are examples of some of the recent studies of Chronicles that are attentive to stylistic and rhetorical concerns: R.L. Braun, 'The Significance of 1 Chronicles 22, 28, & 29 for the Structure and Theology of the Work of the Chronicler' (ThD dissertation, Concordia Seminary, 1971); H.G.M. Williamson, 'Sources and Redaction in the Chronicler's Genealogy of Judah', *JBL* 98 (1979),

study falls into the last-named category and will attempt to show how an appreciation of the Chronicler's literary artistry and rhetoric may advance the critical interpretation of the books. Although this point could be illustrated from a number of texts in Chronicles, the report of Amaziah's reign in 2 Chronicles 25 has been selected as a largely neglected text that is nevertheless representative of the Chronicler's work and has been found useful recently for historical reconstruction.[4] I will begin by comparing the accounts of Amaziah's reign in 2 Kings 14 and 2 Chronicles 25 and follow with an analysis of the structure and rhetoric of the Chronicler's account.

A Comparison of 2 Chronicles 25 with 2 Kings 14

For the purposes of the present study, it will be assumed that the primary source for the Chronicler's composition was the Deuteronomistic History, and consequently, differences between the two may serve to highlight the Chronicler's thought and style.[5] Although there are a few minor omissions and numerous alterations in the Chronicler's use of his *Vorlage*, most striking are the following four additions: (1) the details regarding Amaziah's preparations for, assault against, and victory over Edom/Seir, including the references to Amaziah's enlistment and dismissal of mercenaries, who later attacked Judean cities (vv. 5-11a, 12-13); (2) the description of Amaziah's idolatry and the prophet's rebuke against Amaziah for it (vv. 14-16); (3) the reason for Amaziah's failure to accept Joash's

---

pp. 351-59; R.B. Dillard, 'The Literary Structure of the Chronicler's Solomon Narrative', *JSOT* 30 (1984), pp. 85-93; M.A. Throntveit, *When Kings Speak: Royal Speech and Royal Prayer in Chronicles* (SBLDS, 93; Atlanta: Scholars Press, 1987); L.C. Allen, 'Kerygmatic Units in 1 & 2 Chronicles', *JSOT* 41 (1988), pp. 21-36; and R.K. Duke, *The Persuasive Appeal of the Chronicler: A Rhetorical Analysis* (JSOTSup, 88; Bible and Literature Series, 25; Sheffield: Almond Press, 1990). Duke's study was issued initially as an Emory PhD dissertation under the direction of John H. Hayes and shows the latter's interest in the use of classical Greek rhetoric to illumine the biblical materials.

4.   Cf., e.g., J.M. Miller and J.H. Hayes, *A History of Ancient Israel and Judah* (Philadelphia: Westminster, 1986), pp. 305-307; B.Z. Luria, 'Amaziah, King of Judah, and the Gods of Edom', *BethM* 30 (1984–85), pp. 353-60 (Hebrew).

5.   While additional sources were probably available to the Chronicler, their precise nature and extent are unknown. See R.W. Klein, 'Chronicles, Book of 1-2', *ABD* 1 (1992), pp. 996-97.

rebuke (v. 20b); and (4) the designation of the time when the conspiracy against Amaziah began (v. 27a).

The first of these additions lays the foundation for much of the narrative that follows. It was in the mustering of his forces for war with Edom that Amaziah hired Israelite mercenaries, thereby polluting the 'holiness' of his war and initiating a sequence of events that culminated in battle between Israel and Judah (vv. 21-22). The prophetic rebuke against Amaziah for enlisting Israelite mercenaries serves a typical function in Chronicles[6] by moving the king to reconsider and repent of his sin, thereby laying the groundwork for Judah's victory over Edom (vv. 11-12). Amaziah's repentance, however, led him to release the Israelite mercenaries from his service (v. 10), and this provoked the disappointed Israelite troops to attack certain villages of Judah (v. 13), thus providing the motivation for Amaziah's later challenge to Joash and Israel to face the army of Judah in battle (v. 17). This series of additions supplied critical motivations for several figures in the narrative to behave as they did. While the author of 2 Kings 14 merely reported that Amaziah attacked and defeated Edom, capturing Sela and renaming it Jokthe-el (v. 7), the Chronicler used Amaziah's war with Edom as the occasion for building an elaborate structure that gave greater coherence to the narrative as a whole and ample documentation for the theological points that he wanted to score.

The second of the four additions (vv. 14-16) was critical for the Chronicler's understanding and presentation of Amaziah's reign, since it served as the pivot on which the narrative of 2 Chronicles 25 turned.[7] The substance of the addition is entirely absent in 2 Kings 14 and appears even more striking in its setting in Chronicles by virtue of the fact that it is 'incredibly unmotivated', viz., it seems illogical for Amaziah to have worshiped the idols of the foe whom he had just defeated in battle.[8] All of these considerations converge to mark vv. 14-16 as the most critical episode in Amaziah's reign for the

6. Cf. R. Micheel, *Die Seher- und Prophetenüberlieferungen in der Chronik* (BBET, 18; Frankfurt am Main: Peter Lang, 1983), and J.D. Newsome, 'The Chronicler's View of Prophecy' (PhD dissertation, Vanderbilt University, 1973).

7. See below under 'Structure'.

8. S.J. De Vries, *1 and 2 Chronicles* (FOTL, 11; Grand Rapids: Eerdmans, 1989), p. 351. Cf. R.B. Dillard, *2 Chronicles* (WBC, 15; Waco, TX: Word Books, 1987), p. 201.

Chronicler. Moreover, the absence of this section in 2 Kings 14 illustrates a crucial difference between the two reports of Amaziah's reign: the Deuteronomistic historian's report is brief, enigmatic, and loosely structured, while the Chronicler's account is longer, superficially reasonable (except, perhaps, for the motive for Amaziah's idolatry), and tightly structured.

The third addition (v. 20b) serves two functions: (1) it asserts the sovereignty and power of God to punish human sin, and (2) it connects Joash's victory over Amaziah with the latter's idolatry. In a way that is similar to the Chronicler's report of the reign of Joash, Amaziah's father (2 Chronicles 24), Amaziah's sin is punished by a military defeat and the subsequent conspiracy and assassination.

The final addition to the narrative of 2 Kings 14 by the Chronicler (v. 27a) concerns the occasion of the conspiracy against Amaziah. While 2 Kgs 14.19 gives no reason for the rebellion against Amaziah, the Chronicler explicitly connects the conspiracy with the king's idolatry. In this instance, as well, the Chronicler has supplemented the report of his source in order to provide a rationale for his characters' actions.

The Structure: Concentric[9]

The Deuteronomistic historian's account of Amaziah's reign arrays the four events in the king's life like beads on a string: they follow in chronological succession and are somewhat connected to one another by the thread of human causation that the reader may imagine behind

---

9. Although some scholars would use the term 'chiasmus' to describe the ABCB′A′ structure that is proposed here for 2 Chronicles 25, the designation 'concentric' has been chosen. Following the remarks of S. Bar-Efrat (*Narrative Art in the Bible* [JSOTSup, 70; Sheffield: JSOT Press, 1989], pp. 93-140) and others, the following distinction is observed: in chiasmus there is an equal pairing of elements (e.g., ABA′B′), but in concentric structure there is a central element that separates the paired elements (e.g., ABCA′B′). Contrary to the assertion by Y.T. Radday ('Chiasmus in Hebrew Biblical Narrative', in J.W. Welch (ed.), *Chiasmus in Antiquity* [Hildesheim: Gerstenberg, 1981], p. 52) that chiasmus—by which he includes both chiasmus and concentric structure—is virtually absent in Chronicles because of the late date of composition of the work, recent research has found numerous examples of chiasmus and concentric structure in the Chronicler's history (see, e.g., De Vries, *1 and 2 Chronicles*, pp. 350-52; Dillard, *2 Chronicles*, pp. 5-7; Williamson, 'Sources and Redaction', pp. 351-59).

the events. The structure of the Chronicler's narrative, however, is wholly different—in spite of the fact that it presents the same four events in their Deuteronomistic sequence. By inserting additional material and providing theological commentary, the Chronicler has woven a tightly knit narrative with a concentric arrangement, whose components are clearly related to one another.[10]

A   Introduction of Amaziah's reign (1-4)
    1   Chronological & genealogical information (1)
        a Accession age & duration of reign (1a)
        b Name of mother (1b)
    2   Theological assessment of his reign (2)
    3   Death of assassins with theological rationale (3-4)
        a Execution of the assassins (3)
        b Theological justification (4)
B   War with Edom (5-13)
    1   Mustering of army (5-6)
        a Mustering of Judah & Benjamin (5)
        b Enlistment of Israelite mercenaries (6)
    2   Man of God's rebuke & Amaziah's response (7-10)
        a Man of God's rebuke (7-8)
        b Amaziah's response (9-10)
            i   Amaziah's question about wages paid (9a)
            ii Man of God's reassurance (9b)
            iii Amaziah's dismissal of mercenaries (10)
    3   Judah's victory over Edom (11-12)
        a Judah's victory over Edom in battle (11)
        b Aftermath (12)
    4   Israelite mercenaries' attack on Judean cities (13)
C   Amaziah's idolatry (14-16)
    1   Amaziah's worship of Edomite gods (14)

10. An important aspect of the Chronicler's effort to structure 2 Chronicles 25 is related to his theology of retribution. The Chronicler periodizes the reign of Amaziah to show an initial period of faithfulness to God, which is rewarded, and then a period of unfaithfulness, which is punished. D. Mathias has identified the Chronicler's use of this technique in the accounts for Rehoboam, Asa, Joash, and Amaziah: 'Die Geschichte der Chronikforschung im 19. Jahrhundert unter besonderer Berücksichtigung der exegetischen Behandlung der Prophetennachrichten des chronistischen Geschichtswerkes' (PhD dissertation, Karl-Marx-Universität, 1977), pp. 265-71.

    2   Prophet's rebuke & Amaziah's response (15-16)
       a Prophet's rebuke (15)
       b Amaziah's rejection (16a)
       c Prophet's prediction of Amaziah's death (16b)
B′   War with Israel (17-24)
     1′ Amaziah's challenge to Joash (17)
     2′ Joash's rebuke & Amaziah's response (18-20)
       a′ Joash's rebuke (18-19)
       b′ Amaziah's response (20)
         i′ Amaziah's rejection (20a)
         ii′ Theological rationale (20b)
     3′ Israel defeats Judah (21-24)
       a′ Joash's victory over Amaziah (21-22)
       b′ Aftermath (23-24)
A′   Conclusion of Amaziah's reign (25-28)
     1′ Chronological & source information (25-26)
       a′ Amaziah outlived Joash of Israel by 15 years (25)
       b′ Source citation (26)
     2′ Death of Amaziah with theological rationale (27-28)

The recognition of the concentric arrangement of 2 Chronicles 25 permits several observations. First, it is clear that the chief event in Amaziah's reign according to the Deuteronomistic History was the war with Israel, and this posed the greatest difficulty for the Chronicler. By inserting the two episodes that involved prophetic rebukes (B and C) before the presentation of the war with Israel, however, the Chronicler was able to cast a different light on the report about the conflict with Israel. Furthermore, it is no longer Amaziah's struggle with Joash that occupies center stage in the narrative; it is his struggle with God—his idolatry—that is the focus of attention, and the battle with Israel is the immediate consequence of his unfaithfulness to God. Therefore, by the positioning of his insertions, the Chronicler has reframed the war with Israel and radically altered its significance.

Secondly, the correspondence between the introduction (A) and conclusion (A′) suggests the relevance of Deut. 24.16 for Amaziah's own life. In this connection, the verse from Deuteronomy, which aptly captures the essence of the Chronicler's 'short-term retribution dogma',[11] is made to interpret the reign of Amaziah.[12]

---

11. On the idea of retribution in Chronicles, see R.B. Dillard, 'Reward and Punishment in Chronicles: The Theology of Immediate Retribution', *WTJ* 46 (1984),

Thirdly, there is the correspondence between the battle with Edom (vv. 5-13) and that with Israel (vv. 17-24). The element in the former that finds no correspondence in the latter is the reference to Israelite mercenaries plundering Judah. As the distinctive element in B, therefore, it is highlighted and anticipates B′. Furthermore, a dramatic change has taken place in the disposition of Amaziah between the two sections. In vv. 5-13, the king submitted to the prophetic rebuke—albeit reluctantly—but in vv. 17-24, he defiantly rejected the prophet's words. These antithetical responses are mirrored in the consequences of each: Judah was victorious in the first but thoroughly defeated in the second. Moreover, Amaziah's 'ally' in B became his opponent in B′.

Finally, it is clear that vv. 14-16 played the pivotal role in the Chronicler's interpretation of Amaziah's reign. In C, one meets the second of three instances in which Amaziah was rebuked for wrongdoing, but it is the first time that he rejected the rebuke. While Amaziah's acceptance of the rebuke in B is followed by military victory, and defeat follows his rejection of the rebuke in B′, the notice in C that Amaziah rejected the rebuke is followed by the announcement that God would destroy the king. Just as B4 connects with B′, so C2c, the last element in C, anticipates the next-section-plus-one, A′2′. Therefore, C is the pivotal section in the chapter and discloses the fate of Amaziah.[13]

pp. 164-72; and Japhet, *Ideology*, pp. 150-76.

12. See below under 'Rhetoric'.

13. The Chronicler's arrangement of Joash's reign in 2 Chronicles 24 parallels this in that it has the king's reign turn on the report of Jehoiada's death. (Cf. M.P. Graham, 'The Composition of 2 Chronicles 24', in E. Ferguson [ed.], *Christian Teaching: Studies in Honor of Lemoine G. Lewis* [Abilene, TX.: ACU, 1981], pp. 139-40.) Another example of concentric structure in 2 Chronicles 25 is found in vv. 27-28, where the Chronicler substituted the qal impf 3mpl of *qbr* (v. 28) for the niphal impf 3msg form of the verb in 2 Kgs 14.20. By this alteration the Chronicler was able to create a concentric pattern of 3mpl verbs that describes the actions of certain unnamed people in Jerusalem toward Amaziah.

A	They *conspired* against Amaziah, who then fled to Lachish
B	They *sent* after Amaziah to Lachich
C	They *killed* Amaziah there
B′	They *carried* him on horses
A′	They *buried* him (2 Kgs 14.20 reads, 'he *was* buried')

The Rhetoric: Irony

The Chronicler's narrative about Amaziah is replete with irony.[14] Although there is one example of 'situation irony', viz., an instance in which 'a character in the narrative recognizes the irony' of a situation (v. 15),[15] for the most part, it is 'dramatic irony' that one meets in the Chronicler's description of Amaziah's reign. In this category, it is only the reader who recognizes the irony of the situation.[16] In 2 Chronicles 25, this is the case as the foolish and hapless King Amaziah is observed striving to discharge his royal duties. At each juncture in the narrative, however, there is incongruity and disparity: because the king did not act 'with a blameless heart' (v. 2), his actions were incongruous with his role as king of God's people, and there was often disparity between the king's intentions and his achievements. Moreover, Amaziah's own words and actions often betrayed his weaknesses and failures. The result of it all is a tragic and ironic image of the king.

The Chronicler identified Amaziah from the beginning as a king, and consequently, one expects to read of his royal exploits. Kings were to be great men, whose achievements were marked by wisdom, skill, and courage—they were born and equipped for success. Models of such for the Chronicler were David and Solomon.[17] Such was not

---

14. At the end of his treatment of 2 Chronicles 25, Dillard (*2 Chronicles*, p. 203) characterizes it as a 'study in opposites' and notes several of the contrasts that are described in this paper as instances of irony. In spite of the numerous studies that have been done on the subject of irony, however, there are still disagreements about what constitutes it, how its appearances in literature should be categorized, and what terminology best describes its various manifestations. See, for example, the discussions by E.M. Good, *Irony in the Old Testament* (Philadelphia: Westminster, 1965), pp. 13-31; D.C. Muecke, *The Compass of Irony* (London: Methuen, 1969), pp. 14-22; and L.R. Klein, *The Triumph of Irony in the Book of Judges* (JSOTSup, 68; Bible and Literature Series, 14; Sheffield: Almond Press, 1988), pp. 195-99. For the purposes of the present study, the analysis and terminology of Klein will be adopted.

15. Klein, *Triumph of Irony*, p. 197.

16. Klein, *Triumph of Irony*, p. 197; Muecke (*Compass of Irony*, pp. 100-15) uses the designation 'ironic situations' and finds five subcategories: (1) irony of simple incongruity, (2) irony of events, (3) dramatic irony, (4) irony of self-betrayal, and (5) irony of dilemma.

17. Japhet, *Ideology*, pp. 467-88.

to be the case with Amaziah. As Good explains, 'irony in tragedy lies in seeing the truly great fall beneath destiny, because they sought to be too great. The word for it is hybris, overstepping the proper bounds. The downfall inspires pity and terror.'[18] In the narrative at hand, Amaziah took the initiative repeatedly and vigorously asserted his will in foreign and domestic affairs, whether political, military, religious, or judicial, but the end was disaster. As for hubris, one need look no further than Joash's fable, which suggested that Amaziah was little more than a thistle before the cedars of Lebanon. Examples of such irony in the present chapter may be traced through each of its five major divisions.

The Chronicler begins his account of Amaziah's reign (vv. 1-4) by portraying the king in his role as the wise and just judge: his first act as king was to have his father's assassins executed.[19] The quotation of Deut. 24.16 ostensibly serves to affirm the rectitude of what Amaziah did and to depict him as a king who exercised restraint, that is, his desire for vengeance did not lead him to bloody excess. In fact, however, the citation of Deuteronomy serves a more significant purpose: it illuminates and interprets the outcome of Amaziah's reign. Amaziah was assassinated at the end of the Chronicler's narrative 'for his own sin'. It is ironic that the text from Deuteronomy, apparently cited to praise Amaziah, serves to underscore the justice of God's subsequent decision to destroy the king. Amaziah's text for dealing with his subjects became God's text for dealing with him: Amaziah was not destroyed because of his father Joash's sin, but because of his own.

The second block of text (vv. 5-13) takes up the military function of the king: as the skillful and courageous warrior who subdued foreign powers, Amaziah's first act was to prepare for war against Edom, Judah's neighbor to the south. Amaziah mustered an army of 300,000 soldiers from Judah and then hired 100,000 mercenaries from Israel,

---

18. Good, *Irony in the Old Testament*, pp. 14-18.

19. Japhet (*Ideology*, pp. 165-66) notes that the Chronicler has changed the hophal of Deuteronomy and Kings to the qal and concludes that this changes the juridical import ('shall be put to death') of the latter two books to a general principle regarding punishment by God ('shall die'). I. Gabriel (*Friede über Israel* [ÖBS, 10; Klosterneuburg: Verlag Österreichisches Katholisches Bibelwerk, 1990], p. 149) proceeds from Japhet's observation to note that Deut. 24.16 becomes the rule by which the individual kings from Joram to Joash are assessed in Chronicles.

Judah's neighbor to the north. Three aspects in this episode exhibit irony. First, while 300,000 Judean troops should have been more than adequate to subdue Edom (10,000 Edomites eventually fell in battle and 10,000 more were captured and executed), the fearful Amaziah hired additional troops from Israel. This was hardly how one would have expected a courageous king to proceed, much less a king who acted according to the stipulations of holy war and trusted God for victory.[20] A second instance of irony in this episode appears in that Israel—the people to whom Amaziah turned for help—became Judah's most potent enemy, while Edom—the people whom Amaziah feared to attack without the help of Israelite mercenaries—was overcome by Judah alone, though with the help of God rather than Israelite mercenaries. The irony lies in Amaziah's appeal for aid from the very power that would later plunder him twice (vv. 13, 24) and dismantle Jerusalem's defenses. Finally, the king was reluctant to acquiesce to the demand of the 'man of God', who urged him to dismiss the Israelite mercenaries, because Amaziah was unwilling to lose the hundred talents of silver that had already been paid. While he finally submitted to the prophet's instructions, there is no hint that he expected the mercenaries to exact subsequently the remainder of their wages (the plunder anticipated from victory over Edom).[21] The irony lies in Amaziah's concern for losing a hundred talents of silver, while the entire success of the Edomite campaign hung in the balance, and in the fact that he never anticipated the angry reaction of the Israelite troops, who had been deprived of their plunder.[22]

20. Cf. G. von Rad, *Holy War in Ancient Israel* (Grand Rapids: Eerdmans, 1991 [German original, 1951]). For the Chronicler's use of military *topoi* to advance his theology, see Welten, *Geschichte*, and for the most recent extensive analysis of the Chronicler's treatment of warfare, see D.L. Gard, 'Warfare in Chronicles' (PhD dissertation, Notre Dame, 1991).

21. The variety of opinion about the time of Israel's attack—whether the mercenaries raided Judah on their march home or took advantage of Amaziah's distraction with Edom to plunder his cities—is discussed most recently by Dillard, *2 Chronicles*, pp. 200-201.

22. R. Mason (*Preaching the Tradition: Homily and Hermeneutics After the Exile* [Cambridge: Cambridge University Press, 1990], pp. 83-86) suggests two further instances of irony in this text. First, in v. 7 there is a wordplay on 'with' ('*im*), and it may be that the Chronicler intended his reader to understand that for God to be 'with' the army of Amaziah could mean 'with for the purpose of destroying' the army. Next, the statement by the man of God in v. 8 should be understood ironically and

In the third division (vv. 14-16), it is in his role as founder or patron of the cult that Amaziah established Edomite worship in Jerusalem (v. 14). This was a perverse and foolish thing in the Chronicler's view and provided the occasion for irony in three aspects of the description. First, he installed a foreign cult, rather than a Yahwistic cult, and so departed sharply from the examples of great and faithful kings such as David and Solomon. Secondly, the cult that he established was that of the enemy whom he had just defeated. The reader is invited to wonder why Amaziah would want to worship a deity that was so manifestly inferior to the God of Judah. Finally, while one may interpret Amaziah's worship of Edomite gods as his attempt to secure victory for his anticipated campaign against Israel, it would be this very idolatry that would drive God from his camp and insure his defeat.[23]

In the fourth block of text (vv. 17-24), Amaziah undertook a second military adventure: he summoned Joash and Israel to battle, refused to listen to Joash's warning, and proceeded to be defeated. Irony may be detected in several aspects of this episode as well. First, his ally in v. 6 has now become his enemy. Secondly, it is ironic that Amaziah demanded that Joash meet him in battle, when Amaziah had been abandoned by God—the very one who had given him victory against Edom in vv. 11-12—and was naturally inferior in military power to Israel. One expects the advantaged (rather than the disadvantaged) party to be eager for battle. It is also ironic that while Amaziah clearly saw himself in control of matters, refusing the admonition of Joash and willing the battle with Israel, in fact it was God who had determined that Amaziah would ignore Joash's fable and insist on war. Further examples of irony in the episode may be seen in Israel, the nation abandoned by God (v. 7), defeating Judah, God's elect, and carrying away as plunder not only the vessels that had been used in the worship of Yahweh, but also those used in the worship of 'Obed-edom'.[24]

---

may be paraphrased, 'If you go [viz., with Israelite help] act as resolutely as you will in what you imagine to be God's service, God will in fact be against you.'

23. 'It is ironic when we meet what we set out to avoid, especially when the means we take to avoid something turns out to be the very means of bringing about what we sought to avoid.' Muecke, *Compass of Irony*, p. 102.

24. While the Chronicler may have added 'with Obed-edom' in v. 24 to indicate that the Temple treasure was still under the supervision of the family of Obed-edom

In the final section (vv. 25-28), it is ironic that while most kings of Judah fled to Jerusalem for refuge when threatened, since it was the capital and national stronghold, as well as the place of God's presence (e.g., Rehoboam in 2 Chron. 12.5), Amaziah fled from Jerusalem to Lachish, where he was assassinated. Moreover, while most kings went forth from Jerusalem on horses to battle, Amaziah is carried into Jerusalem on horses, a king slain by his own people rather than by foreign soldiers.

Conclusions

It is clear from the foregoing that literary style and rhetoric have been used by the Chronicler in a skillful way to transform the Deuteronomistic historian's account into a balanced, persuasive, and theologically consistent narrative. While some of the most recent commentaries and other studies of Chronicles have indicated that such intentional structuring and argument as are found in 2 Chronicles 25 have parallels elsewhere in the Chronicler's history,[25] it is my hope that researchers will focus greater attention on the Chronicler's literary and rhetorical techniques in order to enrich subsequent interpretation of his work.[26]

(cf. 1 Chron. 13.13-14; 15.18, 21, 24; 16.5, 38; 26.4, 8, 15), the phrase reminds the reader of Amaziah's earlier worship of Edomite gods, the very idolatry that brought about the present distress and plundering: by surrendering himself to the cult of Edom, Amaziah effectively surrendered (the furnishings of) the cult of Yahweh to his foes.

25. See n. 3.

26. Although literary and rhetorical studies of Chronicles cannot settle conclusively issues of historical reconstruction, they cannot be ignored. Luria ('Amaziah'), for example, has argued that 2 Chron. 25.14 indicates that Israel and Edom worshipped the same God. While this thesis may indeed be plausible on the basis of other considerations, 2 Chron. 25.14 offers slim support. Aside from the obvious fact that the Chronicler sees no connection between the objects of Israelite and Edomite worship, it is possible—even probable, in my opinion—that vv. 14-16 were composed by the Chronicler for entirely stylistic, rhetorical, and theological purposes and have no basis in the historical events of Amaziah's reign.

JOAB AND DAVID: TIES OF BLOOD AND POWER

D.G. Schley

Introduction

The prominence of David in 1 Samuel 16–1 Kings 2 has diverted scholarly attention from the roles played by other key figures of the era. What authority, for example, was wielded in the Davidic state by prophets such as Gad and, more importantly, Nathan? While the biblical writers offer little with which one might answer such questions, Nathan's role as ringleader in the intrigue leading to Solomon's succession points to his considerable personal authority. Nevertheless, the writers of the Davidic narratives gave scant attention to Nathan, aside from his roles in the condemnation of David for Uriah's death (2 Samuel 12) and the accession of Solomon to the throne (1 Kings 1–2).

There is, however, an even more prominent figure in these narratives, Joab the son of Zeruiah. Joab commands David's troops from the time of the king's reign in Hebron. He acts with considerable independence and even countermands David's orders with impunity, killing Abner the son of Ner. Joab is established in the narrative thereafter as David's ruthless, independent, and highly successful general. (A report in 1 Chron. 11.4-9 ties Joab's ascendancy to his successful assault on Jerusalem via the water tunnel [contra 2 Sam. 5.6-10].) Later, he executes the king's rebellious son, Absalom (2 Sam. 18.9-15), and treacherously murders his own kinsman and successor, Amasa the son of Jether (2 Sam. 19.11-15; 20.4-10). On the less sordid side, Joab was responsible for the conquest of the Ammonites and their capital city (2 Samuel 10-12) and for the suppression of the revolts of Absalom (2 Samuel 16–18) and Sheba (2 Samuel 20). Joab figures in other key passages as well, but the examples just cited illustrate his importance in the Davidic monarchy.

Where modern scholarship has assumed that one can reconstruct the history of Israel from the biblical text at all, the tendency has been to neglect Joab and so to exaggerate and romanticize David's power and authority as king.[1] Consequently, the purpose of this paper will be to shed light on Joab and his role in the Davidic state, the fellow whom Wellhausen called 'the most deserving man in the realm'.[2] This should illuminate the nature and distribution of royal authority under King David.

As with many Near Eastern monarchs, David's authority rested ultimately on his role as a successful military commander who had subjugated Israel's enemies. Moreover, David relied more on military prowess to support his authority than had Saul, simply because he had usurped the throne of the popular warrior-king. Throughout his reign, in fact, David seems to have done his best to cut off Saul's male line (cf. 2 Sam. 9.1; 16.7; 19.28; 21.7, 8). Still, David was unable to maintain direct control over his army, and this contributed to a conflict within his administration. By placing the command of the army under his nephew, Joab, David lost to his kinsman early on much of his effective authority. Joab—no obedient servant content merely to do the king's bidding—could not be restrained in the exercise of his authority as he saw fit, although his loyalty to David's throne appears beyond question. The ensuing conflict between these two men, blood relatives and fellow soldiers, is the subject of this study.

The Sources and Validity of the Historical Approach

The treatments of Rost and Gronbaek seemed to establish a consensus as to the historicity of the Davidic narratives.[3] Three major sources had been included in the longer narrative of the united monarchy: (1) the Ark Narrative (1 Samuel 4–6; 2 Samuel 6), (2) the History of David's Rise (1 Samuel 16–2 Samuel 5), and (3) the Throne Succession Narrative (2 Samuel 10–20; 1 Kings 1–2). Although

---

1. Perhaps the most historically realistic treatment of David is found in J. Wellhausen's *Israelitische und jüdische Geschichte* (Berlin: Reimer, 1897), pp. 63-64.

2. Wellhausen, *Israelitische und jüdische Geschichte*, p. 65.

3. L. Rost, *Die Überlieferung der Thronnachfolge Davids* (Stuttgart: Kohlhammer, 1926); J.H. Gronbaek, *Die Geschichte vom Aufstieg Davids* (ATDan, 10; Copenhagen: Prostant Apud Munksgaard, 1971).

composed of earlier sources and archival materials, these narratives
were regarded as substantially historical in both intent and substance,
and nearly contemporary in origin. Even Wellhausen had been of this
opinion, and Noth accepted it as one of the basic elements in his
analysis of the Deuteronomistic History.[4]

Since this earlier consensus regarding the historical reliability of the
Davidic narratives has recently come under heavy attack, it is
necessary to address that issue before attempting any serious historical
reconstruction. Criticisms of the consensus have come from three
major directions: (1) what may be called the Deuteronomistic line of
criticism, which argues that the Davidic narratives are substantially a
Deuteronomistic construct (e.g., Carlson);[5] (2) the wisdom
(Whybray)[6] and folkloristic (Gunn)[7] lines of critique; and (3) Van
Seters's critique of historical skepticism.[8]

The Deuteronomistic critique runs essentially as follows: the
Davidic narratives are arranged according to the pattern of 'David
under the blessing' and 'David under the curse', which has been
derived from the blessing–curse motif established in the book of
Deuteronomy. To this may be added Carlson's own claim that the
Succession Narrative, in particular, is characterized by a
'Deuteronomistic indicator', that is, the Hebrew phrase, *wayhî 'aḥărê-
kēn* ('and it came to pass afterwards that').[9] This phrase is one of a
number of widely distributed and similar expressions, such as
wĕ'aḥărê-kēn ('and afterwards') and *wayhî 'aḥărê* '('and it came to

4.   J. Wellhausen, *Die Composition des Hexateuchs* (Berlin: de Gruyter, 4th
edn, 1963), pp. 235-63; M. Noth, *The Deuteronomistic History* (JSOTSup, 15;
Sheffield: JSOT Press, 2nd edn, 1991), pp. 86-91.

5.   R.A. Carlson, *David, The Chosen King* (Stockholm: Almqvist & Wicksell,
1964).

6.   R.N. Whybray, *The Succession Narrative: A Study of II Samuel 9–20 and
I Kings 1–2* (SBT, 2nd ser., 9; Naperville, IL: Alec R. Allenson, 1968).

7.   D.M. Gunn, *The Story of King David* (JSOTSup, 6; Sheffield: JSOT Press,
1978).

8.   J. Van Seters, *In Search of History* (New Haven: Yale University Press,
1983), most recently. Along the same lines are P.R. Davies, *In Search of 'Ancient
Israel'* (JSOTSup, 148; Sheffield: JSOT Press, 1992), and T.L. Thompson, *The
Early History of the Israelite People, From the Written and the Archaeological
Sources* (Leiden: Brill, 1992).

9.   Carlson, *David*, pp. 41-49, 140ff.

pass afterwards'),[10] which are general stylistic expressions marking an episodic shift in a longer narrative sequence.[11] The wide distribution of such expressions precludes treating them as in any way specifically Deuteronomistic, more especially since there is a dearth of instances of this expression in the Deuteronomistic texts outside of 2 Samuel. Finally, the blessing–curse motif can hardly be ascribed to the so-called 'Deuteronomistic Historian', since the motif is as old as Hammurabi, whose famous code concludes with just such an arrangement. Thus, while there may be more Deuteronomistic editing in the Davidic narratives than Noth believed, there is not so much as many have come to assume.[12]

Whybray's view that these materials basically constitute a wisdom story with didactic purposes[13] fails to allow for the fact that the writing and study of history have rarely, if ever, been dissociated from the teaching of implicit moral lessons. Thucydides, who sought to expunge the traditional 'romantic element' in recounting the past, still thought that history bore lessons for the future. Thus, he wrote for all time.[14] Livy, the Roman historian of Hannibal's wars, wrote a work of great literary—though less historical—merit with a moral purpose:

10. D.G. Schley, 'Joab and David: Ties of Blood and Power' (MA thesis, Emory University, 1980), p. 17.

11. Cf. the five instances in the patriarchal narratives (Gen. 15.14; 23.19; 25.26; 32.21; 45.15) and the three in the Priestly material of Numbers (4.15; 8.15, 22). As a separate expression, *wayhî 'aḥarê-kēn* occurs primarily in the books of Samuel—in 2 Samuel in particular (2.1; 8.1; 10.1; 13.1; 21.18), and in those passages in Chronicles taken from 2 Samuel (1 Chron. 18.1 = 2 Sam. 8.1; 1 Chron. 19.1 = 2 Sam. 10.1; 1 Chron. 20.4 = 2 Sam. 21.18). This expression was employed in the Succession Narrative on account of the clear-cut episodic arrangement of that material. In point of fact, only five of the thirteen instances where the expression, *wayhî 'aḥarê-kēn*, is used occur outside of 2 Samuel, and only two of these (Judg. 16.4 and 2 Kgs 6.24) are found in clearly Deuteronomistic contexts.

12. See esp. T. Veijola, *Die ewige Dynastie. David und die Entstehung seiner Dynastie nach der deuteronomistichen Darstellung* (Toimituksia-Suomalaisen Tiedeakatemian, Annales Academiae Scientarum Fennicae, ser. B, 193; Helsinki: Suomalainen Tiedeakatemia, 1975).

13. Whybray, *Succession Narrative*, p. 72.

14. Thucydides, *The Complete Writings of Thucydides: The Peloponnesian War* (trans. R. Crawley; New York: Modern Library, 1951), pp. 14-15 (Bk. I, ch. 1).

> The study of history is the best medicine for a sick mind; for in history
> you have a record of the infinite variety of human experience plainly set
> out for all to see: and in that record you can find for yourself and your
> country both examples and warnings: fine things to take as models, base
> things, rotten through and through, to avoid.[15]

Whybray's apparent view, that historiography cannot be coupled with
didactic purpose, runs contrary to the entire history of this genre.[16]
Thus, the didactic and wisdom interests of the Davidic narratives
merely reflect the common view in antiquity that the writing of
history provides an essential forum for the discussion of the nature of
human institutions, behavior, and proper conduct—political, moral,
and personal. These are the proper concerns not only of the histories
of Livy, Thucydides, and a host of other writers, ancient and modern,
but also of the authors of the Davidic narratives, the Deuteronomistic
History, and the Chronicler's history.

Regarding Gunn's argument that the Davidic narratives correspond
to the genre of the traditional story rather than historiography, two
observations are in order. First, the traditional story elements outlined
in *The Story of King David* are undeniable and compelling.[17]
Secondly, Gunn's explanation of this is unconvincing.[18] Rather than
identify the narratives themselves as only a 'traditional story', it is
possible to argue that these elements derive from the fact that the
narratives were written under the predominant influence of oral story
forms. The only clearly identifiable history writing in Israel prior to
the Davidic monarchy was the history of Saul, now preserved in only
fragmentary and reworked form in 1 Samuel 1–14.[19] This work itself
contained a number of stories that may be counted as no more than
folklore,[20] and historiography did not free itself entirely from its oral

15. Livy, *The War with Hannibal* (trans. A. de Selincourt; Harmondsworht:
Penguin Books, 1972), p. 15.

16. In the modern period, when there has been a concerted attempt to take such a
dry and lifeless approach to the study and writing of history, interest in the latter as
an informative discipline has nearly died, and most people today consider the past
dead, for all practical purposes.

17. Gunn, *Story*, pp. 37-62.

18. Gunn, *Story*, pp. 61-62.

19. Cf. D.G. Schley, *Shiloh: A Biblical City in Tradition and History* (JSOTSup,
63; Sheffield: JSOT Press, 1989), pp. 139-63; and J.M. Miller and J.H. Hayes, *A
History of Ancient Israel and Judah* (Philadelphia: Westminster, 1986), pp. 124-35.

20. Cf. J.M. Miller, 'Saul's Rise to Power: Some Observations Concerning

story-telling heritage until the classical period. Only then did history emerge as a separate literary genre with Thucydides' masterpiece. Even Herodotus stood under the influence of oral story-telling.

The final critique is found in Van Seters's *In Search of History*. Van Seters argues that the depiction of David in the Succession Narrative is so deeply in conflict with the Deuteronomistic historian's view of David as the ideal king, that the Succession Narrative must be a later work. He also maintains that

> there is no reason to believe that any other sources, traditional or archival, were at the author's disposal when he composed the various scenes and episodes of his work. They may all be contrived. The notion of an eyewitness account of events needs to be abandoned and with it the standard reconstruction of the rise of history writing in Israel.[21]

To this critique a number of objections can be raised. First, the tone of both the History of David's Rise and the Succession Narrative are apologetic with regard to David's conduct. From a rhetorical standpoint, the sons of Zeruiah are made to bear the charge of bloodguilt in David's stead for the entire reign. This is nowhere more obvious than in the infamous 'Godfather scene' (1 Kgs 2.5-9), where David instructs Solomon to exact vengeance on Joab for precisely this reason. The same apologetic tendency is evident in other passages as well, notably 2 Sam. 16.5-14 and 19.21-23, where David denounces the ruthlessness of Abishai, Joab's brother, and the sons of Zeruiah generally. Indeed, both the History of David's Rise and the Succession Narrative are concerned to answer the charges against David that he participated in the overthrow and extermination of the house of Saul and that he was an impious king. These charges were not issues in the reigns of Solomon and Rehoboam, where the corvée was the principle cause of dissent, and so they cannot be attributed to those reigns.[22] In

I Sam 9:1–10:16; 10:26–11:15 and 13:2–14:46', *CBQ* 36 (1974), pp. 157-74.

21. Van Seters, *In Search*, pp. 290-91.

22. As has been done by T.N.D. Mettinger in his otherwise excellent work, *King and Messiah: The Civil and Sacral Legitimation of the Israelite Kings* (ConBOT, 8; Lund: Gleerup, 1976), pp. 40-41. Mettinger's argument (following that of A.R.L. Ward, 'The Story of David's Rise: A Traditio-historical Study of I Samuel XV4-II Samuel V' [PhD dissertation, Vanderbilt University, 1967]) is that the view of Saul as ruler of Judah and Israel in the Davidic narratives must be a retrojection from a period when the Davidides were appealing to Saul's rule over Judah and Israel as the basis for their own claim to rule the two entities. On this point two

an insidious way, since these charges related directly to David's person, they had to be refuted by specific reference to his own personal actions or deflected to some other culprit. Thus, the sons of Zeruiah have been made the villains of David's reign by the writer of the Succession Narrative, who ascribes to them David's bloodguilt for the demise of the house of Saul. While Van Seters is correct in assigning the accounts of the war with Ishbosheth and the murder of Abner by Joab to the Succession Narrative,[23] he overlooks the rhetorical purpose of these texts: to exonerate David from public charges of complicity in the fall of Saul's house. The best explanation for the negative portrayal of David in the Succession Narrative is not that this is the contrivance of a later age. Who in Judea would have accepted such a portrait after the promulgation of the Deuteronomistic History with its theology of David as the ideal king? Possibly the best explanation for the Succession Narrative's dark portrayal of David is that the writing was so close to the time of the actual events that there was no other choice but to depict them honestly. David's actions, his impotence as a king, father, and ultimately, as a male, were matters of public knowledge. The most that could be done by a sympathetic writer was to advance some kind of explanation that could soften or deflect the worst of the charges.

The argument that the Deuteronomistic History was incapable of including a diverse number of perspectives within his historical framework runs counter to the very nature of his work. As Noth recognized, the Deuteronomistic historian's principal contribution to the books of the Former Prophets was his composition of a 'framework work', found basically in long interpretive passages, often in the form of speeches by major figures (e.g., Josh. 1; 23; Judg. 2.6-3.6; 11.12-27; 1 Sam. 12.6-18).[24] The Deuteronomistic historian was

things should be noted. First, the Davidic editors of the earlier Saulide sources worked to one end: to minimize Saul's stature as king. Thus, those positive elements which remain, e.g., Saul's valor as a warrior (1 Sam. 14.52) and the extension of his power into Judah, could only have been retained because they were undeniable. Secondly, there is material that is proper to the apologetic of Rehoboam's reign to be found in passages that glorify Solomon's, such as 1 Kgs 4.20-21 and 10.26-29 (on this, see D.G. Schley, 'I Kings 10:26-29: A Reconsideration', *JBL* 106 [1987], pp. 595-601).

23. Van Seters, *In Search*, pp. 282-83.

24. See Noth, *Deuteronomistic History*, pp. 18-20. For the most recent treatment of the Deuteronomistic History, see S.L. McKenzie, 'The Deuteronomistic History',

far less preoccupied with the material consistency of his final edition than he was with arranging the traditions and sources of Israelite history and putting these in the proper theological-historical interpretive framework. Noth's demonstration of this reality made his thesis of the Deuteronomistic History plausible, and a similar recognition stands as the fundament of pentateuchal source criticism as well.

Van Seters's contention that there is no evidence for the presence of contemporary or archival materials in the Davidic narratives is unconvincing. There is considerable evidence for the existence of an earlier Saulide history, taken over and recast by the Davidic writers,[25] and the summary of Saul's reign in 1 Sam. 14.47-52, which includes the list of his officials, together with similar lists for David and Solomon (2 Sam. 8.15-18; 20.23-26; 1 Kgs 4.1-6), are probably archival in origin. If not, they are at least a special stylistic feature of early monarchical historiography, being recorded only for the reigns of these three kings. Furthermore, the style of warfare employed by Saul and David, which utilized heavily armed infantry, was abandoned a generation later in favor of the standard Near Eastern reliance on chariotry (something apparently of little use to David; cf. 2 Sam. 8.4). The writing of contrived history is invariably done according to the cultural norms of the later writer's own age and is characterized by anachronisms. Thus, one would expect a work of the Persian Period to describe David as a commander of chariotry, not of mercenary infantry. Yet, there is little in any of these narratives that is anachronistic. In fact, their primary characteristic is their depiction of Israel and its institutions in a way that deviates so markedly from the culture of Palestine of the later Iron Age. The stories of Elijah, Elisha, and Jehu, for example, assume the existence of chariot armies in the same way that the Davidic narratives assume the prevalence of small, elite bodies of infantry. Similarly, the Davidic narratives assume a world of competing petty kingdoms in Palestine, Philistia, Syria, and the Transjordan—a world that only briefly existed, from the decline of the great empires at the end of the Late Bronze Age to the rise of Assyria after 935 BCE. Indeed, this world of petty states

ABD 2 (1992), pp. 160-68, with extensive bibliography; *idem, The Trouble with Kings: The Composition of the Books of Kings in the Deuteronomistic History* (VTSup, 42; Leiden: Brill, 1992).

25. See nn. 15 and 16.

allowed Israel to emerge as an independent, monarchical state. Nowhere in the Davidic narratives does one glimpse the homogeneous world of the Persian Empire, created by centuries of deportations and resettlements under the successive empires of Assyria and Babylon. Instead, the setting assumed for the Davidic narratives is exactly what one finds in the early Iron Age; there is no reason to postulate any other. Only a contrived, tendentious argumentation can produce the conclusion that such clearly historically conditioned narratives are themselves post-Deuteronomistic fictions.

Thus, the ensuing discussion of the role of Joab and the military in David's reign proceeds on the assumption that the Davidic narratives are genuine works of history. On the basis of the social and political world that the narratives reflect, it is further assumed that they date from Iron Age I, that is, from the latter part of Saul's reign to the beginning or middle of Solomon's. Although it cannot be demonstrated that they comprise eyewitness accounts, it is likely that they preserve archival materials. At the same time, one must recognize that they were written with didactic and apologetic purposes and that the influence of oral story-telling techniques may have introduced certain fictional elements (which may be difficult to detect) into the narrative.

Joab and David

Joab was the son of David's sister, Zeruiah, and he had two brothers, Abishai and Asahel (1 Chron. 2.15-16). All three emerge early in the Davidic narratives, and their blood ties with David were no doubt the reason for their close relationship with him. Although Joab is not mentioned by name until 1 Sam. 26.6, one may suppose that he was with those who joined David when the condottiere fled from Saul to the cave of Adullam (1 Sam. 22.1-2), since the text lists 'all his father's house' among those who joined David at this juncture. During the war with the remnants of Saul's house, Joab commanded David's personal troops and used his position to eliminate Abner, the son of Ner, Saul's uncle and the real power behind the throne of Ishbosheth, the surviving son and successor to Saul (2 Sam. 2.12–4.12). Although David blames Joab publicly for this treacherous action, the latter retains his position and later directs David's retainers (and perhaps the Israelite levies) in the war against the Ammonites (2 Samuel 10–12).

In fact, during the rest of the Succession Narrative, David never again appears as head of the army, and Joab emerges as the leading power in the kingdom, working with his brother, Abishai. Asahel had died at the hand of Abner during the war with Saul's house (2 Sam. 2.23).

At the same time, the writer also reveals a growing enmity between the sons of Zeruiah and David. Thus, David's earlier instruction to Abishai not to stretch out his hand against the Lord's anointed (1 Sam. 26.6-12) is transformed into an open rebuke of the sons of Zeruiah generally in 2 Sam. 16.9-14. That Joab personally executed the king's rebellious son Absalom (2 Sam. 18.9-15) leads to further conflict between the two men, and Joab threatens open revolt if David does not acknowledge the victory over Absalom and his followers (2 Sam. 19.1-8b). Subsequently, David replaces Joab with another kinsman, Amasa, who was Joab's first cousin (2 Sam. 17.25) and the commander of Absalom's troops during the revolt (2 Sam. 19.11-15). When still another revolt erupts under Sheba ben Bichri, Amasa fails to call out the Judean levies, and Joab and Abishai lead out David's mercenaries to war. When he meets Amasa upon the road, Joab treacherously slays him, whereupon one of Joab's own men takes his stand over the fallen Amasa and demands that the levies commit themselves to Joab's leadership (2 Sam. 20.1-13). Thus, the Succession Narrative concludes with Joab firmly in command of the military and supported by his brother, Abishai.

During the final years of David's reign, however, there is no further mention of Abishai, and Joab's last surviving brother does not appear in the palace intrigue that led to Solomon's coronation and Joab's death (1 Kings 1-2). Joab's relationship to David thus poses a number of intriguing questions about David's reign: What was the nature of David's military establishment, and what role did Joab play in it? Was he primarily the commander of the levies, as has long been maintained,[26] or was his role more important than this? What role did Abishai play, and why was he not present to come to the aid of his brother during Solomon's coup?

To answer these queries in order, David's military was based primarily on a private corps of mercenary troops loyal to his throne.

---

26. Cf. M. Noth, *Geschichte Israels* (Göttingen: Vandenhoeck & Ruprecht, 6th edn, 1966), p. 182; *idem*, *Israelitische und jüdische Geschichte*, pp. 63-64; J. Bright, *A History of Israel* (Philadelphia: Westminster, 3rd edn, 1983), p. 205 n. 49.

Of these, there were several distinct bodies: (1) the Cherethites and Pelethites, probably a company of Aegean warriors;[27] (2) six hundred Philistines, the men of Gath, under David's friend Ittai; (3) the *šālîšîm*, an elite corps of troops numbering between thirty and forty and probably organized in squads of three;[28] (4) the *mišmaʿat*, or bodyguard, later commanded by Joab's enemy, Benaiah (2 Sam. 23.23; 1 Kgs 2.35; 4.4);[29] and (5) probably a wide assortment of loyalists who had served David from the beginning of his career under Saul. These mercenaries constituted the heart of David's army and served in lieu of the levies in all but special circumstances.

The precise role of the levies in David's military is unclear. The report in 1 Chronicles 27 of David's monthly levies of 24,000 troops each is probably only a fictional ideal, perhaps even written under the impress of the massive armies of the Persian Empire. The greatest force ever fielded by the Athenian Empire included only 4,000 heavily armed hoplites and 300 cavalry,[30] though as many as 45,000 additional auxiliaries from Athens's vassals may also have been on hand. That David's Israel ever had at its disposal 288,000 men, in monthly shifts of 24,000 native Israelite and Judean troops, conflicts both with what we know of analogous—or even greater—military organizations and with the Davidic narratives themselves, in which the levies play scarcely any role.[31] The most striking feature of David's mercenary force is the large proportion of foreigners named, as any study of the lists will reveal.

As for his relationship to David's military organization, Joab appears to have divided the command of the professional troops with his brother Abishai in the early stages of the Ammonite war (2 Samuel 10.6-14), with Joab acting as commander-in-chief. There

27. Bright, *History*, p. 205; and C.S. Ehrlich, 'Cherethites', *ABD* 1 (1992), pp. 898-99; *idem*, 'Pelethites', *ABD* 5 (1992), p. 219.

28. This group was commanded by Abishai, Joab's brother, and membership was based on the performance of especially valiant deeds; cf. 2 Sam. 23.8-23. D.G. Schley, 'The *Šālîšîm*: Officers or Special Three-Man Squads?' *VT* 40 (1990), pp. 321-27; *idem*, 'David's Champions', *ABD* 2 (1992), pp. 49-52.

29. Benaiah had come to command the Cherethites and Pelethites by the end of David's reign (2 Sam. 8.18), but his greatest service came as commander-in-chief under Solomon, in place of Joab (1 Kgs 2.35; 4.4).

30. Thucydides, *Peloponnesian War*, p. 355 (Bk. VI, ch. 18).

31. Contra N. Na'aman, 'The List of David's Officers (*šālîšîm*)', *VT* 38 (1988), pp. 71-79.

may have been some participation of the levies during the siege of Rabbah-Ammon (2 Sam. 11.11; 12.26-31). This may be the implication of Uriah's statement in 2 Sam. 11.11, and it is simply a fact of military operations that sieges require a considerable surplus of troops. The one clear reference to the Israelite levies in the Davidic narratives comes during the revolt of Sheba ben Bichri, when Amasa fails to call them out by the appointed time, and David is forced to turn again to his private force of mercenaries and loyalists under the command of the sons of Zeruiah. This evidence suggests that David made little use of the Israelite levies and relied, instead, on various private mercenary corps, many of which were not even Israelite (e.g., the men of Gath, the Cherethites and Pelethites).

The reason for this policy was simple: David's predecessor, Saul, had surrounded himself with a corps of picked loyalists but ultimately relied on the levies in pitched battles. This was especially the case in his victory over the Ammonites (1 Sam. 11.1-11), but it was also true of his defeat on Mt Gilboa. According to the account of Saul's last battle in 1 Samuel 31, the Israelite levies fled the field of battle and then watched from across the Jezreel Valley, as Saul and his men fell under the Philistine attack. David, perhaps even a silent witness to the affair, learned the obvious lesson, and so throughout his reign, he relied on a private army, commanded by his hardened, experienced, and probably hated nephews, the sons of Zeruiah.

The bi-partite structure typically assigned to David's military—the basic divisions being the levies and the retainers—is the product of the later, postexilic age, when David's reign was idealized as the 'golden age' of Israelite history.

As for Joab's role in this scheme, it is clear that he was not the commander of the levies, as has often been maintained, but the commander-in-chief of all David's military, including the professional troops. Joab exercised this authority during David's reign at Hebron, but his power grew stronger during the Philistine wars, when, according to one tradition, David had to relinquish his status as battlefield commander, because he no longer had the strength to fight (2 Sam. 21.15-17).[32] The incidental evidence of the narratives shows considerable prestige accruing to Joab from the time of the Ammonite war on (2 Samuel 10–12). Thus, Joab had to admonish David to take part in

32. It is interesting that David's deliverance from a towering Philistine, one of the last of the Rephaim, is attributed to Abishai, Joab's brother.

the final storming of Rabbah, lest Joab himself receive credit for the victory (2 Sam. 12.26-31). In the story of Uriah, moreover, as the Hittite addresses David, he refers to Joab—not David—as 'my lord' (*'ădōnî*; 2 Sam. 11.11)! The list of *šālîšîm*, in addition, includes the name of Joab's armor-bearer, Naharai the Beerothite (2 Sam. 23.37; 1 Chron. 11.39), while the account of Joab's slaying of Absalom ascribes to the general at least ten 'armor-bearers' (2 Sam. 18.15).

This evidence indicates that Joab enhanced his own personal power and prestige in the kingdom through his position as its leading military figure. One of the king's fundamental obligations in the ancient Orient was the defense of his land and people. By relinquishing this function to Joab, David assured his nephew of a nearly unassailable position in the realm. Joab's rebuke to David following Absalom's revolt demonstrates as nowhere else his independence from the king. David's subsequent attempt to replace Joab with Amasa, and the later appointment of Benaiah to command of the Cherethites and Pelethites, can be taken as attempts by David to weaken Joab's position within the military.

The greatest blow to Joab's status, however, may have come with the (unreported) death of Abishai, which probably occurred before Solomon's coup and is the most likely reason for his absence in the affair. The narrative's frequent condemnation of the 'sons of Zeruiah' is a tacit recognition of the two brothers' successful alliance in controlling David's military, often in opposition to the king's wishes. The death of Abishai, incidentally omitted from the narrative, was the necessary precondition for Joab's doom, for together, the two commanded too much military and public prestige to be removed by force.

Thus, one of the critical subplots in the Succession Narrative is the struggle for control of the military, which proceeded quietly but determinedly throughout the latter half of David's reign between King David and his ruthless but gifted and loyal nephews, the sons of Zeruiah. To this must also be added the observation that David's throne could probably have been maintained by no one else and in no other way than by their ruthlessness. The deep-rooted suspicion against him, revealed in two major revolts, is proof enough of this. But as 'familiarity breeds contempt', so David's nephews came to assert their increasing autonomy from the aged and inactive monarch. Nonetheless, David understood the implications of Joab's independence too well to allow him to continue unchecked. The old king's deathbed order to Solomon—to bring Joab down to the grave 'with blood'—was David's final revenge on the man he could never control and his final move to secure the throne for Solomon. The evidence of Joab's value to David's administration, however, can be seen in the fate of Solomon's kingdom: the military under Benaiah's command was unable to preserve David's conquests, and consequently, the empire fell apart during Solomon's later years. Solomon found in Benaiah loyalty but neither the sagacity nor the decisiveness to employ the army as effectively as his predecessor. Despite Joab's tragic end, he had rendered David indispensable, if bitter, service. Joab had often despised his monarch's will; he had deliberately, if sadly (cf. 2 Sam. 18.19-23), countermanded the king's orders not to kill the rebellious Absalom. In all this, Joab had exercised his authority without excuse or apology. For this service he was repaid with a judicious execution at David's orders, an execution that David himself did not have the temerity to implement. Thus David provided Solomon with a loyal servant in Benaiah, but never again would one be found to serve the Davidic throne who had the strength to defy an errant royal will when necessary, yet who would not covet the throne for himself.

Because of the power and authority that Joab had accrued, David may have been little more than a titular monarch in his later years. For this same reason, however, he was able to bequeath the kingdom to his son intact. One might conclude from this that Joab's example of service to the throne, even at the cost of his life, should have been honored, as Wellhausen certainly thought,[33] but it was not. Instead, one finds in the wisdom literature numerous references to the necessity of avoiding the wrath of the king (Prov. 16.14, 15; 19.12; 20.28; 24. 21-22; 25.6-7).[34] Joab ignored these traditional teachings to his own peril. His refusal to leave the altar in the face of death, however, indicates that Joab died in his integrity, forcing Benaiah to defile the holy place with his blood.

It was probably one of the virtues of David's reign that he was surrounded by strong, independent lieutenants such as Joab, Abishai, and Nathan—men who could not be cowed, were possessed of their

33. Wellhausen, *Israelitische und jüdische Geschichte*, p. 65.
34. Similar proverbs may be found in W.G. Lambert, *Babylonian Wisdom Literature* (Oxford: Clarendon Press, 1982), pp. 233-34.

own integrity, and were willing to rely on their own judgment. Subsequent rulers, such as Solomon and Rehoboam, however, gathered around themselves servile courtiers who would do their every bidding and who, especially in Rehoboam's case, would say what the king wanted to hear. Such was the logic of the monarchy, and the value of the institution was diminished as a result.

History, Literature, and Apologetic

One now arrives at the question of what relationship exists between the historical elements of these narratives and their literary and apologetic ones. To this I would propose that the history serves as the real focus of the apologetic concerns, since the authors of the History of David's Rise and Succession Narrative were concerned to refute or deflect historical charges against David and to justify his rule and the bloody succession of Solomon to the throne. Therefore this is to some extent propagandistic history, especially in the case of Saul's reign, which is depicted with neither ark nor priesthood, and hence, without sacral legitimacy. Yet this picture is almost certainly false.[35] Moreover, the narratives have been composed in a style heavily influenced by oral story-telling, about which Gunn's work is an excellent guide.[36] In this connection, most of the historical elements, on which a reconstruction of the relationship between David and Joab depends, are assumed and only incidentally mentioned in the course of the story of how David became king and Solomon—rather than his older brothers—inherited the throne.

Moreover, Solomon needed to justify the execution of Joab—the commander of David's armies, the victor of great battles, the preserver of David's throne, the wise leader who had maintained the peace of Israel—until his death the most illustrious man of the realm. Thus the lengthy progression to the 'Godfather scene' and its aftermath was necessary to justify the outrages that accompanied Solomon's seizure of the throne at the expense of his older brother, Adonijah, and his execution of Joab at the altar. A basic purpose of ancient historical texts was to serve as propaganda for the victorious regime, and this function cannot be overlooked in reading the Davidic history.

35. See Schley, *Shiloh*, pp. 139-63.
36. Gunn, *Story*.

The most tendentious material in this regard comes with the writer's casting of Joab and Abishai as the typological wisdom figures—men of rashness and violence. Their ways are to be rejected in favor of David's prudence and a willingness to let the Lord act. David, who accepts as the just recompense for his deeds both cursing (2 Sam. 16.9-14) and the death of his son (2 Sam. 12.15-23), exemplifies humble submission to the divine will and the rejection of vengeance, up to a point.[37] One may ask whether the distinctions between these men, who were both antagonists and cohorts, were really so clear. The writer's ambivalence towards Joab and David's dependence on Joab's valor and loyalty are evident throughout the Succession Narrative, even as he uses the sons of Zeruiah as his scapegoats. Examples of this ambivalence appear in the depiction of Joab's integrity in killing Absalom and accepting responsibility for it (2 Sam. 18.14-15, 19-23) and in the account of Joab's death, when he forces his enemy, Benaiah, to slay him at the altar. Here, the dialogue—whether absolutely historical or not—serves to express and develop Joab's character. Hence, Joab's responses to these challenges say as much about the author's view of the old warrior's integrity as they do about the actual events, and perhaps even more.

In conclusion, the literary and apologetic purpose of the writer of the Succession Narrative, to justify Solomon's coup and to exculpate David in the demise of the house of Saul, does not lead him to assassinate the character of the sons of Zeruiah. Rather, it is the emphasis that he places on their ruthlessness which comes into focus, an emphasis that may, after all, be accurate. One is thus left to decide on the truthfulness of an otherwise plausible account, and the decision rests on one's own estimate of the tendentiousness of the writer. Moreover, it seems clear that the author of the Succession Narrative was as sympathetic in his portrayal of the sons of Zeruiah as one could expect from a partisan of David or Solomon.

37. For a fuller treatment of these points, see D.G. Schley, 'Abishai', *ABD* 1 (1992), pp. 24-26; *idem*, 'Asahel', *ABD* 1 (1992), p. 470; and *idem*, 'Joab', *ABD* 3 (1992), pp. 852-54.

HISTORY AND PROPHETIC TEXTS[*]

Ehud Ben Zvi

Introduction

Prophetic texts are communicative messages and so imply a social discourse, which in turn is an integral part of a social system situated concretely in history. It seems reasonable, therefore, to expect some kind of correspondence between prophetic texts and the political, social, cultural, and religious circumstances at their times of composition. It follows then that historical analysis may contribute to the identification of the most likely historical setting for a particular prophetic text.

This paper deals not only with general methodological issues raised by the correlation of texts with their historical circumstances, but also with the degree of correspondence between particular texts and the historical circumstances during the reigns of Hezekiah and Josiah. First, a historical reconstruction of the two periods will be offered, the focus of which will be on Hezekiah's revolt against Assyria and its aftermath and on Josiah's alleged political independence and territorial expansion. Then on the basis of these reconstructions, another issue will be addressed: the likelihood that these periods provide the most suitable historical background for certain prophetic messages commonly associated with them.

The latter issue is especially important because there is no *a priori*

---

[*] A version of this paper was presented at the 1991 meeting of the SBL (Prophets and History Section) as part of a panel discussion, in which John H. Hayes also took part. It was my pleasure and honor then to sit by my teacher and friend and present my views on the issue side by side with him. This occasion reminded me of the many vivid and inspiring discussions which we had while I was a graduate student at Emory University. I offer this essay as a token of my gratitude to him.

reason to prefer historical circumstances mentioned in the superscription of a prophetic book over other possible historical settings, for such a preference would imply that the superscriptions of prophetic books necessarily point to actual authorship (in its modern sense), and such is not the case.[1] Hence, the historical-critical question is not whether one is somehow able to make sense of a prophetic text within the historical setting mentioned in the superscription of the prophetic book, but whether this setting provides the most reasonable historical background for the message of such a text. At any rate, that historical reconstruction is to be preferred which requires the acceptance of the fewest unproven premises, and a case based on circular reasoning carries no critical weight.

Hezekiah and the Invasion of Sennacherib

Biblical literature in general conveys a quite clear image of Hezekiah and his actions around 701 BCE, as well as of their results. Trusting in the LORD, he rebelled against the dominant military power of his day, Assyria, and the latter's punitive response faltered before the walls of Jerusalem. Despite their overwhelming military power, the Assyrian army was utterly defeated, and Judah was free from the yoke of Assyria forever.[2] The message conveyed is clear: no one can stand against the combination of (1) a pious Davidic king and people ready

1. See my *A Historical-Critical Study of the Book of Zephaniah* (BZAW, 198; Berlin/New York: de Gruyter, 1991), pp. 8-13; and 'Isaiah 1,4-9 and the Events of 701 BCE in Judah. A Question of Premise and Evidence', *SJOT* 5 (1991), pp. 95-111, esp. pp. 108-10.

2. This is certainly the contention of the Deuteronomistic History, in which the last reference to Assyrian presence in Judah appears in 2 Kgs 19.36. The Deuteronomistic History portrays Manasseh, Amon, and Josiah as independent kings who reigned over a country, a claim with serious implications for the understanding of the Deuteronomistic images of Manasseh and Josiah. Cf. N. Na'aman, 'The Kingdom of Judah under Josiah', *TA* 18 (1991), pp. 3-71, esp. pp. 55-56. (This once 'forgotten' issue was emphasized in two papers recently presented in the Hebrew Bible, History and Archaeology Section of the SBL/ASOR [1992] by S.W. Holloway, 'Astral Religion in Assyria and Judah: The Archaeologists' Spade and the Deuteronomists' Pen', and E. Ben Zvi, 'Reconstructing the Historical Manassic Judah'.) Prophetic texts (e.g., Isa. 14.24-27) that are either historically related to the events of 701 or intentionally read against that background, also proclaim that the LORD delivered Judah from the Assyrian yoke, and not that God brought a temporary relief.

to follow him, (2) the special status granted to Jerusalem by the LORD, and (3) God's might and readiness to act in response to the cumulative suffering of Israel.

What does history tell us about this period? First, the background of Hezekiah's revolt seems clear. In 705 Sargon died in Anatolia, thus offering a propitious time for rebellion, as examples from the periods following the death of Shalmanesser V and Ashurbanipal clearly show.[3] Rebels on three fronts sought to capitalize on Assyria's weakened condition: (1) in the north (i.e., the Anatolian front), the ongoing rebellion against Assyria flourished; (2) in the south (i.e., the Babylonian front), Marduk-zakir-shumi seized the throne of Babylon for a month but was deposed by the Chaldean Merodach-Baladan, who also rallied the support of Elam, the eastern superpower of the time; and (3) in the west, a coalition of middle-sized regional states with the support of the southern superpower (i.e., the unified Egypt under the Twenty-fifth Dynasty) revolted against Assyria. The three main leaders of the western revolt were: (1) Sidqa, king of Ashkelon, who controlled the Jaffo area and encircled the province of Ashdod from the north and the south; (2) Luli, king of Tyre, who controlled the Mediterranean coast from Sidon to Acco and Cyprus; and (3) Hezekiah, king of Judah, who was able to influence the political events in the adjacent city-state of Ekron and to conquer Assyrian-ruled territory in Judah's vicinity (e.g., Gath and perhaps the Besor area).

Thus, one may conclude that Hezekiah's anti-Assyrian policies reflect his assessment of the regional balance of power, especially with regard to the capabilities of Assyria and Egypt. Similar considerations seem to have governed the foreign policies of Judah's neighbors as well.

Hezekiah's anti-Assyrian policies failed, however, as is shown by the Assyrian accounts of Sennacherib's third campaign, the archaeological evidence of destruction on levels associated with *lmlk* jars, the so-called A account in 2 Kings, and the historical conditions in Judah and its environs after 701.[4] While the preceding period (i.e., 734–

3. See H. Tadmor, 'Sennacherib's Campaign to Judah: Historical and Historiographical Considerations', *Zion* 50 (1985), p. 68 (Hebrew); 'The Campaigns of Sargon II of Assur: A Chronological Historical Study', *JCS* 12 (1958), p. 97; 'The Sin of Sargon', *ErIsr* 5 (1959), p. 158 (Hebrew).

4. For the account of Sennacherib's third campaign, see D.D. Luckenbill, *The*

701) was characterized by numerous rebellions against Assyria in this area, the period after 701 was marked by almost an uninterrupted Assyrian peace in the region (except for Phoenicia). This new political situation resulted, in part, from agreements between Assyria and local elites and the creation of a delicate, regional balance of power. Sennacherib singled out Judah from the nations in the area for particularly harsh treatment. Judah suffered more extensive destruction, deportation, and loss of territory than her neighbors, and yet the nation's obligation of tribute to Assyria was increased. The result was that Judah's economic and political potential in the region was seriously eroded.

True, despite its military defeat, Judah was not annexed to Assyria. But, as any Judahite well informed of the political affairs of the time could not have failed to recognize, Sennacherib annexed no country in the west and perhaps even reinstated the kingdom of Ashdod. These actions were not haphazard but represented a general policy of developing an area of buffer-states under Assyrian hegemony in the west.[5] Jerusalem was not conquered and razed in 701, but neither were Ashkelon and Tyre, a fact that a well-informed contemporaneous Judahite must have known. Hezekiah remained in Jerusalem and in charge of a regional center of power, but only because he submitted to Assyrian suzerainty, a situation similar to that in Tyre. The goal of the Assyrian policy was certainly not to dethrone a king, but to establish a stable agreement between the Assyrian king (and elite) and the local elites. By keeping Hezekiah on the throne of Judah, in Jerusalem, Assyria actually achieved this political goal, for, as a matter of fact, neither he nor any member of the royal house of Judah rebelled again against Assyria. In any case, Hezekiah was certainly neither the first nor the last representative of a local elite who retained his power after an unsuccessful rebellion against Assyria.[6]

Annals of Sennacherib (OIP, 2; Chicago: University of Chicago Press, 1924), pp. 29-34; *ANET*, pp. 287-88. According to the version of the campaign in Bull IV, Ashkelon also received some of Judah's territories.

5. See, e.g., N. Na'aman, 'Sennacherib's "Letter to God" on his Campaign to Judah', *BASOR* 214 (1974), pp. 35-36; B. Otzen, 'Israel under the Assyrians', in M.T. Larsen (ed.), *Power and Propaganda* (Mesopotamia, 7; Copenhagen: Akademisk Forlag, 1979), pp. 257-58; J.M. Miller and J.H. Hayes, *A History of Ancient Israel and Judah* (Philadelphia: Westminster, 1986), pp. 383-85.

6. E.g., Hiram of Tyre and Hanun, king of Gaza, in the days of Tiglath-pileser III; Baal of Tyre in the days of Essarhadon; Necho I of Sais in the days of

An analysis of the literary aspects and the historical-political references in prophetic texts indicates that both those who composed them and their audiences were well-educated and well-informed people. Although they would have been disheartened by the reduced status of Judah in the post-701 period (see above), they would have understood that they were living in an Assyrian vassal state that was too weak and isolated to regain its independence.

Had Hezekiah been victorious over Assyria, it would be easy to correlate well-educated, post-701 Judahite writers and their historical addressees with texts claiming that the Assyrians were defeated in Judah, that the Assyrian hegemony over Judah ended in 701 (as the book of Kings maintains), and that Hezekiah succeeded in his rebellion because of his trust in the LORD. Indeed, when the historical memories faded and people came to believe that Hezekiah had actually succeeded, it became possible to glorify Hezekiah, who emerged as the Chronicler's favorite Judahite king and a quasi-messianic figure later on.[7] Is it reasonable, however, to assume that well-educated Judahites, such as the authors of prophetic texts and their audiences who lived in the aftermath of the 701 revolt, were convinced that such was the case? Although one cannot rule out such a possibility, it seems very unlikely. It would be somewhat analogous to assuming the existence of writers living immediately after 598, in Jerusalem, and whose message to their historical community is that the Babylonian hegemony has ended because the rebellion against Babylon had been successful.

The fact was that Hezekiah was not victorious, nor was there any reasonable political scenario that could have led his contemporaries to expect an Assyrian defeat in Judah (e.g., Isa. 14.24-27 and 31.4-9) soon after 701. Thus, if one claims that these texts proclaiming such a defeat were integral to the social discourse of the period, one must

Ashurbanipal; and Luli in 701.

7. See, P.R. Ackroyd, 'The Biblical Interpretation of the Reigns of Ahaz and Hezekiah', in W.B. Barrik and J.R. Spencer (eds.), *In the Shelter of Elyon: Essays in Honor of G.W. Ahlström* (JSOTSup, 31; Sheffield: JSOT Press, 1984), pp. 247-59, and the bibliography cited there; cf. R.E. Clements, 'The Immanuel Prophecy of Isa. 7.10-17 and its Messianic Interpretation', in E. Blum, C. Macholz, and E.W. Stegemann (eds.), *Die Hebräische Bibel und ihre zweifache Nachgeschichte: Festschrift für Rolf Rendtorff* (Neukirchen-Vluyn: Neukirchener Verlag, 1990), pp. 225-40. Some talmudic texts point to a similar image (e.g., *b. Pes.* 119a; *b. Sanh.* 94 a-b, 99a).

consider them as examples of an underground apocalyptic/proto-apocalyptic (cf. Isa. 31.8) reaction to the circumstances following 701.

Although this interpretation solves the problem of the dissonance between historical circumstances and the message of these texts, it requires a new non-superfluous premise, that is, that there were Isaianic groups producing apocalyptic/proto-apocalyptic literature at that time. Moreover, this premise is in fact based on the assumption that these texts were written and read in the aftermath of Sennacherib's campaign to Judah. Therefore, in order to avoid circular reasoning, one must demonstrate—without the support of the *ad hoc* unproven premise mentioned (and in spite of its necessary character)—that these texts were most likely composed at that time.

A qualification of the last statement, however, seems in order. Certainly, if there is a convincing argument for the historical existence of the mentioned Isaianic groups, then the necessary premise would not be an unproven, *ad hoc* premise. This being so, the critical issue seems to be the existence of *independent* evidence supporting the historicity of the premise that is needed to resolve the tension between the historical circumstances of the period and the message of these texts. The stress is, of course, on the word 'independent', for neither the texts nor their message can be used to demonstrate the existence of the required Isaianic groups without falling into circular argumentation. But in fact, there is no independent evidence for the existence of such underground, apocalyptic/proto-apocalyptic, Isaianic groups in Sennacherib's Judah. This being the case, and since the burden of proof lies on those who advance this hypothesis, one must reject the hypothesis that relates prophetic texts that announce an imminent Assyrian defeat in the land of Israel to the period just after 701.

During Sennacherib's time a Judahite rebellion against Assyria would have been an unrealistic endeavor because of the lack of Egyptian support. Later on, however, Assyria entered into war with Egypt, and this may have provided a more favorable setting for anti-Assyrian forces and texts.

But the fact is that there is no evidence that Judah revolted against Assyria during the Egyptian wars of Esarhaddon and Ashurbanipal or at any time until the end of the Assyrian hegemony in the region.[8] On the contrary, all available evidence portrays Judah as a loyal vassal. In

8. The only possible source is the historically questionable account in 2 Chron. 33.10-13, which does not even mention the term 'rebellion'.

this respect, it is worth noting that scholars generally interpret similar data involving Judah's neighbors as an indication of uninterrupted, faithful vassaldom to Assyria. In his classic article on Philistia under Assyrian rule, for example, Tadmor summarizes Gaza's political record after the deportation of Hanun in 720: 'she (Gaza) seemed to have learned her lesson well, and henceforth, despite the unrest which continued to prevail in Palestine during the reigns of Sargon and his successors, remained loyal to Assyria'.[9] Most scholars assume on the basis of similar evidence that Ammon, Moab, Edom, and Ekron were faithful Assyrian vassals too.[10] Their reasoning is straightforward: if the few pieces of clear evidence point to submissive vassalage, then one should assume that this was the ongoing situation. Those who propose failed revolts, then, must accept the burden of proof. Since the same rule applies to the study of Judah's history, one must conclude that it was most likely a loyal Assyrian vassal from 701 until the Assyrian hegemony ended.

This being so, it is reasonable to assume that if clearly anti-Assyrian texts such as Isa. 10.24-27, 14.24-27, and 31.8-9 were composed during Manasseh's reign (c. 697–642),[11] they do not likely represent the official policy of the court, nor were they intended for public reading. These texts, therefore, can only represent the work and social discourse of underground anti-Assyrian circles. Although one cannot rule out the existence of such groups, nor that they produced such texts, it must be noticed that this reconstruction rests on two *necessary* premises: (1) such groups existed, and (2) the texts mentioned belonged to the social discourse of these groups.

Thus, the situation is similar to the one discussed above. To show that such texts were integral to the discourse of the Manassic period,

---

9. H. Tadmor, 'Philistia under Assyrian Rule', *BA* 29 (1966), p. 91.

10. E.g., C.M. Bennet, 'Excavations at Buseirah (Biblical Bozrah)', in J.F.A. Sawyer and D.J.A. Clines (eds.), *Midian, Moab and Edom: The History and Archaeology of Late Bronze and Iron Age Jordan and North-west Arabia* (JSOTSup, 24; Sheffield: JSOT Press, 1983), pp. 16-17; J.R. Bartlett, *Edom and the Edomites* (JSOTSup, 77; Sheffield: JSOT Press, 1989), pp. 137-40; R. Haak, 'Prophets and History: Zephaniah', yet unpublished; S. Gittin, 'Urban Growth and Decline at Ekron in the Iron II Period', *BA* 50 (1987), pp. 206-22. Cf. D.L. Christensen, *Transformations of the War Oracle in Old Testament Prophecy* (HDR, 3; Missoula, MT: Scholars Press, 1975), p. 86.

11. Although there is no consensus concerning the precise extent of Manasseh's reign, most set it somewhere between 699 and 640.

one must demonstrate that the two necessary premises are supported by independent evidence or that such a proposal is the most likely, in spite of the fact that it requires the validity of these two premises, for—all things being equal—the more unproven hypotheses one must assume, the less compelling one's proposal becomes.

The Reign of Josiah

The reign of Josiah (639–609),[12] especially after his eighteenth year (622 BCE; see 2 Kgs 22.3), is usually considered not only a period of religious/cultic reform but also a time of political liberation, revitalized nationalism, and territorial expansion, that is, a period in which Judah attempted to recreate the (historical or literary) Davidic empire. This is not only the general image suggested by biblical texts but also a common scholarly historical reconstruction, clearly exemplified in the works of Bright, Cross, Malamat, Naveh, Weinfeld, and many others.[13]

This understanding of the period, in turn, has strongly influenced the interpretation of prophetic texts. For instance, Blenkinsopp characterized Nahum as 'the spokesman for the Temple cult in the service of the (Josianic) nationalistic revival';[14] Christensen interpreted Zeph. 2.4-15 as a theological basis for Josiah's program of political expansion;[15] and Sweeney recently wrote that the purpose of

12. As for the dates of Josiah's reign, see, e.g., Miller and Hayes, *History*, p. 377.

13. E.g., J. Bright, *A History of Israel* (Philadelphia: Westminster, 2nd edn, 1972), p. 316; F.M. Cross and D.N. Freedman, 'Josiah's Revolt Against Assyria', *JNES* 12 (1953), pp. 56-58; A. Malamat 'Josiah's Bid for Armageddon', *JANESCU* 5 (1973), pp. 267-79; 'The Kingdom of Judah Between Egypt and Babylon: A Small State Within a Great Power Confrontation', in W. Claasen (ed.), *Text and Context: Old Testament and Semitic Studies for F.C. Fensham* (JSOTSup, 48; Sheffield: JSOT Press, 1988), pp. 117-29; Y. Naveh, 'A Hebrew Letter from the Seventh Century B.C.', *IEJ* 10 (1960), pp. 129-39; M. Weinfeld, 'The Awakening of the National Consciousness in Israel in the Seventh Century BCE', in *Oz l'David* (Pirsume ha-Hevrah le-Heker ha-Miqra be-Yisrael, 15; Jerusalem: Kiryat Sefer, 1964), pp. 401-20 (Hebrew).

14. See J. Blenkinsopp, *A History of Prophecy in Israel* (Philadelphia: Westminster, 1983), p. 149.

15. D.L. Christensen, 'Zephaniah 2: 4-15: A Theological Basis for Josiah's Program of Political Expansion', *CBQ* 46 (1984), pp. 669-82.

the book of Zephaniah was 'to garner support for King Josiah's program of religious and national restoration in the late seventh century B.C.E'.[16] In addition, it seems almost impossible to dissociate this reconstruction of Josiah's reign from the argument in favor of a Josianic/Assyrian redaction in the book of Isaiah, as well as that in favor of a Josianic redaction of the book of Kings, and perhaps of most of the Deuteronomistic History.[17]

The historical basis of this glorious image of the Josianic kingdom has been challenged at several points recently.[18] First, there is no evidence pointing to tensions between Josiah and the Transjordanian kingdoms, and certainly not to Judahite territorial conquests.[19] Prophetic texts such as Zeph. 2.8-10 or Jer. 49.1-5 are irrelevant to

16. M.A. Sweeney, 'A Form Critical Reassessment of the Book of Zephaniah', *CBQ* 53 (1991), pp. 388-408 (p. 406).

17. See, e.g., F.M. Cross, *Canaanite Myth and Hebrew Epic* (Cambridge, MA: Harvard University Press, 1973), pp. 274-89; R.D. Nelson, *The Double Redaction of the Deuteronomistic History* (JSOTSup, 18; Sheffield: JSOT Press, 1981), esp. pp. 120-23; S.L. McKenzie, *The Trouble with Kings: The Composition of the Book of Kings in the Deuteronomistic History* (VTSup, 42; Leiden: Brill, 1991), esp. pp. 117-34; R.E. Clements, *Isaiah 1–39* (NCB; Grand Rapids: Eerdmans; London: Marshall, Morgan & Scott, 1982), esp. pp. 5-8; H. Barth, *Die Jesaja-Worte in der Josiazeit: Israel und Assur als Thema einer produktiven Neuinterpretation der Jesajasüberlieferung* (WMANT, 48; Neukirchen–Vluyn: Neukirchener Verlag, 1977), *passim*.

18. E.g., Miller and Hayes, *History*, pp. 383-85, 401; N. Na'aman, 'The Negev in the Last Days of the Kingdom of Judah', *Cathedra* 41 (1986), pp. 4-15, esp. pp. 13-14; *idem*, 'Kingdom of Judah', pp. 3-71; G.W. Ahlström, 'Prophetical Echoes of Assyrian Growth and Decline', in H. Behrens, D. Loding, and M.T. Roth (eds.), *Dumu-e2-dub-ba-a: Studies in Honor of Åke W. Sjøberg* (Occasional Publications of the Samuel Noah Kramer Fund, 11; Philadelphia: Samuel Noah Kramer Fund, University Museum, 1989), pp. 1-6; cf. *idem*, 'King Josiah and the DWD of Amos vi.10', *JSS* 26 (1981), p. 8 n. 3; D. Edelman, 'The Manassite Genealogy in 1 Chronicles 7:14-19: Form and Source', *CBQ* 53 (1991), p. 197; Ben Zvi, *Zephaniah*, p. 299.

19. Contra M. Noth, 'Israelitische Stämme zwischen Ammon und Moab', *ZAW* 60 (1944), pp. 11-57; H.L. Ginsberg, 'Judah and the Transjordan States from 734 to 582 B.C.E.', in S. Lieberman (ed.), *Alexander Marx Jubilee Volume* (New York: Jewish Theological Seminary of America, 1950), pp. 347-68; and Y. Aharoni, *The Land of the Bible: A Historical Geography* (trans. and ed. A.F. Rainey; Philadelphia: Westminster, 1979), pp. 402-404, among others. But see, e.g., Z. Kallai, *Historical Geography of the Bible. The Tribal Territories of Israel* (Jerusalem: Magnes, 1986), pp. 413-14; and Na'aman, 'Kingdom of Judah', p. 42.

the argument, unless one demonstrates independently that they were most likely composed during Josiah's reign to legitimize his movements into the Transjordan.[20]

Secondly, one cannot learn from the report of Josiah's death at the hands of Necho at Megiddo in 2 Kgs 23.29 (cf., however, 2 Chron. 35.20-24) that Megiddo or any Assyrian province was annexed to Judah nor that Josiah planned to attack Necho. The use of the expression *hlk lqr't*-X (2 Kgs 23.29) does not necessarily connote hostile intentions (see, e.g., 2 Kgs 8.8; 16.10).[21]

Thirdly, there is no clear evidence that Josiah conquered Philistine territories. The ostracon from Mesad Hashavyahu has been interpreted as pointing to Josiah's rule over the place,[22] but also to the opposite situation, that is, to the vassalage of contemporaneous Judah.[23] Certainly, the text of the ostracon demonstrates neither that the region was included in the realm of Judah nor that it was conquered by Josiah. Moreover, one can hardly assume actual Judahite domination of the seacoast from 616 to 610/609 (Josiah's last year), since the Egyptian army would not have campaigned in Northern Syria while

20. See Christensen, *Transformations*, pp. 154-63, 224-27; *idem*, 'Zephaniah 2:4-15'.

21. Necho's motive for killing Josiah is unknown. Cf. Miller and Hayes, *History*, p. 402; M. Cogan and H. Tadmor, *II Kings* (AB, 11; Garden City, NY: Doubleday, 1988), pp. 300-301; Na'aman, 'Kingdom of Judah', pp. 53-55. It is noteworthy that there is no evidence that Ashuruballit II survived the 609 campaign.

22. For example, J. Naveh ('The Excavations of Mesad Hashavyahu. Preliminary Report', *IEJ* 12 [1962], pp. 97-99) proposed that Josiah conquered the place after the fortress was established by the Greek mercenaries of Psammetichus I (c. 630–625) and that it was eventually abandoned in 609. The fortress may have been destroyed during the campaign of 604. See Na'aman, 'Kingdom of Judah', p. 47, and the bibliography cited there.

23. See Miller and Hayes, *History*, p. 389; Na'aman, 'Negev', pp. 12-14; *idem*, 'Kingdom of Judah', pp. 44-47. The usual dating of the ostracon to the reign of Josiah rather than to that of Jehoiakim, who was an Egyptian vassal until 604, rests on two questionable assumptions: (1) the conviction that the document demonstrates Judahite rule over Mesad Hashavyahu and (2) the assumed Josianic expansion of Judah to the Philistine coast. See, e.g., Cross, 'Epigraphic Notes', pp. 35-36; J.D. Amusin and M.L. Heltzer, 'The Inscription from Mesad Hashavyahu', *IEJ* 14 (1964), p. 149.

the coastal area—the main military route to and from Egypt—was in alien hands.[24]

Fourthly, the exact time at which Saitic Egypt gained independence from Assyria is unknown but cannot have been later than 643, and probably not earlier than 658–656 (i.e., during the reign of Manasseh).[25] It is worth noting that Assyria remained the major power in the west, even after 656, and that the transition from Assyrian to Egyptian (Saitic) hegemony probably occurred after 627. Moreover, this transition was generally peaceful, and Egypt acted as the successor state of the Assyrian Empire in the west and its main ally, rather than its enemy.[26] Although one may imagine that there were certain tensions in this transition, the fact remains that there is no evidence of direct conflict between Egypt and Assyria, nor of actions of war fought by proxy.[27] The contrast between this transition

24. See, e.g., A.J. Spalinger, 'Psammetichus, King of Egypt: II', *JARCE* 15 (1978), p. 52.

25. Prism A (643–642 BCE) shows that Saitic Egypt was independent of Assyria. Moreover, if Gyges' dispatch of Lydian troops to Egypt is seen as an indication of Egypt's independence (A II, 113-15), then it cannot postdate 644, for in this year Gyges was killed. More likely, Gyges sent mercenaries to Egypt c. 662–658, that is, after the defeat of the first Cimmerian invasion and before their second attack in 657. Psammetichus I gained control of Thebes in 657 and unified Egypt by 656. Taking into consideration Psammetichus's cautious policies, it is unlikely that he broke with Ashurbanipal before 656. Moreover, neither the Assyrian evidence claims that Egypt entered into any alliance against Assyria nor do Egyptian traditions describe the rise of the independent Egypt of the Saitic dynasty as a 'war of liberation' against Assyria. See A.J. Spalinger, 'Psammetichus, King of Egypt: I', *JARCE* 13 (1976), pp. 133-47; *idem*, 'The Date of the Death of Gyges and its Historical Implications', *JAOS* 98 (1978), pp. 400-409.

26. For the general date and character of the transition, see, e.g., R.D. Nelson, 'Realpolitik in Judah (687–609 BCE)', in W.H. Hallo, J.C. Moyer, and L.G. Perdue (eds.), *Scripture in Context II* (Winona Lake, IN: Eisenbrauns, 1983), pp. 177-89; Na'aman, 'Kingdom of Judah', 34-36; *idem*, 'Chronology and History in the Late Assyrian Empire (631-619 B. C.)', *ZA* 81 (1991), pp. 243-67, esp. 263-64. Na'aman suggests that Assyria retreated from the west and concluded an alliance with Saitic Egypt as late as 622.

27. Haak ('Prophets and History: Zephaniah') maintains that such a period of tension existed between 649 and 633 and that it provided a window of opportunity (from 640, the first year of Josiah, to 633) for the proclamation of Zephaniah's prophecy against the nations (including Assyria). Significantly, the Gezer document of 649 demonstrates that Assyria still controlled the area. The Assyrian campaigns against the Arabs/Arabians (probably 645) and against Ushu and Akko (644; Prism

and that from Egyptian to Babylonian hegemony cannot be sharper. Significantly, it seems that regional elites preferred to remain in the 'old' Assyrian-Egyptian political realm rather than be included in the 'new' one of Babylon.

Fifthly, there is no evidence pointing to any Judahite revolt against Assyria or any attempt to preempt Egyptian dominance. Moreover, were such attempts made, they would have been an exception to the general behavior of the regional elites. Most regional rebellions in times of transition involved more than a single country, and any revolt against a superpower seems very unlikely without the support of another superpower. Thus, a revolt would not have occurred against Assyria before the transition (because Saitic Egypt was Assyria's ally) nor any time after the first successes of the Babylonian revolt (when Egypt was active in the area). Furthermore, since Judah was a vassal state before and after the transition, one should assume that Josiah moved directly from Assyrian to Egyptian vassalage, rather than hypothesize a revolt for which there is no independent evidence.

Sixthly, the only clear action outside the traditional borders of Judah that can be attributed to Josiah is the destruction of the cultic center at Beth-El and perhaps some shrines in Samaria (2 Kgs 23.15-20). Although the book of Kings does not mention any permanent expansion of the kingdom of Judah beyond the 'from Geba to Beer-sheba' (2 Kgs 23.8) borders, Alt may be correct in relating the city list in Josh. 18.21-28—which includes Beth-El—to Josianic Judah.[28] If so, it would suggest that the territory of Judah expanded a few miles north and east of Jerusalem. Perhaps, it also included Lod, Ono, and Haddid, but not Ekron.[29] In any case, the extent of Josiah's kingdom

A [also represented by the Rassam cylinder] mentions both campaigns and was probably written by 643) point to Assyrian control of the area even later. The 'annalistic' literature of the period shows no indication of any Western revolt from 644 to 639, the date of the latest prism (the Babylon Prism). In the votive inscription to Marduk, written later, the enemy is Lygdamis, the Scythian, not Egypt or any Western country (Spalinger, 'Psammeticus, King of Egypt: I', p. 136).

28. A. Alt, 'Judas Gaue unter Josia', *PJ* 21 (1925), pp. 100-16 (= *KS*, II, pp. 276-88).

29. Ekron (cf. Josh. 15.46; 19.43) was an independent kingdom in the early Babylonian period (see B. Porten, 'The Identity of King Adon', *BA* 44 [1981], pp. 36-52; and Gittin, 'Urban Growth', esp. p. 221 n. 9). People from Beth-El, Jericho (a former Israelite city), Ein Gedi, Lod, Ono, and Haddid are mentioned

seems to be nearer the Persian province of Yehud (except in the south) than Davidic Israel.[30]

Finally, the possible annexation of a few miles of Assyrian territory north and east of Jerusalem may be understandable from the perspective of a mini-successor state, that is, a small friendly state that inherits a small territory close to its borders and its capital during the political reorganization of the area. In fact, a comparison between the extent of the territory that passed to Egyptian hands, the major successor state, and that which may have passed to Judahite hands seems to shed some light on Judah's actual weight in the new regional balance of power. It is worth stressing in this respect that the arguments in favor of this Josianic expansion seem to presuppose that the new hegemonic power gave its assent to this slight enlargement of Judah's borders. At the very least, it is clear that even when Necho killed the king of Judah and removed his successor, he did not take away the new Judahite territories.

Therefore, it is most likely that there was no Josianic empire nor independent Judah during Josiah's days, nor was there any uprising against Assyria. In addition, there is no clear evidence of hostile relations between Judah and its western or eastern neighbors at that time.

Clearly, this conclusion calls into question many of the correlations that have been proposed between prophetic texts and the historical circumstances of Josiah's reign. A comprehensive analysis of the

among those Judahites who returned from the exile (see Ezra 2.28, 33, 34 // Neh. 7.32, 36, 37), and their cities were included in the realm of Persian Yehud (see Neh. 3.2; 11.31). Since the Persians generally followed the administrative arrangements of the Babylonians, one may assume that these cities were also included in the Babylonian Judah. See Miller and Hayes, *History*, p. 401; Ahlström, 'Prophetical Echoes'.

30. Such a position is congruent with the general absence of 'rossete' jars from areas not included in the proposed realm of Josianic Judah. See Na'aman, 'Kingdom of Judah', pp. 31-33. The geographical distribution of the 'rossete' jars, however, cannot be expected to indicate the exact borders of Josianic Judah, because (1) by chance they may have not appeared in places within Josianic Judah, and (2) goods may have traveled the short distances involved in crossing the borders of Judah, especially towards its neighbors from the north and west. Thus, for instance, a single 'rossete' inscription from Gibeon or Gezer neither proves nor disproves that these cities belonged to Judah during Josiah's days. (The case is similar to that of the *lmlk* inscriptions; from the fact that one *lmlk* stamp was found in Beth-El and another in Ashdod does not follow that Hezekiah conquered both cities.)

affected correlations is beyond the scope of this paper, and it must suffice here to point to a few examples of the most important implications. First, if there was no expansion into Philistia or Transjordan, nor any rebellion against Assyria, it is extremely doubtful that Zeph. 2.4-15 was composed to support Josiah's program of political expansion at the expense of Assyria, particularly in Philistia and Transjordan. Of course, Josiah may have considered the conquest of Philistia and Transjordan, without having ever attempted to do so,[31] but this is certainly a superfluous, *ad hoc* hypothesis, which results from the assumption that Zeph. 2.4-15 belongs to the Josianic period.[32]

Secondly, as for the kind of texts discussed in the previous section, it seems more likely that the historical referent of the texts, which announces that the Assyrian armies will be utterly defeated as they fight against Jerusalem, is a power that was actually about to attack— or had recently attacked—Jerusalem, such as Babylon, rather than actual (as opposed to literary) Assyrians who neither attacked Jerusalem for three generations nor were about to attack it in Josiah's time.[33]

Finally, if during and, to a large extent, due to the Pax Assyriaca, Judah prospered, as archaeological data shows, one cannot assume as self-evident that the Judahite center of power was extremely anxious of Assyria's defeat.[34] Moreover, given the fact that Egypt and Assyria were allies at that time, it is doubtful that a Judahite elite living under Egyptian hegemony would have been free to rejoice at Assyria's fall.[35] Blenkinsopp recognizes, for example, that it is difficult to see

31. Cf. Christensen, 'Zephaniah 2:4-15'; Sweeney, 'Form Critical Reassessment'. Informal conversations with colleagues during the last year suggest a growing tendency towards such proposals.

32. Another necessary assumption is that the text should be interpreted as political propaganda, whose aim was to justify actual or planned territorial conquests.

33. This conclusion strongly weakens the case for an anti-Assyrian, Josianic redaction of the book of Isaiah, including, e.g., Isa. 14.24-27; 30.27-33; 31.8-9.

34. The more doubtful is this 'self-evident' assumption, if one takes into account that the regional centers of power seemed to have preferred the Assyrian-Egyptian system to the Babylonian.

35. Significantly, both proposals are either implied or explicitly claimed in some widespread analyses of the messages of prophetic texts. See, e.g., Blenkinsopp, *History of Prophecy*, pp. 148-49; Clements, *Isaiah 1–39*, p. 252; R.L. Smith, *Micah–Malachi* (WBC, 32; Waco, TX: Word Books, 1984), p. 68.

how Nahum, a spokesman of the Temple, could have proclaimed his anti-Assyrian *massa* before the actual event, because such inflammatory material could have come to the attention of the Assyrians.[36] If this is indeed the case, then can we consider the period of Egyptian dominion over Josianic Judah the most likely occasion for the proclamation of Nahum's prophecy?

Conclusion

To sum up, an analysis of the possible correspondences between prophetic texts and possible historical backgrounds against which these texts may have been written and communicated to their first audiences does help to discern between more and less likely backgrounds.

The present examination has raised serious questions about the validity of assertions regarding the (post-701) Hezekianic or Manassic historical settings of Isaianic texts (i.e., texts included in the book of Isaiah) claiming or proclaiming the complete defeat of the Assyrian army before Jerusalem or in Judah/Israel.

New reconstructions of the historical reign of Josiah have profound implications for the dates and messages of many biblical texts that have been generally associated with the Josianic era. Texts suggesting a policy of territorial expansion towards Transjordanian or Philistine cities, or those suggesting a policy of restoring Judah to its assumed grandeur in David's days, or those (pro)claiming the imminent destruction of the Assyrian armies before Jerusalem, or those expressing extreme joy at the fall of Assyria can no longer be related convincingly to the reign of Josiah on the basis of their 'historical' references.

36. So, Blenkinsopp, *History of Prophecy*, p. 148.

HOSEA AND THE PENTATEUCHAL TRADITIONS
The Case of the Baal of Peor

George R. Boudreau, O.P.

Caution Concerning Pentateuchal Traditions in Hosea

To explain an apparent pentateuchal reference found in the book of Hosea on the basis of the final form of the Pentateuch is at best a hazardous enterprise.[1] While some connection between such references in Hosea and the accounts in the Pentateuch may be justified, the extent and even the direction of such a connection—Which tradition is earlier, and has it influenced the other?—are often most difficult to establish.

The eighth-century prophet Hosea, as opposed to disciples of the prophet and later editors, is credited by most scholars with the so-called pentateuchal references in the book of Hosea. That Hosea is aware of a particular pentateuchal tradition merits closer scrutiny for the following reasons: (1) pentateuchal traditions underwent extensive oral and even written flux before achieving their final, written form; (2) a major development in these traditions occurred from the seventh

---

1. Hosean passages ordinarily associated with pentateuchal texts include: 'How can I make you like Admah! How can I treat you like Zeboiim!' in 11.8 (see the Sodom and Gomorrah tradition in Gen. 19.24-29 and Deut. 29.23); 'In the womb he [Jacob] took his brother by the heel. . . ' and 'Jacob fled to the land of Aram, and there did service for a wife. . . ' in 12.4-5, 13 (see the Jacob cycle in Genesis); phrases such as 'and from Egypt I called my son' and 'by a prophet Yahweh brought Israel up from Egypt' in 11.1b and 12.14 (see the Exodus narrative centered around the prophet Moses); and 'they came to Baal-Peor and separated themselves to the shame' in 9.10 (see Num. 25.1-5 and Deut. 4.3-4). See, for example, the interpretations of these passages in the following commentaries: H.W. Wolff, *Hosea* (Hermeneia; Philadelphia: Fortress Press, 1974); J.L. Mays, *Hosea* (OTL; Philadelphia: Westminster, 1969); and D.K. Stuart, *Hosea–Jonah* (WBC, 31; Waco, TX: Word Books, 1987). Commentators also find references in Hosea to early, non-pentateuchal traditions (e.g., a Gibeah tradition and references to tribal conflicts during the period of the Judges in Hos. 9.9; 10.9 [cf. Judg. 19–21]).

to the fifth centuries BCE—well after Hosea's day; (3) it is possible that the Hosean passages in question referred to eighth-century situations that are no longer known; (4) there are clear differences between the traditions in the Pentateuch and those in Hosea (e.g., Jacob is a negative figure in Hosea but a positive one in the Pentateuch; Jacob weeps in Hos. 12.5 but not in Gen. 32.24-32); (5) some of the important expressions used in the Hosean passages are multivalent (e.g., 'Jacob' does not always refer to the patriarch [see Hos. 12.3]; nor is 'from Egypt' (*mimmiṣrayim*) always a reference to the exodus event [see 11.11]); (6) text-critical difficulties—for which the book of Hosea is notorious—complicate the interpretation of the so-called pentateuchal references in Hosea; and (7) passages in Hosea are often difficult to interpret due to the poetic obscurity of the language. Therefore, it will be argued in this essay that the author of the Baal-Peor text in Hos. 9.10b had a vastly different situation in mind than that described in Num. 25.1b-5 and Deut. 4.3-4.

Numbers 25.1b-5 as an Exilic Composition

There is no dispute in attributing Hos. 9.10 to the prophet Hosea. The verse reads,

> Like grapes in the wilderness
> I found Israel.
> Like a first fruit on the fig tree in its first season,
> I saw your ancestors.
> But they came to Baal-Peor,
> and separated themselves to the shame.
> And they were detestable,
> like the thing they loved.

Since Hos. 9.10 contains the terms *midbār* ('wilderness'), *'ābôt* ('ancestors'), *māṣā'* ('to find'), and *ba'al-pĕ'ôr* ('Baal-Peor'), it is assumed that the author had in mind an earlier oral or written version of the Baal-Peor tradition, such as that found in Num. 25.1-5. This is based on the observation of source critics that the text in Numbers derives from the (pre-Hosean) J or JE sources.[2] Set in the wilderness

---

2. The following illustrates the variety of sources that scholars find in Num. 25.1-5: (1) JE: J. Wellhausen, *Prolegomena to the History of Ancient Israel* (Gloucester, MA: Peter Smith, 1983 [1883]), p. 356; G.B. Gray, *Numbers* (ICC, 4; Edinburgh: T. & T. Clark, 1903), p. 380; and J. de Vaulx, *Les Nombres* (SB; Paris:

period,[3] this Numbers tradition also appears in Deut. 4.3-4.

Further developments in the Baal-Peor tradition are found in Num. 25.6-18 (P); 31.16 (P); and Josh. 22.17 (P), traditions considered too late to have been known by Hosea. Ps. 106.28-31, the last Baal-Peor account to appear in the Old Testament, is a postexilic summary of the entire Numbers 25 account.

Is Num. 25.1-5 a pre-Hosean J or JE account? A detailed analysis of the text[4] suggests that it arose from the Deuteronomistic editor rather than from the compilers of J or JE. This is indicated by the presence of Deuteronomistic vocabulary ('Moab',[5] 'Baal',[6] 'Peor',[7] *ṣmd* [niphal: 'to attach, bind'],[8] *rō'š* ['chief', 'leader'],[9] *yq'* [hiphil: 'to expose?' 'to

Gabalda, 1972), p. 299; (2) J: W. Rudolph, *Der 'Elohist' von Exodus bis Josua* (BZAW, 68; Berlin: A. Töpelmann, 1938), p. 128; and P.J. Budd, *Numbers* (WBC, 5; Waco, TX: Word Books, 1984), p. 276; (3) E: K. Jaroš, *Die Stellung des Elohisten zur kanaanäischen Religion* (Göttingen: Vandenhoeck & Ruprecht, 1974), pp. 390-98; (4) J + 'Lay' Source: O. Eissfeldt, *Hexateuch-Synopse. Die Erzählung der fünf Bücher Mose und des Buches Josua mit dem Anfange des Richterbuches* (Leipzig: Hinrichs, 1922), p. 190; and (5) J + 'Nomadic' Source: G. Fohrer, *Introduction to the Old Testament* (Nashville: Abingdon, 1968 [1965]), pp. 148, 162.

3.   Among those who see the Num. 25.1-5 tradition behind Hos. 9.10 are: W.R. Harper, *Amos and Hosea* (ICC, 23; New York: Charles Scribner's Sons, 1905), pp. 336-37; S.L. Brown, *The Book of Hosea* (Westminster Commentaries; London: Methuen, 1932), pp. 82-83; Wolff, *Hosea*, p. 165; J.M. Ward, *Hosea: A Theological Commentary* (New York: Harper & Row, 1966), p. 167; Mays, *Hosea*, p. 133; H. McKeating, *The Books of Amos, Hosea and Micah* (CBC; Cambridge: Cambridge University Press, 1971), p. 129; and Stuart, *Hosea-Jonah*, p. 151.

4.   V. 1a ('And Israel dwelt in Shittim') is a Priestly connective that was added to the Peor account when the Balaam material was inserted into the book of Numbers. See G.R. Boudreau, 'A Study of the Traditio-historical Development of the Baal of Peor Tradition' (PhD dissertation, Emory University, 1991), pp. 238-58.

5.   Appears 43 times in Deuteronomistic material, once in Gen. 19.37 (possibly not J), 24 times in passages of disputed sources (Numbers 21-24 [22 times]; Gen. 36.35; and Exod. 15.15), and in P passages.

6.   The god Baal appears 55 times in Deuteronomistic material, but there are no occurrences in J, JE, or P texts.

7.   Six times in Deuteronomistic material, once in Num. 23.28 (disputed source), and four times in P passages.

8.   While the niphal of this verb does not appear elsewhere in J, JE, D, Deuteronomistic, or P material, the pual form is attested once in 2 Sam. 20.8 (Deuteronomistic), and the noun *ṣemed* appears eight times in Deuteronomistic texts.

9.   Thirteen times in D-Deuteronomistic passages, once in Exod. 18.25 (source disputed), and in P material. JE prefers the term *sar* in designating a leader.

hang?'],[10] *ḥārôn* ['burning (wrath)'],[11] and *šōpēṭ* ['judge'])[12] and themes that permeate the Deuteronomistic History (Israel involved with the Baal cult; Israel bowing down before, worshiping, serving, and following after other gods; Israel 'sacrificing' [*zbḥ*] to other gods; the kindling of Yahweh's anger; Israel eating in honor of other gods; and Israel 'playing the harlot' [*znh*]). Except for the fourth theme, those mentioned rarely occur, if at all, in J or JE material.[13]

The tradition described in Num. 25.1b-5 closely resembles that found in Deut. 4.3-4. The latter passage stems from a late exilic Deuteronomistic editor's hand.[14] These two pentateuchal passages are the earliest narrative accounts of the Baal-Peor incident, and yet, by virtue of their Deuteronomistic provenance, it is possible that both were composed as late as the exilic period, two centuries after Hosea's career.[15]

Incongruities between Hosea 9.10b and the Numbers 25.1b-5 and Deuteronomy 4.3-4 Tradition

If it is indeed the case that Num. 25.1b-5 derived from the Deuteronomistic editor, and not from the J or JE source, then it is possible that the tradition reflected in Num. 25.1b-5 and Deut. 4.3-4 arose after the eighth century and was unknown to the author of Hos. 9.10. With this possibility in mind, the question is posed anew: is

10. The verbal root *yqʻ* appears four times in Deuteronomistic material (twice in its hiphil form [2 Sam. 21.6, 9], once in its hophal form [2 Sam. 21.13], and once in an emended archaic hophal form [1 Sam. 31.10]). There are no JE or P occurrences of the hiphil/hophal form.

11. See Deut. 13.18 (D); 1 Sam. 28.18 (Deuteronomistic); and 2 Kgs 23.26 (Deuteronomistic). The term also occurs in Exod. 15.7; 32.12; Num. 32.14; and Josh. 7.26, all passages attesting Deuteronomistic influence. There are no clear JE occurrences, and the term does not appear in the P material.

12. Twenty-two times in D-Deuteronomistic material, only twice in JE material (Gen. 18.25; Exod. 2.14), and never in P material.

13. For further particulars, see Boudreau, 'Baal of Peor Tradition', pp. 48-75.

14. See B.R. Moore, 'The Scribal Contribution to Dt 4.1-40' (PhD dissertation, University of Notre Dame, 1976), pp. 30-36; and A.D.H. Mayes, 'Deuteronomy 4 and the Literary Criticism of Deuteronomy', *JBL* 100 (1981), pp. 23-51; *idem, The Story of Israel between Settlement and Exile: A Redactional Study of the Deuteronomistic History* (London: SCM Press, 1983), pp. 22-39.

15. A more precise dating of Num. 25.1b-5 is beyond the scope of this article. See ch. 3 of Boudreau, 'Baal of Peor Tradition', which promotes a late exilic dating.

Hos. 9.10b a reference to a pre-conquest, Mosaic, wilderness period tradition, whether in oral or written form, such as that in Num. 25.1b-5 or Deut. 4.3-4? There are several reasons to conclude that the answer is 'no' and that Hos. 9.10b alludes to a completely different tradition or event.

The Ideal Wilderness
According to the book of Hosea, Israel's sinfulness began in the settlement period after the ideal wilderness period. The references to 'country', 'altars', and 'improved pillars' in Hos. 10.1b-c all indicate sinfulness during the settlement period. This is in sharp contrast to v. 1a, which describes Israel in the previous wilderness period as a luxuriant vine, and to the positive view of the wilderness found in 2.16, where Hosea promises to allure his wife into the wilderness and speak tenderly to her.[16] Moreover, Hos. 13.1a ('Ephraim...was exalted in Israel') suggests that the ideal, sinless period extended to the early settlement period. This is followed in vv. 1b-2 by a sinful era that continued to Hosea's time. In light of these passages,[17] therefore, it is unlikely that the sinful situation described in Hos. 9.10b refers to a pre-settlement, wilderness event such as the one described in Num. 25.1b-5 and Deut. 4.3-4.

The Settlement in the Land
Well-attested in both the Deuteronomistic History and the prophets is the 'ideal era' oracle of reproach, the genre of Hos. 9.10-14.[18] Its form is as follows:

1.   Yahweh and the Israelites have an ideal initial relationship (v. 10a).

16. B.S. Childs, *The Book of Exodus* (OTL; Philadelphia: Westminster, 1974), p. 256.
17. Note also Hos. 11.1-2. Although a distinction between the wilderness and settlement eras is not stated explicitly, the initial, ideal period before Israel was called out of Egypt in 11.1 ('When Israel was a child. . . ') is contrasted in 11.2 with Israel's sinfulness after this call took place. Therefore, Hos. 11.1 may be assigned to the wilderness era, and 11.2 to that of the settlement.
18. See Deut. 32.10-33; 2 Kgs 17.7-18; Jer. 2.2b-37; 7.21-34; 9.12-15; 11.7-17; 16.11-13; 34.13-22; Ezek. 16 (allowing for an initial period of Israelite corruption before the ideal period); and Hos. 10.1-6; 11.1-7; 13.1-3.

2. The Israelite ancestors forsake Yahweh during a later period (v. 10b).
3. The present generation imitates the sinfulness of the Israelite ancestors. (Understood in v. 10b? See 'Sinfulness Past and Present' below.)
4. The consequence is punishment of the present generation (vv. 11-14).

The focus in this section is on the second element in the form. Is the 'later period' in it the pre-conquest wilderness period or some other era in Israelite history?

An investigation of this genre as it occurs in the Old Testament reveals that the sinfulness mentioned in the second form element arises in Israelite life at some point after the settlement. Note, for example, the descriptions of Israelite sins in Hos. 10.1 (altars and the nation of Israel are mentioned); 13.1 (Ephraim is already part of Israel); 2 Kgs 17.8-11 (mention is made of kings of Israel, towns, watchtowers, fortified cities, and nations driven from the land); Jer. 2.4, 7 (sins begin only when the Israelites have entered the land); Ezek. 16.15-34 (shrines have been built, streets exist, and Egyptians, Philistines, Assyrians, and Chaldeans have been wooed); and Deut. 32.13-14 (the sinful period is preceded by an initial, ideal settlement period in which land, crops, honey, oil, flocks, wheat, and grapes are mentioned).[19]

By virtue of form, therefore, the Baal-Peor reference in Hos. 9.10b alludes to an incident that occurred during the settlement period. The Num. 25.1b-5 and Deut. 4.3-4 incident, on the other hand, occurred during the pre-settlement period.

Sinfulness Past and Present
At first glance, it would appear that form element three of the ideal era oracle of reproach (the sinfulness of Israel in Hosea's day) is missing from Hos. 9.10-14. However, the following three observations suggest that both the second and third form elements are contained in v. 10b. First, it would be surprising for the book of Hosea, so thoroughly permeated with references to the sinfulness of the present generation of Israelites, to omit an element as crucial as

19. Note further examples of the jump to a later post-wilderness period in 2 Kgs 17.14 and Jer. 7.24. The transitionary connective *wĕ* is usually expressed in English as 'but [they]'.

the third form element in vv. 10-14 by jumping, without explanation, from the sinfulness of a past generation directly to the punishment of the present generation. Secondly, in addition to Hos. 9.10-14, the ideal era oracle of reproach genre occurs in three other passages in the book: 10.1-6; 11.1-7; and 13.1-3. In all three cases, the sins of earlier generations are identical to the sins of Hosea's generation. Finally, Hos. 9.10-17 forms a unit that consists of two parallel oracles of reproach: vv. 10-14 and vv. 15-17. Within this unit, the 'Baal-Peor shame' (v. 10b) is parallel to the 'Gilgal evil' (v. 15). Hos. 4.15, 12.12, Amos 4.4, and 5.5 reveal that Gilgal was the seat of shameful sacrificial practices during the eighth century. Could one then conclude that the 'Baal-Peor shame' also occurred in the eighth century?

These three observations indicate that 'Baal-Peor shame' in v. 10b should be interpreted with reference to Israelite sinfulness, which is not only past but also present, as present as the 'Gilgal evil'. 'They came to Baal-Peor, and they were continuing to come to Baal-Peor.' True to the book of Hosea's general message and its use of the ideal era oracle of reproach genre, v. 10b refers to a past situation in which the present generation plays a direct, if not identical, participatory role. The Mosaic Baal-Peor incident, on the other hand, was an isolated event that pre-dated Hosea's generation by at least five centuries.

Vocabulary and Content

In the pentateuchal accounts, the term Israel and the designation 'Baal-Peor' are the only expressions that reappear in Hos. 9.10. However, 'Israel' more narrowly denotes 'Ephraim' (the northern kingdom) in Hosea, while in the pentateuchal context of Num. 25.1b-5 (see vv. 3-5) and Deut. 4.3-4 (see v. 1), it refers to the people who will inhabit the territory of what will become both the northern and southern kingdoms. In 9.10b, 'Baal-Peor' is a place name,[20] while in Num. 25.3, 5, it designates the deity, 'the Baal of Peor'. In

---

20. The syntax of the phrase *hēmmâ bā'û ba'al-pĕ'ôr* ('But they came to Baal-Peor') indicates that Baal-Peor is a place name: no preposition follows the verb *bw'*. See, e.g., Deut. 1.7; Judg. 17.8; 1 Sam. 10.5; Jer. 26.21; 34.3; Amos 4.4; and Ruth 1.19, 22. Baal-Peor is not a person; in such a case the syntax typically includes the preposition *'el-* after the verb *bw'*. See, e.g., Exod. 2.18; 5.23; Num. 22.14; Josh. 2.23; 1 Sam. 19.18; 21.11; 1 Kgs 2.19; Isa. 39.3; and Jer. 40.6.

Deut. 4.3-4, it is used for both place and deity.

If all three texts indeed refer to the same event, as is usually assumed, it is surprising that there is not more shared vocabulary. Why, for example, did the author of Hosea, otherwise prone to the use of sexual imagery,[21] use the verb *nzr* ('to separate oneself to') in Hos. 9.10b, instead of the verb *ṣmd* (see Num. 25.3, 5) with its sexual overtones?[22] One obvious answer is that he was unfamiliar with the Num. 25.1b-5 tradition and intended to rebuke something other than sexual misconduct here. Note that the book of Hosea is not concerned about Israelite men having sex with foreign women. Although Hos. 7.8 suggests this issue, alliances with foreign powers is the real concern.

Apart from the fact that Hos. 9.10b deals with 'a sinful incident at Baal-Peor', one would be hard-pressed to find other relations between the content of the text from Hosea and the Num. 25.1b-5 and Deut. 4.3-4 tradition. In the Hosean account, there is no mention of a divine slaughter or any past punishment, and furthermore, the name of Moses is neither connected with this tradition nor mentioned elsewhere in the book of Hosea (cf. Num. 25.4-5; Deut. 1.1; 4.3).

Hosea 9.10b in its Eighth-Century Context

The sin that Hos. 9.10b condemns, therefore, must have begun after Israel entered the land and must have continued into Hosea's own day. What past and present sin does Hosea have in mind here? The words and phrases that are most helpful in answering this question are: 'Baal-Peor', 'they separated themselves (*nzr*) to the shame (*bōšet*)', and 'detestable things (*šiqqûṣîm*)'. Unfortunately, these expressions are not attested elsewhere in the book of Hosea.

The term *bōšet* had as general a use during biblical times as our term 'shame' has today.[23] In the case of *šiqqûṣîm*, however, the

---

21. See Hos. 1.2-3; 2.4, 6, 9, 12, 14; 3.1, 3; 4.2, 10, 12-15, 18; 5.3, 4; 7.4; and 9.1.

22. J. Milgrom, *Numbers* (JPS Torah Commentary; Philadelphia: Jewish Publication Society, 1990), pp. 212-13. Milgrom also notes (*Numbers*, p. 323) the sexual connotation of a cognate Akkadian term in an old, bilingual Mesopotamian text: 'A girl who did not reach her bloom. . . a boy who remained unyoked (*etlu la tsum[mudu]*.' Cf. '*ṣummudu*', *CAD* 16 (1962), p. 247.

23. See S.J. De Vries, 'Shame', *IDB* 4 (1962), pp. 305-306.

context is often that of idolatry.[24] Mention of 'Baal-Peor', as opposed to the more geographical appellation 'Beth-Peor',[25] along with the reference to a 'separation of oneself to the shame', further suggests that idolatry is the sin condemned in Hos. 9.10b.

There is scriptural evidence that Peor was a northern Moabite town. It is attested in Deut. 3.29; 4.46; 34.6; and Josh. 13.20 as 'Beth-Peor', and in Deut. 4.3a as 'Baal-Peor'. Josh. 13.20 includes Peor in its Reubenite (i.e., northern Moabite plateau) city-list. That the four references from Deuteronomy—all exilic[26]—allude to this Transjordanian site is suggested by the location of the Israelite camp throughout Deuteronomy (i.e., east of the Jordan River) and the Moabite incident recounted in Num. 25.1b-5 (i.e., Israel's worship of the Baal of Peor while encamped east of the Jordan River).

That this Peor is the one mentioned by Hosea in 9.10b may be impossible to establish.[27] Increasing the likelihood of such an identification, however, is the assertion of some scholars that the place names found in Josh. 13.17-20 are part of a pre-exilic, Reubenite tribal or administrative town-list.[28] While Gray considers the list to be more generally from the monarchy,[29] Kallai's careful study of Reubenite/Gadite history concludes that this list must be dated

24. E.g., Deut. 29.16; 2 Kgs 23.24; Jer. 4.1; 7.30; 13.27; and Ezek. 20.7, 8.

25. Deut. 3.29; 4.46; 34.6; and Josh. 13.20. Variations in ancient Israelite place names containing 'Beth' (Beth-Peor, Baal-Peor, Peor) are common (e.g., Baal-Meon [Num. 32.38; Jer. 48.23; Ezek. 25.9; and 1 Chron. 5.8], Beth-Baal-Meon [Josh. 13.17], and Beon [Num. 32.3]; and Bamoth-Baal [Josh. 13.17], Beth-Bamoth [Mesha Inscription], and Bamoth [Num. 21.19, 20]).

26. Deut. 3.29; 4.46; and 34.6 occur in the exilic framework of the book, and as indicated in the previous section, Deut. 4.3-4 stems from a late exilic Deuteronomistic editor's hand. For a comprehensive discussion of the Deuteronomistic editing of Deuteronomy, see M. Noth, *The Deuteronomistic History* (JSOTSup, 15; Sheffield: JSOT Press, 1981 [1943]); Mayes, *Story of Israel*, pp. 22-39; and *idem*, *Deuteronomy* (NCB; Greenwood, SC: Attic, 1979), pp. 41-55, 117-18, 411.

27. Hos. 9.10b itself does not provide evidence that 'Baal-Peor' is located in northern Moabite territory. Furthermore, as shown in the previous section, Hos. 9.10b is not a reference to the Mosaic incident described in the Num. 25.1b-5 and Deut. 4.3-4 tradition.

28. See the discussion in Mayes, *Story of Israel*, pp. 53-55.

29. J. Gray, *Joshua, Judges, and Ruth* (NCB; Greenwood, SC: Attic, rev. edn, 1977 [1967]), p. 105.

to the close of David's and the beginning of Solomon's reigns.[30] Traditionally, every mention of Peor in the Old Testament assumes the same Transjordanian site: a town east of the northern tip of the Dead Sea and at the northwestern edge of the northern Moabite plateau in the Reubenite hill country of the Pisgah/Nebo mountain range.[31]

The history of northern Moab before Hosea's time is difficult to reconstruct. When would Israel have inhabited this region, and what events in Peor's history would have resulted in Israelite ancestors 'separating themselves to the shame' and 'becoming detestable as the thing they loved' so that there were repercussions for Hosea's generation?

Non-biblical evidence is of little help in showing Israel's involvement in this area before the mid-ninth century. From the ninth century, however, the Mesha Inscription mentions that 'Omri, King of Israel' humbled Moab (or at least northern Moab), but that Mesha, king of Moab, later triumphed over Omri's son. Therefore, it would appear that northern Moab was ruled and probably even inhabited by Israelites during the early Omride period. The four Omrides (Omri,

---

30. Z. Kallai, *Historical Geography of the Bible: The Tribal Territories of Israel* (Jerusalem: Magnes, 1986), p. 322.

31. Since the fourth century CE, the main contenders have been Khirbet el-Mehatta and Khirbet Ayun Musa, both located in the Wadi Ayun Musa Valley which runs from the northern Moabite plateau down toward the northern tip of the Dead Sea. Representative of those promoting Khirbet el-Mehatta is A. Musil, *Arabia Petraea: I - Moab* (Vienna: Adolf Holzhausen, 1907), pp. 344, 348. For Khirbet Ayun Musa, see O. Henke 'Zur Lage von Beth Peor', *ZDPV* 75 (1959), pp. 161-63. Although no extensive archaeological excavations have been performed at either site, pottery dating to the Iron Age has been found in both places. At Khirbet el-Mehatta, Henke found a few probable Iron Age sherds ('Zur Lage', p. 161), and the Heshbon Survey Team found Iron Age II/Persian and possible Hellenistic pottery. See R. Ibach, Jr, *Hesban 5: Archaeological Survey of the Hesban Region* (ed. Ø.S. LaBianca; Berrien Springs, MI: Andrews University, 1987), p. 16. At Khirbet Ayun Musa, N. Glueck found sherds dating possibly to late Iron Age I-II. See N. Glueck, *Explorations in Eastern Palestine* (ed. M. Burrows and E.A. Speiser; AASOR, 15; New Haven: University of Pennsylvania Press, 1935), II, pp. 110-11; and *Exploration in Eastern Palestine* (AASOR, 18-19; New Haven: ASOR, 1939), III, pp. 251-66. The Heshbon Survey Team (see *Hesban 5*, p. 160) found Early Bronze, Iron Age Ia, Ib, Ic, II, and Iron Age II/Persian pottery but noted that the area in which the pottery was found (around the springs) does not appear to have been an occupational site.

Ahab, Ahaziah, and Jehoram) ruled Israel from c. 880 until c. 840.

Under close examination, however, the biblical accounts give us additional information concerning Mesha's reclamation of this territory. 2 Kgs 1.1 and 3.4-27 indicate that Mesha had to pay tribute to the king of Israel, that Mesha rebelled against the king of Israel, that the king of Israel was an Omride, that the king of Israel approached Kir-hareseth in Moab, and finally that the Israelite troops returned home after an unsuccessful campaign against Mesha.[32]

An investigation of other biblical texts indicates several more occasions after Israel's settlement in Palestine in which at least part of Moab may have been ruled by Israel: Num. 24.17-18; 1 Sam. 14.47; 22.3-4; 2 Sam. 8.2, 11-12; 23.20; 24.5; 1 Kgs 4.9; 11.1-8; and 1 Chron. 5.10. All of these biblical passages, however, present strong literary and/or textual difficulties that diminish their usefulness for the reconstruction of Israelite history and illumination of Israel's political dominance over Moab.[33] On the other hand, these passages, and many others,[34] suggest that there were dealings between Israel/Judah and Moab, whether adversarial or peaceful, before the time of the Omrides[35] and that they continued long after Mesha's revolt.

Given such close contact between Israel and Moab through the years, it is even likely that people of Israelite ancestry had, by the eighth century, inhabited Moabite territory for many generations, changing allegiance when necessary, and adopting the religious practices of their new rulers.

32. See J.M. Miller and J.H. Hayes, *A History of Ancient Israel and Judah* (Philadelphia: Westminster, 1986), pp. 253-55, 264. This summary of the Omride period is based largely on the work of J.M. Miller, 'The Fall of the House of Ahab', *VT* 17 (1967), pp. 307-24; S.J. De Vries, *Prophet against Prophet: The Role of the Micaiah Narrative (I Kings 22) in the Development of Early Prophetic Tradition* (Grand Rapids: Eerdmans, 1978); and J.R. Bartlett, 'The "United" Campaign against Moab in 2 Kings 3:4-27', in J.F.A. Sawyer and D.J.A. Clines (eds.), *Midian, Moab, and Edom: The History and Archaeology of Late Bronze and Iron Age Jordan and North West Arabia* (JSOTSup, 24; Sheffield: JSOT Press, 1983), pp. 135-46.

33. See Boudreau, 'Baal of Peor Tradition', p. 175 n. 32.

34. See Gen. 19.30-38; Num. 21.21-30; Deuteronomy 2; Judges 11; 2 Kgs 13.20-21; 24.2; Jer. 27.3; 40.11-12; Ruth 1.4; 4.13-22; and 1 Chron. 5.17; 8.8-10.

35. The Mesha Inscription itself reads, 'Now the men of [the Israelite tribe of] Gad had always dwelt in the land of Ataroth [present-day Atarus, c. 13 km NNW of Dhiban in the northern Moabite plateau], and the king of Israel built Ataroth for them. . . ' See *ANET*, p. 320.

The book of Hosea is permeated with references to eighth-century Israelite apostasy,[36] idolatry,[37] and following after and sacrificing to Baal.[38] Shrines at Bethel/Beth-aven (4.15; 10.5; 12.5) and Gilgal (4.15; 9.15; 12.12) were centers of these abominable practices. References in 9.10b to *šiqqûṣîm* and to 'Baal' in the place name, as well as the parallel mention of the Gilgal shrine in v. 15, suggest that Israelites living in the Transjordan were also going to the Peor shrine to worship Baal. Hos. 9.10b reminds the prophet's audience that the present idolatry at Peor continues the practice of earlier generations.

Conclusion

The foregoing analysis of Hos. 9.10b cautions strongly against making too close an identification between allusions in the book of Hosea and traditions appearing in the Pentateuch. Unlike the Num. 25.1b-5 and Deut. 4.3-4 tradition, Hos. 9.10b concerns Israelite idolatry at Peor after the settlement. Originating perhaps at some long-forgotten point in the past, this idolatry continued to Hosea's day, as Israelites separated themselves from Yahweh, frequented the shrine at Peor, and became as detestable as the Baal they worshiped there.

36. Cf. Hos. 1.2 (see 1.9); 3.1 (see 4.1, 6, 7); 4.12, 13, 19; 5.4; 7.7, 10, 13, 14; 8.1, 14; 9.1; 10.1, 2, 8; 12.12; 13.2; and 14.1.
37. Cf. Hos. 4.12, 17; 8.4, 5; 10.5; 11.2; 13.2; and 14.9.
38. Cf. Hos. 2.10, 15, 18, 19; 11.2; and 13.1.

PROBLEMS OF TEXT AND TRANSLATION IN ISAIAH 10.13bb*

Stuart A. Irvine

Isaiah 10.13bb is part of a larger speech composed by Isaiah and placed in the mouth of the Assyrian king (10.8-9, 11, 13-14).[1] The speech illustrates the arrogance of the king by having him describe his military conquests as the achievements of his own initiative and power. In v. 13bb, according to the MT, the king boasts, *wĕ'ôrîd ka'bîr yôšĕbîm*. Most commentators repoint the verb as *wā'ôrîd*, so that it fits with the other imperfect consecutive and perfect forms in vv. 13 and 14.[2] As for *ka'bîr*, scholars who follow the kethib usually vocalize the consonants as *kĕ'abbîr*. With these small changes, the line would mean, 'and I [the Assyrian king] brought down inhabitants (rulers) like a mighty one'.[3]

---

* I wish to pay special tribute to my friend and former teacher, John Hayes. In recent years he has urged greater caution in textual emendation, and I have tried to follow his lead. I also wish to thank William Brown (Union Theological Seminary in Virginia) and Marvin Sweeney (University of Miami) for commenting on earlier drafts of this essay. It should not be assumed that they agree with my arguments or conclusions.

1. Commentators generally regard vv. 10 and 12 as secondary additions. The authenticity of v. 11, on the other hand, is widely debated. For a brief survey of scholarly opinion, see H. Wildberger, *Isaiah 1–12* (Continental Commentaries; Minneapolis: Augsburg Fortress, 1991), pp. 413-14. As for v. 13bb, most commentators think it is original; cf., however, G. Fohrer, *Das Buch Jesaja* (Zürcher Bibelkommentare; 2 vols.; Zurich/Stuttgart: Zwingli, 2nd edn, 1966), I, p. 154; and F. Huber, *Jahwe, Juda und die anderen Völker beim Propheten Jesaja* (BZAW, 137; Berlin/New York: de Gruyter, 1976), p. 41 n. 10.

2. Similarly, *wĕ'āsîr* in v. 13ba is usually repointed as *wā'āsîr*. Cf., however, F. Delitzsch, *Biblical Commentary on the Prophecies of Isaiah* (Clark's Foreign Theological Library, 4th ser., 14-15; Edinburgh: T. & T. Clark, 1879), I, p. 269. He retains *wĕ'āsîr* and *wĕ'ôrîd* and construes the imperfect forms as expressions of past iterative action.

3. The repointing of the MT as *wā'ôrîd kĕ'abbîr yôšĕbîm* goes back at least to

This reconstruction of the text, however, has not gone unchallenged. Clements, for example, observes that the MT of 10.13bb 'appears to be in a very disturbed state',[4] and Kaiser that it 'is evidently corrupt, and a line has fallen out'.[5] Wildberger argues the same and suggests restoring, *wā'ôrîd be'āpār 'ārîm*... *yôšĕbêhem*...('I strike down into the dust the cities...their inhabitants...').[6] This reading partly follows an earlier proposal by Marti, who restored the Hebrew more fully: *wā'ôrîd bā'ēper 'ārîm ûbe'āpār kol-yôšĕbêhem* ('and I brought down cities into ashes, and into dust all their inhabitants [all enthroned in them]').[7] Duhm reconstructed the text similarly: *wā'ôrîd bā'ēper he'ārîm ûbe'āpār yôšĕbîm* ('and I brought down into ashes the cities and into the dust the enthroned').[8]

Duhm, Marti, and Wildberger offer a number of reasons for emending the MT so extensively. First, in comparison to the bi-cola in vv. 13a and 13ba, v. 13bb is strikingly short. Secondly, with the verb *wā'ôrîd* (hiphil of *yrd*), one would expect some indication of direction, e.g., *lā'āreṣ* ('to the ground'), *bā'ēper* ('into ashes'), or *be'āpār* ('into dust'); cf. Isa. 47.1. Thirdly, reference to the king's 'might' in v. 13bb is unnecessary, since the beginning of the verse already emphasizes his strength (*bĕkōaḥ yādî*, 'by the power of my

A. Dillmann (*Der Prophet Jesaja* [KEHAT, 5; Leipzig: S. Hirzel, 5th edn, 1890], p. 108).

4.   *Isaiah 1–39* (NCB; Grand Rapids: Eerdmans; London: Marshall, Morgan & Scott, 1980), p. 113. For similar statements, see J. Skinner, *The Book of the Prophet Isaiah, Chapters I–XXXIX* (CBSC; Cambridge: Cambridge University Press, 2nd edn, 1915), p. 96; B.S. Childs, *Isaiah and the Assyrian Crisis* (SBT, 3; London: SCM Press, 1967), p. 40; and W. Dietrich, *Jesaja und die Politik* (BEvT, 74; Munich: Chr. Kaiser, 1976), p. 119 n. 26.

5.   *Isaiah 1–12* (OTL; Philadelphia: Westminster, 2nd edn, 1983), p. 229 n. 10.

6.   *Isaiah 1–12*, p. 413. Clements quotes this translation as a possibility (*Isaiah 1–39*, p. 113).

7.   *Das Buch Jesaja* (KHCAT, 10; Tübingen: Mohr, 1900), p. 104.

8.   *Das Buch Jesaia* (Göttingen: Vandenhoeck & Ruprecht, 5th edn, 1968), p. 100. In the first edition of this commentary (1892), Duhm had suggested adding *l'rṣ* before or after *yôšĕbîm* ('to the earth the enthroned'), or reading *yôšĕbê kol-hā'āres* ('the enthroned of all the earth'). Cf. H. Donner, *Israel unter den Völkern. Die Stellung der klassischen Propheten des 8. Jahrhunderts v. Chr. zur Aussenpolitik der Könige von Israel und Juda* (VTSup, 11; Leiden: Brill, 1964), p. 143. Donner refers to the 'brilliant conjecture' of Duhm and proposes only a slight modification: *wā'ôrîd bā'ēper he 'ārîm . . . yôšĕbê hā'āreṣ*.

hands'). Thus, the kethib *k'byr* (vocalized *kĕ'abbîr*, 'like a mighty one') and the qere *kabbîr* ('a mighty one') are equally suspect. Fourthly, the LXX translation of v. 13bb reads, *kai seisō poleis katoikoumenas* ('and I will shake inhabited cities').[9] The Targum reads, *w'ḥytyt btqwp yt ytby krkyn tqypyn* ('and I have brought down by strength the inhabitants of strong cities').[10] The mention of 'cities' in the Greek and Aramaic translations suggests *'ārîm* or *he'ārîm* as the accusative object of the verb in the Hebrew text.[11] Fifthly, it is easy to imagine how *[he]'ārîm ûbe'āpār* could have dropped out of the original Hebrew text through haplography.

Several of these arguments may be questioned. Since an indication of direction does not invariably accompany hiphil forms of *yrd* in the Hebrew Bible (e.g., Prov. 21.22 and Pss. 56.8; 59.12), it is not necessary to restore *bā'ēper* or *be'āpār* after the verb in Isa. 10.13bb. Moreover, none of the ancient versions clearly supports the emendation. As for *kĕ'abbîr* or *kabbîr* repeating the idea of the king's 'might', such repetition might be appropriate in a speech that aims to illustrate the extreme hubris of the Assyrian ruler. Furthermore, as will be seen below, the kethib *k'byr* may in fact have special connotations that add to the thought of the verse.

The witness of the LXX merits closer study. The future tense of *seisō* is of less concern here than the choice of the verb itself.[12] *seiein*

---

9.   In some editions of the LXX, this sentence comes at the beginning of v. 14. See, e.g., J. Ziegler (ed.), *Isaias* (Septuaginta, Vetus Testamentum Graecum, 14; Göttingen: Vandenhoeck & Ruprecht, 2nd edn, 1967); cf. A. Rahlfs, *Septuaginta* (Stuttgart: Württembergische Bibelanstalt, 8th edn, 1965).

10.   The Aramaic word *kerak* usually refers to fortified cities specifically; see M. Jastrow, *Dictionary of the Targumim, the Talmud Babli and Yerushalmi, and the Midrashic Literature* (2 vols.; New York: Pardes, 1950), I, p. 669. B. Chilton thus translates *krkyn tqypyn* as 'strong fortresses' (*The Isaiah Targum* [Aramaic Bible, 11; Wilmington, DE: Michael Glazier, 1987], p. 25).

11.   Cf. the Peshitta: *wĕkabšet mĕdînātâ dĕjatĕbān* ('and I subdued inhabited cities'). Wildberger refers to the Syriac text but seems to give it little weight in the debate over Isa. 10.13bb. On the text-critical value of the Peshitta's reading, see n. 29.

12.   The Greek translators chose to render all the verbs in vv. 13-14 in the future tense, and this served their broader purpose in 10.5-19, that is, to make the point that Yahweh will not allow the Assyrian king to do what he intends. In this connection, note the LXX's addition at the beginning of v. 16: *kai ouch houtos* ('and it shall not be so').

means 'shake' and, in the active voice with an accusative object, it usually translates hiphil forms of *rgz* and *r'š* (Isa. 14.16; Job 9.6; Hag. 2.7, 22). In contrast, hiphil forms of *yrd* are usually rendered by other Greek verbs: *katagein* (36 times), *katabibanein* (8 times), *katapherein* (5 times), *katarrein* (3 Kgdms 2.33 only), and *katachalan* (Josh. 2.15 only).[13] If one assumes that the LXX's *seisō* translates a hiphil of *rgz* or *r'š* in Isa. 10.13bb, it would be difficult to account for the hiphil of *yrd* in the MT. On the other hand, if the LXX translators found *wě'ôrîd* or *wā'ôrîd* in their *Vorlage*, they did not render the verb literally.[14]

The LXX continues with the accusative *poleis katoikoumenas* ('inhabited cities').[15] A straightforward retroversion of the clause would probably yield *'ārîm yôšěbîm*,[16] and this reading is far shorter than Duhm and Marti's reconstruction, *bā'eper [he]'ārîm ûbe'āpār yôšěbîm/yôšěbêhem*. The *Vorlage* of the LXX may already have been

13. In the book of Isaiah specifically, the LXX translators use *katagein* in 63.6 (MT *wě'ôrîd*) and *katabainein* in 14.15 (MT *tûrād*, a hophal of *yrd*). In 43.14ba, the verb of the LXX, *epegerō* ('and I will stir up'), contrasts with the verb of the MT, *wěhôradtî* ('and I have brought down'). Here, the Greek text may genuinely attest a Hebrew variant, perhaps *wěha'îrōtî* (the hiphil of *'ûr*, 'rouse, stir up').

14. Cf. the later Greek translations of Aquila and Symmachus. Instead of *seiein*, they use the verb *katagein*, which closely matches the hiphil of *yrd* in the MT.

15. Cf. again the later Greek translations: *hōs dunatos tous katoikountas* (Aquila and Symmachus) and *hōs kratei tous katoikountas* (Theodotian). These adhere closely to the MT.

16. Cf. S. Olofsson, *God Is My Rock: A Study of Translation Technique and Theological Exegesis in the Septuagint* (ConBOT, 31; Stockholm: Almqvist & Wiksell, 1990), pp. 91-92. He states that 'in Is 10:13 K the translator has misunderstood the Hebrew *k'byr* and rendered it by *polis*, which probably reflects *byrh* in his Hebrew text'. The noun *bîrâ* occurs 17 times in the MT, all in the books of Esther, Daniel, Nehemiah, and 1 Chronicles. It generally means 'castle, palace', but it sometimes refers to a fortress or temple within a city, including Jerusalem (1 Chron. 29.1; Neh. 2.8; 7.2). The LXX renders the word by *polis* in Esth. 1.2, 5; 2.3, 5, 8; 9.6, 11, 12; and Dan. 8.2. If the *Vorlage* of the LXX contained *k'br* in Isa. 10.13, the Greek translators would have understood it easily. They encountered *'byr* in Isa. 1.24 and 49.26, and rendered the word in those passages as *ischuos* and *ischuontes*. Thus, they knew the basic meaning of *'byr* ('strong'). The translators may have found *k'byr* in 10.13 but chose to play on the word, rendering it as though it were *bîrâ*. Ancient translators might resort to this kind of wordplay if the exegetical/theological payoff were significant. It does not appear to be so in this instance.

a corruption of the fuller text that these scholars propose. It is difficult to imagine, however, the scribal error that would have left *[he]'ārîm* in the *Vorlage* of the LXX without the *bā'ēper* and *ûbe'āpār* that supposedly preceded and followed *[he]'ārîm* in the original Hebrew text.

In light of these remarks, it is worthwhile to consider whether inner-translational factors might adequately explain the LXX's deviation from the MT in Isa. 10.13bb.[17] The Greek version of the passage is possibly a free translation of a Hebrew text that matched the MT closely,[18] a suggestion based on five observations.

First, the kethib-qere of the MT (*kĕ'abbîr* and *kabbîr*) might preserve two ancient textual variants.[19] If the *Vorlage* of the LXX followed the qere, it would have read, *wĕ'ôrîd/wā'ôrîd kabbîr yôšĕbîm*.

Secondly, the Greek translators presumably construed *kabbîr*

---

17. See E. Tov, *The Text-critical Use of the Septuagint in Biblical Research* (Jerusalem Biblical Studies, 3; Jerusalem: Simor, 1981), p. 74. He advises, 'When analyzing the LXX translation for text-critical purposes, one should first attempt to view deviations as the result of inner-translational factors. Only after all possible translational explanations have been dismissed should one turn to the assumption that the translation represents a different reading from MT.' Further, 'the more one knows about the nature of the translation, and the more thoroughly inner-translational deviations are analyzed, the less one is inclined to ascribe translational deviations to Hebrew variants' (p. 80).

18. The LXX of Isaiah is, on the whole, 'free, paraphrastic and strongly affected by the exegetical understanding and translation techniques of the translator and his personality as well as the Sitz im Leben of the version as regards both time and place...'. (Olofsson, *God Is My Rock*, p. 88). For similar descriptions, see A. van der Kooij, *Die alten Textzeugen des Jesajabuches. Ein Beitrag zur Textgeschichte des Alten Testaments* (OBO, 35; Göttingen: Vandenhoeck & Ruprecht, 1981), pp. 33-34, 65-71, 112; I.L. Seeligmann, *The Septuagint Version of Isaiah: A Discussion of its Problems* (Leiden: Brill, 1948), pp. 38-60, 95-121; J. Ziegler, *Untersuchungen zur Septuaginta des Buches Isaias* (ATAbh, 12/3; Münster: Aschendorff, 1934), pp. 8, 13, 46-47, 56-60, 83. Cf. J. de Waard, 'Old Greek Translation Techniques and the Modern Translator', *BT* 41 (1990), pp. 311-19.

19. This explanation might apply to most instances of the kethib-qere. See H.M. Orlinsky, 'The Origin of the Kethib-Qere System: A New Approach', in G.W. Anderson *et al.* (eds.), *Congress Volume: Oxford, 1959* (VTSup, 7; Leiden: Brill, 1960), pp. 184-92; A. Sperber, *A Historical Grammar of Biblical Hebrew* (Leiden: Brill, 1966), pp. 493-506; also G.E. Weil, 'Qere-kethib', *IDBSup* (1976), pp. 721-23.

yôšĕbîm as a construct chain—'a great (number) of inhabitants'—and took the phrase as the object of the preceding verb.[20]

Thirdly, for guidance in rendering *kabbîr yôšĕbîm*, the translators probably looked to the immediate context. Verses 9-11 in the MT contain an impressive list of cities that had fallen, or would fall, to the Assyrian king—Carchemish, Calno, Arpad, Hamath, Damascus, Samaria, and Jerusalem.[21] The Greek translators understandably assumed a similar sense in v. 13bb and thus paraphased *kabbîr yôšĕbîm* as *poleis katoikoumenas* ('inhabited cities').

Fourthly, as suggested above, although the translators may have found a hiphil of *yrd* ('bring down') in their *Vorlage*, they chose to construe the action of the Assyrian king as a matter of 'shaking' (*seisō*) cities. Their decision can be understood, in part, as an attempt to heighten the king's arrogance. The Hebrew Bible often speaks of Yahweh 'shaking' (*r'š* or *rgz*) the heavens and the earth, and the LXX typically uses the verb *seiein* in such contexts.[22] By having the Assyrian king boast of 'shaking' cities in Isa. 10.13bb, the Greek translators portrayed him as a blasphemer who claimed for himself the power that Yahweh alone exercised.[23] Their interpretation accords well with the overall purpose of vv. 5-15, namely, to illustrate and denounce the hubris of the king.

20. The quantitative nuance of *kabbîr* ('much, many, great') is attested in Isa. 16.14 and Job 31.25. Note, too, the verbal root *kbr* ('be numerous'), which means in the hiphil, 'make much, many' (see KB, p. 422; Job 35.16; 36.31).

21. The series in the LXX is slightly different: 'the country above Babylon', Chalanne 'where the tower was built', Arabia, Damascus, Samaria, and Jerusalem. The departures from the MT probably reflect the limited geographical knowledge of the Greek translators (see Seeligmann, *The Septuagint Version of Isaiah*, pp. 77-79; cf. van der Kooij, *Die alten Textzeugen des Jesajabuches*, pp. 35-38). They equated Calno with Chalanne 'in the land of Shinar' (Gen. 10.10 in the LXX) and identified the city specifically as the place of the infamous tower described in Gen. 11.1-10. As for Arpad and Hamath, the translators apparently knew very little about their location and so guessed that the broad designation, Arabia, might cover both cities. (Cf. the LXX of Isa. 11.11, where Arabia seems to replace Hamath. That Arabia might also cover Arpad could have been inferred from the pairing of the city with Hamath in Isa. 10.9 and elsewhere.) As for Carchemish, the translators probably surmised from the context that the city lay somewhere north of Chalanne, 'where the tower was built'. They thus referred vaguely to 'the country above Babylon'.

22. See, e.g., Judg. 5.4; 2 Kgdms 22.8; Job 9.6; Ps. 67(68).9; Joel 4(3).16; Nah. 1.5; Hag. 1.6, 21; Isa. 13.13; 24.18.

23. Cf. the similar braggadocio of the king of 'Babylon' in Isa. 14.13-14.

Fifthly, while the sense of the immediate context guided the LXX translation of 10.13bb, the thought and language of a more distant passage, 14.16-17, may have been a factor as well.[24] Here the people respond to the death of the king of 'Babylon', and according to the MT they ask, 'Is this the man who made the earth tremble (*margîz hā'āreṣ*), who shook kingdoms (*mar'îš mamlākôt*), who made the world like a desert and overthrew its cities (*wĕ'ārāyw hārās*)?' The LXX reading is close: 'This is the man who troubled the earth (*ho anthrōpos ho paroxunōn tēn gēn*), who shook kings (*seiōn basileis*), who made the whole world desolate and destroyed its cities (*kai tas poleis autou katheilen*). . . .' The talk of 'shaking kings/kingdoms' and 'overthrowing/destroying cities' in 14.16-17 probably influenced the translators' choice of *seisō* and *poleis* in 10.13bb.[25]

The Targum's translation of Isa. 10.13bb requires more attention, too.[26] The verb *w'ḥytyt* ('and I have brought down') presupposes the hiphil of *yrd* and thus approximates the *wĕ'ôrîd* of the MT. The Aramaic text continues with *btqyp yt ytby krkyn tqypyn* ('by strength the inhabitants of strong cities'). This reading, like the LXX, mentions 'cities', but like the MT, it also refers explicitly to the 'strength' of the Assyrian king.

The Targum in v. 13b possibly rests on a Hebrew text that differed only slightly from the MT. This proposal requires one to assume again that the kethib-qere of the MT preserves two textual variants, *kĕ'abbîr* and *kabbîr*. While the *Vorlage* of the LXX contained the qere, as suggested above, the Hebrew text behind the Targum may have included both variants side-by-side.[27] Thus, it would have read,

---

24. This suggestion fits the exegetical character of the LXX generally. See Tov, *The Text-critical Use of the Septuagint*, pp. 82-83. Tov distinguishes between linguistic and contextual exegesis but then states, 'In a way, all forms of exegesis might be called "contextual exegesis", because the translators' concept of "context" was wider than ours. They referred to the relationship between the words not only in their immediate, but also in remote, contexts. Furthermore, the translation might contain any idea the source text called to mind.'

25. For a different explanation, see Seeligmann, *The Septuagint Version of Isaiah*, p. 81; and van der Kooij, *Die alten Textzeugen des Jesajabuches*, pp. 34-38.

26. For a recent discussion of the translation technique, provenance, and text-critical value of the Isaiah Targum generally, see van der Kooij, *Die alten Textzeugen des Jesajabuches*, pp. 161-213.

27. The conflation of variant readings is common in the MT and in the ancient versions. For examples, see P.K. McCarter, *Textual Criticism* (Guides to Biblical

wā'ôrîd kĕ'abbîr kabbîr yôšĕbîm.[28] Presumably the translators paraphrased *kĕ'abbîr* ('like a mighty one') with *btqwp* ('by strength') and then construed *kabbîr yôšĕbîm* in the same way as the LXX, that is, as a reference to the cities mentioned earlier in vv. 8-11.

To summarize: the translations of Isa. 10.13bb in the LXX and the Targum may be paraphrastic renderings of Hebrew texts that closely approximated the wording of the MT. The ancient versions do not clearly support the reconstruction(s) of the passage that Duhm, Marti, and Wildberger propose.[29] What remains of their case is the legitimate observation that v. 13bb is short in comparison to the bicola of vv. 13a and 13ba—an argument that carries little weight by itself.

The rest of this study focuses on the translation and meaning of the MT. The predominance of perfect and imperfect consecutive forms in 10.13-14 certainly justifies repointing *wĕ'ôrîd* as *wā'ôrîd* ('I have brought down') at the beginning of v. 13bb. The change, furthermore, is supported by the Targum's *w'hytyt*, the Vulgate's *detraxi* ('I have pulled down'), and *katēgagon* ('I brought down') in the later Greek translations of Aquila and Symmachus.[30] As for the participle

---

Scholarship, Old Testament Guides; Philadelphia: Fortress, 1986), pp. 36-37.

28. Alternatively, one could suppose that the Targum translators found only one of the variants in their Hebrew text, but being familiar with the other variant, they chose to reckon with both in their translation.

29. The Peshitta seems to support the reconstruction(s), but the long and complex history of this version may impair its text-critical value. The original Peshitta was not a new translation but a revision of an older Syriac version. The latter, in turn, probably rested on an ancient Palestinian Targum. Furthermore, the LXX also exercised considerable influence on the Peshitta. For a more detailed discussion of the Syriac translation, see A. Vööbus, 'Syriac Versions', *IDBSup* (1976), pp. 848-54; also E. Würthwein, *The Text of the Old Testament* (Grand Rapids: Eerdmans, 1979), pp. 80-83. According to Vööbus (p. 849), the Isaiah scroll from Qumran 'has close affinities with the Peshitta and confirms its value as a witness to the text'. However, in Isa. 10.13bb specifically, 1QIsa[a] has a lacuna and so does not support any of the ancient versions. The Syriac *mĕdînātâ dĕjatĕbān* ('inhabited cities') probably reflects a dependence on the Targum tradition and the LXX. As for the verb, *wĕkabšeṭ* ('subdue'), it may attest a form of *kbš* in the ancient Palestinian Targum. The Aramaic verb, in turn, could have rendered the Hebrew *w'rd* (= *w'wryd* in the MT, spelled defectively), taken as a form of *rdd* ('beat out/down, subdue') or *rdh* ('rule, dominate').

30. It remains unclear why the Masoretes vocalized the Hebrew verb as they did. Their concern to protect the pointing is indicated by the circulus over the word and by

yôšĕbîm at the end of the line, both 'inhabitants' and 'rulers' are possible translations. The Vulgate chooses the latter (*in sublimi residentes*, 'them that sit on high'), and the modern translations of the NIV and RSV prefer it as well. Duhm reasons that the preceding verb *wā'ôrîd* refers more naturally to exalted individuals than to the general population.[31] 'Inhabitants', however, is not out of the question, and the KJV, NEB, JB, and TEV choose it.

As suggested above, the qere *kabbîr* and the kethib *kĕ'abbîr* are probably ancient variants. Which is preferable, and how should it be translated? Among the modern translations of Isa. 10.13, only the JPSV seems to follow the qere: 'and [I] exiled their vast populations'. This rendering, like the LXX, apparently construes the adjective *kabbîr* as a substantive in construct with *yôšĕbîm*—literally, 'a great (number) of inhabitants'. *kabbîr* occurs nine other times in the Hebrew Bible, all in the books of Isaiah and Job. It refers to 'mighty' waters and wind (Isa. 17.12; 28.2; Job 8.2), 'much' property or wealth (Job 31.25), 'mighty' and 'aged' people (Job 15.10; 34.24), the small, 'not great' (*lô' kabbîr*), remnant of a country (Isa. 16.14), and 'mighty' God (Job 34.17; 36.5). Only in Job 31.25; 34.17 and 24 does *kabbîr* function as a substantive, and in these passages the term does not stand in construct with another noun. Thus, as a construct chain,

the Masora, which notes that the form occurs only twice, in Isa. 10.13 and 63.6. (See Mm 2434 in G.E. Weil [ed.], *Massora Gedolah iuxta Codicem Leningradensem B 19a* [Rome: Pontificium Institutum Biblicum, 1971], I, p. 274.) It is tempting to guess that the Masoretes wanted to preserve *wĕ'ôrîd* as a way of projecting the actions of the Assyrian king into the future, perhaps anticipating the narrative in Isa. 36–37. This suggestion falters, however, on two observations. First, the Masoretes took no steps to protect the imperfect form, *wĕ'āsîr*, in v. 13ba, which would seem just as crucial to their interpretation. Secondly, they could have easily vocalized *wtmṣ'* in v. 14a as an imperfect verb; instead, they pointed the consonants as an imperfect consecutive (*wattimṣā'*) and thus as a past tense.

The Masoretic protection of *wĕ'ôrîd* may concern the plene spelling of the word, not its imperfect form. A defective spelling, *wĕ'ōrîd*, could be misunderstood and miscopied as *wĕ'ārîd*, from the root *rdd* ('beat out, subdue'). The Syriac verb in the Peshitta of 10.13 might indicate that this scribal error did in fact occur (see n. 29). The Masoretes presumably tried to prevent it by insisting on writing the o-vowel with the *waw*. This proposal, of course, does not explain the imperfect form in 10.13bb, but it does suggest that the Masoretes were more concerned with a different problem.

31. *Das Buch Jesaja*, p. 100; see also Skinner, *Isaiah*, p. 96.

kabbîr yôšěbîm in Isa. 10.13bb has no close parallels elsewhere in the Hebrew Bible.

A more probable rendering of the qere would construe *kabbîr* as an accusative of manner, 'like a mighty one'. This interpretation underlies translations of Isa. 10.13 as quoted in the Mishnah (*Yad.* 4.4).[32] As an accusative of manner, *kabbîr* appears equivalent to *kě'abbîr*, but in fact the meaning of *kabbîr* is blander. The kethib has special connotations that make it a more distinctive reading (see below).[33]

If the qere is not original, it may have arisen in one of two ways. The original reading, *k'byr*, could have become *kbyr*, as the pronunciation of the *alef* gradually weakened in late Hebrew.[34] Alternatively, scribes may have purposefully substituted *kbyr* for *k'byr*, because *k'byr* had overtones that the scribes found theologically offensive.

While the kethib *kě'abbîr* is preferable, its meaning is ambiguous.[35] The RSV, NEB, and TEV read 'like a bull', presumably in part because *'abbîr* elsewhere has the connotation of 'bull' (Ps. 22.13; Isa. 34.7; Jer. 46.15; cf. Pss. 50.13; 68.31).[36] In fact, the word means 'strong, mighty', and it sometimes describes horses (Judg. 5.22; Jer. 8.16; 47.3; 50.11), people (Lam. 1.15; Job 24.22; 34.20; cf. 1 Sam. 21.8; Ps. 76.6; Isa. 46.12), and even angels (Ps. 78.25).[37] Thus, on lexical grounds, *kě'abbîr* in Isa. 10.13 may be translated, 'like a bull'—

---

32. See C. Albeck and H. Yalon, *The Six Orders of the Mishnah Explained and Pointed* (Jerusalem: Bialik Institute; Tel Aviv: Dvir, 1952-59); H. Danby, *The Mishnah* (Oxford: Oxford University Press, 1933); P. Blackman, *Mishnayoth* (7 vols.; New York: Judaica, 2nd edn, 1964); J. Neusner, *The Mishnah: A New Translation* (New Haven: Yale University Press, 1988).

33. In the first edition of his Isaiah commentary (1892), Duhm stated that the kethib and the qere were equally *nichtssagend*. Cf., however, the opinion of Delitzsch: the kethib (vocalized as *kā'abbîr*) is 'to be preferred as more significant' than the qere (*The Prophecies of Isaiah*, I, p. 269).

34. For examples of Hebrew variants resulting from the quiescence of *alef*, see McCarter, *Textual Criticism*, pp. 54-55.

35. Words in First Isaiah often have more than one meaning, and such ambiguity may be purposeful, at least in some instances. See J.J.M. Roberts, 'Double Entendre in First Isaiah', *CBQ* 54 (1992), pp. 39-48.

36. In Pss. 22.13 and 68.31, the word is used figuratively of enemies. The reference in Jer. 46.15 is to the Egyptian bull-god, Apis.

37. See A.S. Kapelrud, "*ābhîr*', *TDOT*, I (1977), pp. 42-44.

though this specific sense is not required—and it could be supported by the fact that bulls figure prominently in Assyrian art as symbols of strength. The simile, 'like a bull', thus would be apt in the mouth of the king in Isa. 10.13.[38] On the other hand, the Akkadian cognate of *'abbîr* is *abāru* ('strength'), and it occurs in the expression *gamir dunni u abāri* ('consummate in power and strength') with reference to Sargon II.[39] Accordingly, the Hebrew *kĕ'abbîr* in Isa. 10.13 could be translated, 'like a mighty one', and understood as imitating the inflated rhetoric of the Assyrian kings in their own inscriptions.

The larger context of Isa. 10.13 allows another interpretation of *kĕ'abbîr*. In v. 15, Isaiah asks rhetorically, 'Shall the axe glorify itself over the one who cuts with it, or the saw magnify itself over the one who wields it?' The question serves to characterize the preceding boast of the Assyrian king as a presumptuous claim to be equal with, or superior to, Yahweh. The whole of the king's speech, of course, implies such a claim, but the simile in v. 13bb, 'like a mighty one', makes the claim more directly. The word *'abbîr* is reminiscent of two divine epithets elsewhere in the Hebrew Bible: 'the Mighty One of Jacob' (*'ăbîr ya'ăqōb*, Gen. 49.24; Ps. 132.2, 5; Isa. 49.26; 60.16) and 'the Mighty One of Israel' (*'ăbîr yiśrā'ēl*, Isa. 1.24).[40] If overtones of these names are intended in Isa. 10.13, the Assyrian king would appear guilty of the most extreme blasphemy: he suggests his equality with Yahweh.[41] Vocalizing the kethib with the definite article

---

38. See Delitzsch, *The Prophecies of Isaiah*, I, p. 269; also Skinner, *Isaiah*, p. 96.

39. See D.G. Lyon, *Keilschrifttexte Sargons Königs von Assyrien (722-705 v. Chr.)* (Assyriologische Bibliothek, 5; Leipzig: J.C. Hinrichs, 1883), p. 30.

40. The distinction between *'ābîr* and *'abbîr* is likely an artificial invention of the Masoretes. See Olofsson, *God Is My Rock*, pp. 90-91; cf. Kapelrud, *"ābhîr'*, p. 42.

41. O. Procksch came close to this interpretation by translating *kĕ'abbîr*, 'like a god' (*Jesaia I* [KAT, 9; Leipzig: A. Deichert, 1930], pp. 162, 167). The interpretation might be supported by Isa. 14.13-14, which ascribes a very similar thought to the king of 'Babylon': 'I will ascend to heaven; above the stars of God I will set my throne on high; I will sit on the mount of assembly in the far north; I will ascend above the heights of the clouds, I will make myself like the Most High' (*'eddammeh lĕ'elyôn*). Commentators debate the authorship of the larger passage (14.4-21), as well as the identity of the king in it. At least some scholars, however, assign an original core of the text to Isaiah and seem to identify the king in it with the Assyrian ruler of 10.5-15. See H. Barth, *Die Jesaja-Worte in der Josiazeit*

(*kā'ăbîr*) would make the comparison explicit: 'Like the Mighty One, I brought down rulers.'[42]

This interpretation has two advantages. First, as mentioned earlier, it might explain how *kabbîr* first arose as a textual variant. Early scribes presumably substituted it for the original *k'byr* to avoid the scandalous analogy between Yahweh and the king of Assyria. (Perhaps for the same reason the later Masoretes preferred *kabbîr* as the form to be read.) Secondly, the interpretation might account for the brevity of v. 13bb. By interrupting the pattern of bi-cola that precede and follow, the line creates a pause and calls attention to itself. This emphasis might have served the rhetorical strategy of Isaiah by allowing the shock-value of the king's self-comparison to Yahweh, 'the Mighty One', to exert its full force on the prophet's audience.

(WMANT, 48; Neukirchen–Vluyn: Neukirchener Verlag, 1977), pp. 26, 135-39; cf. J.H. Hayes and S.A. Irvine, *Isaiah, the Eighth-Century Prophet: His Times and His Preaching* (Nashville: Abingdon, 1987), pp. 226-35.

42. Texts from the Cairo Geniza include an early medieval copy of the Mishnah with Babylonian pointing, and the quotation of Isa. 10.13 in *Yad.* 4.4 attests the reading, *kā'abîr*. See M.H. Goshen-Gottstein (ed.), *The Book of Isaiah* (Hebrew University Bible; Jerusalem: Magnes, 1975).

ISAIAH 8.11 AND ISAIAH'S VISION OF YAHWEH*

Brian C. Jones

Introduction

Isaiah 8.11 introduces the last section of what is commonly thought to be the first version of Isaiah's so-called *Denkschrift* (6.1–8.18): 'For the LORD spoke thus to me while his hand was strong upon me, and warned me not to walk in the way of this people, saying. . . '[1] This paper will examine the verse, paying particular attention to the grammatical and syntactical difficulties connected with the two expressions 'while his hand was strong upon me' and 'warned me not to walk'. On the basis of this analysis, I will offer an interpretation of 8.11-15 and argue that it is intimately connected with the vision account in ch. 6.

Several general issues that arise concerning v. 11 call for discussion. First, the initial *ky* in 8.11 marks a transition from a prophetic speech that details Yahweh's coming judgment to a section in which the prophet recounts God's personal address to him.[2] The *ky* has no clear syntactic connection with the preceding section, and Wildberger suggests that it is 'a redactional transitional element'.[3] Nevertheless, commentators agree that vv. 11-15 belong to the same period of prophetic activity as the preceding material in 7.1–8.10 and form part of the conclusion to this section.[4] Secondly, the standard

* This paper is offered with thanks and appreciation to my teacher John H. Hayes.

1. All translations are from the NRSV unless otherwise indicated.
2. It should be noted, however, that the *ky* is not represented in the LXX and the Syriac. 1QIs^a has an empty space between vv. 10 and 11, probably indicating the beginning of a new section.
3. H. Wildberger, *Isaiah 1–12: A Commentary* (Continental Commentaries; Minneapolis: Fortress Press, 1991), p. 354.
4. O. Kaiser, *Isaiah 1–12* (OTL; Philadelphia: Westminster, 2nd edn, 1983), pp. 190-91.

messenger formula, *kh 'mr yhwh*, is followed by the phrase, *'ly khzqt hyd wysrny mlkt bdrk h'm-hzh*, rather than by the content of the message as is usual in prophetic texts. This modification of the normal form makes it necessary to add *l'mr* at the end of the verse in order to introduce the message itself.[5] Thirdly, 8.11 leads the reader to expect an oracle addressed to Isaiah personally, but in 8.12-13 the verbs and pronominal suffixes are 2mpl.[6] Finally, it is difficult to determine the meaning of Yahweh's word to the prophet. Why is the prophet warned? Who is 'this people'? What events or plans are not to be called 'conspiracy'? These and other questions perplex the reader, and it is with them in mind that we proceed to examine v. 11.

khzqt hyd

The syntactic use of *khzqt* in Isa. 8.11 is unique. Wildberger analyzes the form as a qal infinitive construct, and BDB as a noun construct.[7] The construct form, whether infinitive or noun, occurs with the prefixed preposition *k* in three other Hebrew Bible texts (2 Chron. 12.1; 26.16; and Dan. 11.2). In each it occurs with a 3ms suffix and with reference to a time when a king secured military power. For instance, 2 Chron. 12.1 records, 'When the rule of Rehoboam was established and *he grew strong*, he abandoned the law of the LORD. . . ' The phrase in Isa. 8.11 has no 3ms suffix, refers to divine action toward an individual rather than to human attainment, and comes from a significantly earlier time than the Chronicles or Daniel

5. Elsewhere in Isaiah this standard introduction is never interrupted, nor is it ever followed by *l'mr* (see 7.7; 10.24; 22.15; 28.16; 29.22; 30.15; 37.6, 21, 33; 38.1, 5). The addition of *'ly* ('to me') occurs elsewhere in the book (18.4; 21.16; 31.4).

6. The disruption caused by the second person plural can be explained by the suggestion that here Yahweh addresses Isaiah *and* his disciples (Kaiser, *Isaiah*, p. 190). It may be that vv. 12-15 were composed and delivered independently first and that v. 11 was added by Isaiah later in order to incorporate the material into the larger body of his work. Perhaps the message contained in 8.11-15 was understood by the prophet primarily as a message to himself but secondarily as a message for those he hoped to influence (whether his supposed disciples or some wider audience). Thus, when he expressed the message in public form, he couched it in the second person plural. While such explanations are plausible, there is no direct evidence to support them.

7. Wildberger, *Isaiah*, p. 354; BDB, p. 305.

texts. For these reasons the latter two books shed little light on the phrase in Isaiah.

Textual uncertainty adds to the difficulty of understanding the phrase in Isaiah. A significant number of Hebrew MSS read *bḥzqt* instead of *kḥzqt*.[8] The construction *bḥzqh* occurs five times elsewhere in the Hebrew Bible, always functioning adverbially and specifying emphatic or vigorous action: of political oppression, 'cruelly' (Judg. 4.3); of upbraiding in a tribal dispute, 'violently' (Judg. 8.1); of seizure of sacrificial meat, 'by force' (1 Sam. 2.16); of oppressive rulers, 'with force' (Ezek. 34.4); and of calling on Yahweh, 'mightily' (Jon. 3.8). The idiom is not exactly the same, however, since *bḥzqh* never occurs in these texts in construct with another noun, as is the case in some MSS of Isa. 8.11. Nevertheless, the frequent attestation of *bḥzqh* in a variety of contexts suggests that it is a more likely reading than *kḥzqh*. If 8.11 did not contain *hyd*, we could translate it, 'Yahweh spoke to me forcefully', on the analogy of the use of *bḥzqh* elsewhere. Even with the addition of *hyd*, the phrase is probably best understood adverbially as a reference to the forcefulness of Yahweh's address to the prophet: 'Yahweh spoke to me with the forcefulness of the hand.'

The meaning of this statement is problematic. As Werner has noted, the reference to Yahweh at the beginning of the verse leads us to expect *hyd* with a 3ms suffix.[9] It is clear in the context that the hand is Yahweh's, but the way it is stated is unusually elliptical. Assuming that Yahweh's hand is meant, how are we to understand the phrase? Does it refer to a disciplinary hand? To a coercive hand? Or is the phrase a technical expression for a particular kind of divine address?

It is widely accepted that the phrase is a technical expression for an ecstatic experience during which the prophet receives the divine

8. So Codex Vaticanus and numerous medieval Hebrew MSS (see M.H. Goshen-Gottstein [ed.], *The Book of Isaiah* [Jerusalem: Magnes, 1975], I, p. *l*'). The editors of BHK[3] followed this reading, as did the older commentaries (e.g., G.B. Gray, *A Critical and Exegetical Commentary on the Book of Isaiah, I–XXVII* [ICC, 18.1; Edinburgh: T. & T. Clark, 1912], p. 151). The confusion of *b* and *k* is of course a common error; the similarity is so great that sometimes context and usage would have been the scribe's only guide. In a context as enigmatic as the present one, a disagreement among the MSS is understandable.

9. W. Werner, 'Vom Prophetenwort zur Prophetentheologie: Ein redaktions-kritischer Versuch zu Jes 6,1-8,18', *BZ* 29 (1985), p. 7.

word.[10] This interpretation is based on a comparison with other texts
that deal with prophets and the hand of Yahweh (e.g., 2 Kgs 3.15;
Jer. 15.17; Ezek. 1.3; 3.14, 22; 8.1; 33.22; 37.1; and 40.1). The most
important and abundant comparative material comes from Ezekiel,
whose use of the terminology is fairly consistent. The usual pattern is
the *converted imperfect* (*hyh* 5×, *npl* 1×) + *'ly* + *temporal or spatial
indicator* (e.g., *šm* 3×) + *yd yhwh*. The expression regularly
introduces a vision/audition report (Ezek. 33.22 probably refers to a
previous vision/audition). Ezek. 3.22, for example, records, 'Then the
hand of the LORD was upon me there; and he said to me, "Rise up, go
out into the valley, and there I will speak with you".' Ezek. 3.14 is
particularly important because, of all the cited texts, it alone contains
the term *ḥzqh*:

> *wrwḥ nś'tny wtqḥny w'lk mr bḥmt rwḥy wyd-yhwh 'ly ḥzqh*
> The spirit lifted me up and bore me away; I went in bitterness in the heat
> of my spirit, *the hand of the LORD being strong upon me.*

Although the syntax is quite different from 8.11, the coincidence of
two items of vocabulary has led most commentators to the conclusion
that *kḥzqh hyd* in Isa. 8.11 is an earlier form of the expression found
in Ezek. 3.14.

Since Ezek. 3.14 is the key comparative text, it merits closer
examination. First, we must note that the phrase does not conform to
the usual pattern in Ezekiel as outlined above. It alone contains the
term *ḥzqh*; it has no 'converted' imperfect verb; and it does not
introduce a vision/audition report but rather comes at the end of one.
In fact, Ezek. 3.14 apparently refers to a prolonged state of anger and
bitterness rather than to an ecstatic state.[11] The result of the hand of
Yahweh in the case of 3.14 is that the prophet sits for seven days in

10. E.g., Gray, *Isaiah*, p. 151; Kaiser, *Isaiah*, p. 191; Wildberger, *Isaiah*,
p. 336.

11. The word *mr* ('bitterness') is not found in the LXX or the Syriac versions. It
may have been added as an explanatory gloss (see W. Zimmerli, *Ezekiel 1*
[Hermeneia; Philadelphia: Fortress Press, 1979], p. 94). Nevertheless, *bḥmt rwḥy*
alone suggests that the prophet's emotional state was one of anger and vexation. This
emotional state should be seen not as a part of his ecstatic experience but rather as a
response to it. Verse 16 introduces a new audition, and 3.14 marks the end of the
preceding experience. Thus the phrase 'the hand of the LORD was strong upon me'
refers to his state *after* his call experience, a state that apparently lasted for seven
days.

such a state that those around him are worried. All of this sets 3.14 apart and suggests that the phrase refers to something quite different from the six other texts that refer to the hand of the LORD being upon Ezekiel. For this reason the verse should not be aligned with the other 'hand of the LORD' texts, and it should not be interpreted as an indication of an ecstatic state. From this we learn that although the hand of Yahweh is mentioned often in prophetic experience, it does not always produce the same effect.

Jer. 15.17 supports this conclusion. As in Ezek. 3.14, the effect of the hand of Yahweh is not ecstasy but anger.

> *l'-yšbty bswd-mśḥqym w''lz mpny ydk bdd yšbty ky-z'm ml'tny*
> I did not sit in the company of merrymakers, nor did I rejoice; under the weight of your hand I sat alone, for you had filled me with indignation.

This text also shares with Ezek. 3.14 the element of social isolation. Both Jeremiah and Ezekiel are angry and sit alone because of the hand of Yahweh.

We must conclude that the comparative material does not necessarily indicate that Isa. 8.11 refers to an ecstatic experience. Our best comparative text suggests a powerful experience leading to anger and social isolation. Social isolation of a sort is evident in 8.11 as well. Yahweh's message to Isaiah turns him from 'the way of this people' and prevents him from saying what they say, thus isolating him from 'this people'. There is no obvious indication of the deep anger found in Ezek. 3.14, but we may detect a note of anger in the reference to 'this people' in Isa. 8.11.

Nevertheless, conclusions about similarities between Isa. 8.11 and Ezek. 3.14 must be drawn with caution. The former lacks both the preposition *'l* and a suffix on *yd*. Furthermore, *bḥzqt hyd* in Isa. 8.11 describes not *the state of the prophet* (i.e., of being in the condition of having Yahweh's hand upon him) but rather *the manner of Yahweh's speaking*. Thus, while Ezek. 3.14 may be helpful for comparison, it should not be seen as conclusive evidence for interpretation.

wysrny mlkt bdrk h'm-hzh

The lack of good evidence from other materials for understanding *kḥzqt hyd* suggests that it should be interpreted according to contextual clues as much as possible. One such clue is the verb that follows it, *ysrny*. This term is coordinate with the preceding verb *'mr*, since it shares its subject (Yahweh) and expresses coordinate action: Yahweh's act of speaking *khzqt hyd* is commensurate with the act described by *wysrny mlkt bdrk h'm-hzh*. Unfortunately, the pointing—and hence the root—of *wysrny* is uncertain. The MT points it as a qal imperfect from **ysr* ('to discipline'), which is relatively common in the Hebrew Bible; its qal form occurs nowhere else in biblical Hebrew. The term is usually found in the piel. The text is easily repointed to give the piel perfect with simple *waw*, but this creates an impossible narrative sequence construction.[12] One expects a 'converted' imperfect form, and by repointing the verb as the hiphil *waysirēnî* of **swr* ('to turn someone away from something'), such is achieved. This seems to be the most grammatically plausible construction.[13] Furthermore, this reading is supported by the text of 1QIs^a (*wysyrny*), the Greek text of Symmachus, and the Syriac.

Decisive evidence for reading the hiphil of **swr* comes from an examination of the lexical fields of **ysr* and **swr*. The idea of 'disciplining' (*mlkt bdrk*) is not attested elsewhere in the Hebrew Bible, whereas the idea of 'turning away' (*bdrk mlkt*) is. Isa. 30.11a has the expression in the imperative: 'turn aside from the path' (*swrw mny-drk*). The expression **swr + mn-hdrk* occurs five times in Deuteronomic literature (Deut. 9.12, 16 [= Exod. 32.8]; Deut. 11.28; 31.29; Judg. 2.17; cf. Deut. 5.32; 7.4), and Deut. 9.12-13 is especially interesting, since it states that 'this people' (v. 13) 'turned quickly from the way' (*srw mhr mn-hdrk*). Thus, there is substantial comparative material to support pointing *wysrny* as a 'converted' hiphil imperfect. The phrase, *wysrny mlkt*, should then be translated, 'and he turned me aside from going...' This in turn suggests that the initial phrase, *khzqt hyd*, refers to the strong persuasion used by Yahweh to change the prophet's course.

h'm-hzh

The identity of 'this people' is undoubtedly crucial for understanding the historical situation of Isaiah's ministry. Although it is beyond the scope of the present study to present a full treatment of this term, a few brief comments are in order.[14] 'This people' is predominantly a

---

12. Gray, *Isaiah*, p. 154.

13. So Wildberger, *Isaiah*, p. 355; on this form, cf. Deut. 7.4 and 1 Sam. 18.13.

14. For a full treatment, see J. Boehmer, 'Dieses Volk', *JBL* 45 (1926), pp. 134-48.

negative term in the Hebrew Bible, occurring most frequently in discourse between the prophet (preeminently Moses) and God and denoting the *rebellious* nation of Israel.[15] In Isaiah, 'this people' first occurs in 6.9-10, where it designates the group to whom Isaiah is commanded to prophesy the word of hardening. Thereafter, 'this people' always refers to a group opposed to Yahweh's purposes (8.6, 11, 12; 9.15; 28.11, 14; 29.13, 14), and Isaiah's use of the term is comparable to that of JE and Deuteronomy. Isaiah's position is analogous to that of Moses, and the group designated by 'this people' is analogous to the faithless Israelites of the Sinai and wilderness traditions. 'The way of this people' is the way that fails to trust Yahweh's provision.[16]

Isa. 8.14 and 17 refer to 'both houses of Israel', 'the inhabitants of Jerusalem', and 'the house of Jacob' as the objects of judgment. But it is not clear that 'this people' is to be identified with any of these groups. Those who are judged and those who say 'conspiracy' may be separate groups. Hayes and Irvine argue that 'this people' in Isaiah 6–8 refers to those Judeans who supported the anti-Assyrian coalition led by Syria, as opposed to the Davidic family and its adherents, who refused to join Israel against Assyria.[17] Although other commentators

15. E.g., Exod. 32.21 (E), 31 (J); Num. 11.11-14 (4×, J); 14.11-19 (6×, J); Deut. 9.13, 27; 31.16; Jer. 5.14; 6.19, 21 + 19x (source analysis according to M. Noth, *A History of Pentateuchal Traditions* [Chico, CA: Scholars Press, 1981; reprint of 1972 edn]).

16. See also 8.6, where 'this people' rejects the 'waters of Shiloh which flow gently [or 'secretly', from *l't*, cf. Exod. 7.11, 22], and rejoice over Rezin and the son of Remaliah' (for a defense of this translation, see J.H. Hayes and S.A. Irvine, *Isaiah, the Eighth-Century Prophet: His Times and His Preaching* [Nashville: Abingdon, 1987], pp. 146-47). Is it possible that this is an allusion to the waters that God provides in the wilderness at Massah (*msh*, note verbal echoes in 8.6: *m's* and *mśwś*)? Note also Isa. 28.11, where 'this people' reject the 'rest' (*nwḥ*) offered to them by Yahweh, language reminiscent of wilderness/conquest traditions found in Exod. 33.14 (J); Deut. 3.20; Josh. 1.13, 15.

17. *Isaiah*, p. 110. Hayes and Irvine interpret the 'conspiracy' as a reference to accusations made by other Judeans against Ahaz for his refusal to support Israel in its bid for independence from Assyria (*Isaiah*, pp. 153-56). Other commentators see the conspiracy as some sort of direct threat to Ahaz. It is usually identified with the threat by the coalition in the north to install a certain 'Tabelite' in place of Ahaz (7.5-6; e.g., Wildberger, *Isaiah*, p. 358). But such interpretations make little sense of Yahweh's instruction to Isaiah to oppose 'this people' over this very issue. Are we to think that Isaiah endorsed the attempt to replace Ahaz? This seems unlikely. Yahweh does not

understand the term to refer rather vaguely to all the people of both Israel and Judah,[18] the implication of 8.11 that Isaiah had once 'walked in the way of this people' suggests that they were Judeans.

This concludes the grammatical and syntactical examination of Isa. 8.11. By way of summary, it may be noted that the phrase *khzqt hyd* refers to a manner of address by Yahweh that caused a change in Isaiah's attitude and actions. The expression may also imply the effect of 'the hand' to isolate. The prophet was 'turned aside' from 'the way' of a group referred to as 'this people', who acted faithlessly toward Yahweh. The text does not require this to have been an ecstatic experience, and the comparative material provides no conclusive evidence in the matter. In any case, the focus is not on the experience but on its effect. We may translate the verse as follows: 'For the LORD spoke thus to me with the strength of the hand and turned me aside from going in the way of this people, saying. . . '

The implication of 8.11—obscured in many translations—is that Isaiah had an experience at some point during his public ministry that changed his position on certain issues, especially on the alleged conspiracy. The NRSV, for example, translates, 'For the LORD spoke thus to me while his hand was strong upon me, and warned me not to walk in the way of this people, saying. . . '[19] Most commentators have either missed or dismissed the implication of a radical change. Gray suggests that the verse refers to the prophet's 'inner conflict' and

command Isaiah to support whatever plan or policy 'this people' was calling a conspiracy, but rather Isaiah is commanded to deny that the plan or policy is in fact a conspiracy. What is at issue is the technical or legal status of the plan or policy. Since 8.11 implies that the question was the subject of public discussion, it seems likely that it related to a matter of state policy rather than to a threat to the person of the king.

18. Kaiser, *Isaiah*, p. 131; Wildberger, *Isaiah*, p. 271. Gray notes the problem of identifying 'this people' either with Judah or Israel alone or with Israel and Judah together, but he does not resolve it (*Isaiah*, pp. 109-10).

19. The word 'warned' leaves open the question whether Isaiah was already in agreement with 'this people' and was warned to change his position or was warned not to join them. Reading *swr makes this clear: Isaiah was in agreement with 'this people' and experienced a significant reorientation. The NRSV also specifies that the 'hand' is Yahweh's ('his hand') and adds the words 'upon me', which are not in the text. The translators are apparently offering an interpretation of the meaning of *khzqt hyd* in the light of texts that mention the hand of Yahweh as a part of ecstatic experience.

Yahweh's 'warning' to him.[20] Kaiser translates, 'and he warned me not to walk in the way of this people'.[21] Clements gives scant attention to the reading based on the hiphil pointing and chooses instead to interpret the verse as 'a word. . . of assurance' to the prophet, who is discouraged by his own rejection.[22] Wildberger's text-critical work leads him to read the hiphil of *swr* and translate, 'For thus said Yahweh to me, as the hand grabbed hold and restrained me from going in the way of this people' (*und mich davon abhielt, den Weg dieses Volkes zu gehen*). He does not, however, understand this to refer to a significant change of course in the prophet's work.[23]

Few commentators have chosen to emend the text to read the hiphil of *swr*, and few have considered the idea that 8.11 indicates that Isaiah radically reoriented his position on certain issues sometime during his public ministry. The implication that the prophet walked in the way of 'this people' for a time and then experienced a dramatic change fits poorly with the usual understanding of his life and work. Such a radical reorientation *during* his public ministry raises theological problems for the view that the prophets, as God's messengers, flawlessly delivered the divine word.[24] Isa. 8.11, however, suggests that the prophet underwent just such a change of mind and message.

20. Gray, *Isaiah*, p. 151.

21. Kaiser, *Isaiah*, p. 191.

22. R.E. Clements, *Isaiah 1–39* (NCB; London: Marshall, Morgan & Scott; Grand Rapids: Eerdmans, 1980), p. 99.

23. Wildberger, *Isaiah*, p. 354. German from *Jesaja* (BKAT, 10; Neukirchen–Vluyn: Neukirchener Verlag, 1978), p. 334. K. Jeppesen, arguing on other grounds than I have, reads 8.11 as a reference to Yahweh's correcting the prophet's course when he had 'swerved from the path set for prophets by Yahweh' ('Call and Frustration, A New Understanding of Isaiah viii 21-22', *VT* 32 [1982], pp. 149 and 155). He correctly points out indications in the text that the prophet may have struggled before accepting God's way and that he suffered social isolation for his views.

24. Jer. 15.19 implies that Jeremiah turned from the way that Yahweh had set for him. But as R.P. Carroll (*Jeremiah* [OTL; Philadelphia: Westminster, 1986], p. 334) argues, this is probably nothing more than a rhetorical flourish in the argument between Yahweh and Jeremiah and should not be taken as an indication of a serious lapse on the part of the prophet. For an illuminating treatment of the multifaceted relationship between the prophets and God, see Y. Muffs, *Love and Joy: Law, Language, and Religion in Ancient Israel* (New York/Jerusalem: Jewish Theological Seminary of America, 1992), pp. 9-48.

Isaiah 8.11 and 6.1-13

If indeed Isaiah did experience a radical reorientation during his ministry, we might expect that references to it would appear elsewhere in the book as well. This final section will argue that Isaiah's vision, recorded in ch. 6, reflects this same experience of reorientation, an experience that he underwent during, rather than at the beginning of, his public work.

The vision account in ch. 6 and the narrative in 8.11-15 are connected by verbal and conceptual similarities. The difficult phrase, *khzqt hyd*, would serve nicely as a starting point and as primary evidence for connecting the two passages, if only it were clear that it referred to an ecstatic or visionary experience. At the very least, the expression refers to an experience in which Isaiah was powerfully addressed by God and consequently reoriented in his thinking and speaking. It seems likely that the experience is retold as an apology for his change of position on certain political issues and for his disengagement from 'the way of this people'. This reorientation was surely no small event in the prophet's life but represented a profound change. It is quite plausible to identify the change mentioned briefly in 8.11-15 with the transforming experience mentioned in ch. 6. This is especially attractive if, as will be argued below, the vision in the Temple is a record of an experience that the prophet had during, rather than at the beginning of, his ministry.

Thematic links provide significant evidence for connecting the two texts. Isaiah 6 states that in the year of King Uzziah's death, Isaiah had a vision of Yahweh, enthroned and exalted, and heard the seraphim call, 'Holy, Holy, Holy is Yahweh Sebaoth.' This experience caused him to realize the uncleanness of his own lips and his precarious position, as one who was 'dwelling among a people of unclean lips'. Several connections to the themes in 8.11-15 are apparent. First, Isaiah's former alignment with (expressed as 'dwelling among') a 'people of unclean lips' (6.5) is analogous to the implication of 8.11 that he once followed the 'way of this people'. In 8.11 this alignment took the form of 'saying' the same thing that the people 'say'. In 6.5 the focus on the lips of both the prophet and the people also points to speech as the crux of the uncleanness: his unclean lips said what their unclean lips said. Secondly, in Isaiah 8 the act of calling some policy or decision a 'conspiracy' is equated with a failure to 'call holy' or 'sanctify' (*tqdyšw*) Yahweh Sebaoth.[25] Isa. 8.12b-13 focuses on this failure to respect or fear correctly. In like manner, the vision report in ch. 6 focuses on Yahweh's holiness and the awe inspired thereby. Isaiah realizes that his lips and those of his associates are impure, because their words did not properly acknowledge God's holiness. Thus, both texts emphasize incorrect speech and the holiness of Yahweh Sebaoth. Thirdly, the command in 8.12-13, 'Do not fear what it fears, or be in dread. But the LORD of hosts, him you shall regard as holy; let him be your fear, and let him be your dread,' corresponds to the prophet's response of fear when he sees Yahweh: 'Woe is me! I am lost' (6.5). The vision inspires fear and dread in the prophet. From his experience of Yahweh's awe-inspiring holiness, Isaiah realizes his uncleanness and need for purification. His purification, in turn, implies a fundamental change in orientation. Fourthly, just as 8.11 suggests the setting apart and isolation of the prophet as a result of Yahweh's word to him, so too the vision of Yahweh in ch. 6 sets the prophet apart. He alone has his sin removed, and he is established as one with a message that is destined to be rejected. The nature of his proclamation shows that he is no longer one who 'dwells among a people', but one who is radically opposed to 'this people'. The change from 'a people' (6.5) to 'this people' (6.9-10) is significant. Isaiah sees himself no longer as identified with the people of unclean lips, but as alienated from them. Yahweh's speeches—both in 6.9-10 and in 8.12—use 'this people' to designate a group following a course counter to his purposes. Isaiah's use of 'this people' (8.11) shows that

25. Wildberger (*Isaiah*, pp. 355-58) emends *tqdyšw* in v. 12a to read *tqšyrw*. Likewise, he emends *mqdš* in v. 14a to read *mqšr*. At first glance this is an attractive set of emendations, especially in the case of v. 14a, where the ideas 'sanctuary', 'snare', and 'trap' are apparently used as contextual synonyms. Nevertheless, there is no evidence from other MSS or from the versions for these changes, and the similarity of the terms *qdš* and *qšr* may be due to paronomasia, not corruption. Wildberger's case for emending v. 13a is weak, since the text makes sense as it stands, and **qšr* appears nowhere else in the Hebrew Bible in the hiphil. Emending the text to a *hapax legomenon* form on the basis of contextual considerations alone is not acceptable (see Hayes and Irvine, *Isaiah*, p. 157). The difficulty of the term *mqdš* in v. 14a can be resolved by a less adventurous emendation or by interpretation of the text as it stands. Again, Wildberger's proposed emendation creates a *hapax legomenon* (Hayes and Irvine, *Isaiah*, p. 158). For these reasons the text should not be emended. See also the arguments against emendation in N. Lohfink, 'Isaias 8, 12-14', *BZ* 7 (1963), pp. 98-104.

he has aligned himself with Yahweh's view. Fifthly, the theologically difficult implication of 6.10 that the prophet's task is to instill insensitivity in 'this people' is analogous to the equally difficult statement in 8.14-15 that Yahweh himself will become a 'stone one strikes against; for both houses of Israel he will become a rock one stumbles over—a trap and a snare for the inhabitants of Jerusalem. . . They shall fall and be broken; they shall be snared and taken'. The language of trapping and snaring suggests that Yahweh's action toward the people will be one of deliberate deception: Yahweh will lure them to destruction. Similarly, 6.9-12 indicates that Yahweh's desensitizing message will bring utter destruction on the people.[26] Finally, the expression 'this people' connects the two passages. As mentioned above, the phrase does not occur in Isaiah 1–5; it occurs first in Yahweh's commission to Isaiah in 6.9-10, again in 8.6, and twice in 8.11-12. Three further occurrences are found in 28.11, 14, and 29.13, contexts which have many similarities to ch. 6 and 8.11-15, including the theme of the insensitivity which leads to 'this people's' destruction.

These thematic and verbal connections provide evidence that the reference in 8.11 to being 'turned aside from going in the way of this people' designates the same event recorded in ch. 6. The latter recounts in a traditional genre the experience of reorientation, whereas 8.11 merely alludes to it. Both texts serve to explain and defend a radical change in the prophet's opinions and actions, a change that set him against a group with whom formerly he had agreed.

A crucial question remains to be addressed: Do the two texts under discussion refer to the prophet's initial call or to an experience that he had later in his ministry?[27] Several points support the latter option.

---

26. The ideas of 'snaring' and of the deliberately confusing word of Yahweh are directly linked in 28.13: 'Therefore the word of the LORD will be to them precept upon precept, precept upon precept, line upon line, line upon line, here a little, there a little; that they may go, and fall backward, and be broken, and snared, and taken.' The last clause reads in Hebrew, *lm'n ylkw wkšlw 'ḥwr wnšbrw wnwqšw wnlkdw*, language strongly reminiscent of that found in 8.14-15.

27. The interpretation of Isa. 6 as the prophet's initial call probably has its origins among medieval rabbinic interpreters (see L. Ginzberg, *The Legends of the Jews* [7 vols.; Philadelphia: Jewish Publication Society of America, 1909-38], VI, p. 357 n. 29). Christian interpreters during the Reformation period, including Oecolampadius, Calvin, Zwingli, Luther, and Brenz, understood the chapter as the record of an event during the prophet's ministry. Calvin mentions that 'some'

Isaiah 6 lacks the usual prophetic call formula, 'The word of the LORD came to X' (*hyh + dbr-yhwh*; cf. Jer. 1.4; Ezek. 1.3; and Hos. 1.1). The report of the vision/audition does not appear at the beginning of the book, where one would expect a call narrative, and while it is typical in call narratives for the prophet to be reluctant to accept the call of Yahweh, Isaiah shows no such hesitancy. The probable connection between ch. 6 and 8.11-15 suggests that the placement of ch. 6 is chronologically (and not just thematically) appropriate. The implication of 8.11 that Isaiah aligned himself with 'this people' until his experience of redirection suggests that he held an official role in society prior to the experience. The frequently noted similarities between Isaiah's vision in the Temple (ch. 6) and Micaiah ben Imlah's vision of the enthroned Yahweh (1 Kgs 22) support this view, since Micaiah was already a prophet when he received the vision.

Although many scholars favor the opinion that ch. 6 records Isaiah's call vision, there are a few who have argued that the the vision is placed in the book in its proper chronological sequence.[28] Milgrom, for example, reads ch. 6 sequentially in the book, basing his view on a comparison of the historical and social conditions presupposed in Isaiah 1–5 with what is known about conditions in the time of Uzziah, on an analysis of the change in stylistic usage and thematic content in chs. 6ff, and, most importantly, on the progressive erosion of the prophet's belief in the possibility of repentance:

> since the offer of repentance is contained in the first two chapters alone
> and nowhere else, then i 10-ii 21 is the true beginning of the book and ch.
> vi cannot be Isaiah's inaugural prophecy but belongs thematically where it

interpreters argue that ch. 6 should be placed at the beginning of the book (D.C. Steinmetz, 'John Calvin on Isaiah 6; A Problem in the History of Exegesis', *Int* 36 [1982], pp. 162-63). It is not clear who these 'some' were, but it seems likely that Calvin was familiar with the interpretation from rabbinic sources. By the time of the commentaries of R. Lowth (*Isaiah: A New Translation with a Preliminary Dissertation and Notes, Critical, Philological, and Explanatory* [London: J. Nichols for J. Dodsley, 1778]) and W. Gesenius (*Der Prophet Jesaia* [3 vols. in 4; Leipzig: F.C.W. Vogel, 1821–29]), opinion among Christian interpreters had shifted to favor a view of the chapter as Isaiah's initial call.

28. See Wildberger, *Isaiah*, pp. 256-58. Wildberger sides with those who interpret the chapter as Isaiah's call (cf. pp. 275-78).

is at the culmination of the period of the prophet's ministry when he saw
his hopes for the reformation of his own generation irreparably
shattered. . . [29]

Finally, he suggests that since the contemptuous designation 'this
people' does not occur until ch. 6, it must reflect a change in the
prophet's disposition toward 'this people' after the event described in
ch. 6.[30]

Milgrom's insights and the further evidence offered by 8.11 all
point to the conclusion that both Isaiah 6 and 8.11 refer to an
experience during the course of the prophet's ministry.

Conclusion

This paper has argued that Isa. 8.11 refers to an experience of radical
reorientation during the ministry of Isaiah, an experience that caused

---

29. J. Milgrom, 'Did Isaiah Prophecy During the Reign of Uzziah?', *VT* 14
(1964), pp. 164-82 (172-73). Milgrom was not the first to propose this interpretation. Earlier, it had been defended by C.P. Caspari (*Commentar til de tolv føste
Capitler of Propheten Jesaia* [1867], pp. 240-45), S. Mowinckel (*Profeten Jesaja: en
Bibelstudiebok* [Oslo: H. Aschehoug, 1925], pp. 16, 20ff.), and M.M. Kaplan
('Isaiah 6.11', *JBL* 45 [1926], pp. 251-59). J.J.M. Roberts ('The Divine King and
the Human Community in Isaiah's Vision of the Future', in H.B. Huffmon *et al.*
(eds.), *The Quest for the Kingdom of God: Essays in Honor of George
E. Mendenhall* [Winona Lake, IN: Eisenbrauns, 1983], p. 127 n. 1) has raised
objections to Milgrom's interpretation, arguing, 'The fiery cleansing of Isaiah's sins,
centred on his lips, is surely to be understood as enabling him to take up the
prophetic task'. But as this paper has suggested, the cleansing of Isaiah's lips is an
atonement for past speech that he comes to realize was unclean (this does not
exclude, however, the possibility of an allusion to a lip purification ritual lurking in
the background and influencing the retelling of the event). The traditional response of
a prophet to Yahweh's commission is a confession not of impurity but of inability or
insignificance. Moreover, 6.7 affirms explicitly that the coal purifies Isaiah's lips in
order to remove his guilt; it says nothing of preparing him to deliver the word of
Yahweh, as one might expect if it were his initial call. Roberts also cites Amos's 'call
narrative' as an example of such placed other than at the beginning of the book. But
Amos 7.10-16 must be treated as a unique case inasmuch as it is found in the context
of a narrative account of Amos's confrontation with Amaziah and is thus not strictly
comparable to other call narratives. Amos 7.10-16 is a reminiscence of the prophet's
call, not a formal call narrative.

30. This view is also defended by Hayes and Irvine (*Isaiah*, pp. 108-10), whose
arguments closely follow the line of argument laid out by Milgrom.

him to dissociate himself from the ultimately doomed views and policies of 'this people' and to begin to advocate views and policies that showed proper regard for Yahweh. Thematic and verbal similarities between 8.11-15 and ch. 6 suggest that both texts refer to the same experience of reorientation, though ch. 6 records the event more fully and according to traditional forms. Thus, ch. 6 and 8.11-15 form an inclusio around the material dealing with at least a certain phase of the Syro-Ephraimitic War. The theme of both is the prophet's experience of reorientation and the message of doom for 'this people'.

THE ANCIENT MEANING OF THE LAW OF MOSES*

Phillip R. Callaway

Introduction

It is not the purpose of this study to rehearse the extensive history of scholarship that questions or affirms the Mosaic authorship of pentateuchal or other biblical laws.[1] Nor is it an attempt to date any source of the Pentateuch. Quite simply, the concern is to review the biblical and some postbiblical evidence bearing on the meaning of the Law,[2] and in particular the Law of Moses (and similar variant terms), in order to discover how it functioned, as a categorical term, among the ancient biblical writers of Israelite–Judaean history and law.

The thesis of this essay is that as the law grew from the beginnings

---

*   To see John H. Hayes at work is to see a master among his disciples. In my experience the door to his office has always been open to everyone. One finds him reading widely—from the Hebrew Bible to the history of interpretation—and pecking away at an IBM Selectric II keyboard or writing his latest ideas longhand on a yellow legal pad. Nevertheless, he makes time to discuss academic and personal issues with all who walk through the door. I am honored to offer this study to the one person who has always supported my academic efforts and showed me that the true scholar is always willing to rethink old positions.

1.   J.M. Miller and J.H. Hayes, *A History of Ancient Israel and Judah* (Philadelphia: Westminster, 1986), pp. 393-94, 473. Cf. B. Oded, 'Judah and the Exile', in J.H. Hayes and J.M. Miller (eds.), *Israelite and Judean History* (OTL; Philadelphia: Westminster, 1977), pp. 461, 463; G. Widengren, 'The Persian Period', in J.H. Hayes and J.M. Miller (eds.), *Israelite and Judean History* (OTL; Philadelphia: Westminster, 1977), pp. 514-15. More recently, see J.H. Hayes and P.K. Hooker, *A New Chronology for the Kings of Israel and Judah and Its Implications for Biblical History and Literature* (Atlanta: John Knox, 1988), pp. 75, 87-88, 100.

2.   I shall capitalize the term 'law' throughout, when it seems to reflect a discrete book or scroll. Furthermore, Ezekiel will not be discussed in the present context, although it does play a significant role in the understanding of law in the Bible.

of the Israelite nation up to and beyond the act of biblical canonization, the phrase 'Law of Moses' gradually became a convenient, authoritative rubric under which to subsume a millenium of legal findings.[3] This is not a matter of false attribution in the modern academic sense. Rather, it is somewhat analogous to the concern in the United States of America to determine whether a legal finding is consistent with the words and the spirit of our country's Founding Fathers, for example, James Madison and Thomas Jefferson.

Exodus–Judges

Traditionally, 'Law of Moses' has been understood to refer to the commandments and any other laws that Moses received from God on Mount Sinai and promulgated to the Israelites thereafter.[4] Exod. 24.2-4 reports that Moses then wrote down 'all the words of the Lord'. Thus, even after Moses demolished the first two tablets that God wrote, this record would have been preserved (Exod. 32.20–34.1). What follows through the end of Leviticus is a collection of laws concerning the tabernacle, its furnishings, cases of leprosy, bodily discharges, the Day of Atonement, the impurity of blood, incest, the holy life, the liturgical calendar, and the sabbatical year and jubilees. Lev. 26.46 summarizes the foregoing, 'These are the statutes and ordinances and laws which the Lord made between him and the people of Israel on Mount Sinai by Moses.' Lev. 27.34 is nearly identical.

In Num. 31.21, Eleazar tells the men of war, 'This is the statute of the Law which the Lord has commanded Moses . . . ' Num. 33.2 confirms this tradition that Moses functioned as a recorder of important laws and historical events: 'Moses wrote down their starting

3. The method or approach of this essay owes much to the notion of the recapitulation of tradition and its modification. In particular, the following two works were most influential: J. Weingreen, *From Bible to Mishna* (Manchester: Manchester University Press, 1976), pp. 23-24, 67 (esp. pp. 143-59); and M. Fishbane, 'Torah and Tradition', in D.A. Knight (ed.), *Tradition and Theology in the Old Testament* (Philadelphia: Fortress Press, 1977), pp. 275-300. I first used this kind of analysis in 'Extending Divine Revelation: Micro-Compositional Strategies in the Temple Scroll', in G.J. Brooke (ed.), *Temple Scroll Studies* (JSPSup, 7; Sheffield: JSOT Press, 1989), pp. 149-61.

4. For a helpful survey of the history of interpretation, see C. Houtman, 'Ezra and the Law', *OTS* 21 (1981), pp. 91-103. See also J.H. Hayes, *An Introduction to Old Testament Study* (Nashville: Abingdon, 1979), pp. 157-58.

places, stage by stage, by command of the Lord: and these are their
stages according to their starting places.' The emphasis again falls on
Moses' scribal activity, as in Exod. 24.4.

Num. 36.13 concludes the book with a summarizing statement
similar to earlier ones: 'These are the commandments and the
ordinances which the Lord commanded by Moses to the people of
Israel in the plains of Moab by the Jordan at Jericho.' Therefore,
statements in Exodus, Leviticus, and Numbers indicate that laws were
given at various points along the way from Mount Sinai—even up to
the entry into the Promised Land.

Deut. 1.1 connects with the tradition in Num. 36.13: 'These are all
the words that Moses spoke to all Israel beyond the Jordan in the
wilderness. . . ' Deut. 1.4 goes a step further by presenting Moses as
the earliest interpreter and teacher of the Law (cf. vv. 13-14). He
warns the Israelites not to add to or take away from all the words of
the Law (Deut. 4.2, 5). Despite historical evidence to the contrary,
this warning was intended to suggest a rather early fixation, if not a
canonization, of the letter of the Law.

The warning in Deut. 4.2 applies apparently—in the context of
Deuteronomy—to the laws preserved in that book. Deut. 4.13-14
repeats the story of the two tablets told first in Exodus, but in this
context, the mountain is Horeb. Then follows an exhortation that
details Exod. 20.4 and 34.17. Deut. 4.44-47 seems to conclude a
section ending with the cities of refuge: it includes a historical note in
which Moses addresses the children of Israel 'in the land of Sihon the
king of the Amorites, who lived at Heshbon. . . ' Deut. 5.6-21
preserves the Decalogue (cf. Exod. 20.1-17). Nevertheless, in 10.1-5
Moses ascends the mountain to acquire a second set of tablets. In the
rest of the chapter and in the next the reader is constantly admonished
to obey these commandments.

According to Deut. 11.18-20, the study and practice of the Law is
preserved as a personal matter symbolized by reminders on the
forehead, the hand, the doorpost, and the gate:

> You shall therefore lay up these words of mine in your heart and in your
> soul; and you shall bind them as a sign upon your hand, and they shall be
> as frontlets between your eyes. And you shall teach them to your children,
> talking of them when you are sitting in your house, and when you are
> walking by the way, and when you lie down, and when you rise. And
> you shall write them upon the doorposts of your house and upon your
> gates. . .

The actual legal code finally begins with the centralization of worship in ch. 12 and seems to conclude with Moses' admonition that Israel 'keep the commandments which I command you today' (Deut. 27.1).

Other passages also threaten and summarize. Deut. 28.58 warns, 'If you are not careful to do all the words of this Law which are written in this book. . . the Lord will bring on you and your offspring extraordinary afflictions'. In a further address Moses concludes, 'These are the words of the covenant which the Lord commanded Moses to make with the people of Israel in the land of Moab, besides the covenant which he had made with them at Horeb' (Deut. 28.69 [Eng. 29.1]). Deut. 29.9 and 21 echo this note.

Toward the end of his life, according to Deut. 31.9-13, Moses writes a law requiring the priests, the sons of Levi, and the elders of Israel to read this law to an assembly of men, women, children, and sojourners within their towns at the feast of booths every seventh year (cf. Ezra 3.4; Neh. 8.14-15). This passage reiterates the authority of Moses, his recording of the Law, and the required public proclamations of the Law throughout Israel.

After Moses dies, the Lord commands Joshua, Moses' successor, to cross the Jordan and take possession of the land. Success will be ensured only by strict adherence to the Law of Moses (Josh. 1.7-9): 'Only be strong and very courageous; being careful to do according to all the Law which Moses my servant commanded you.. . . The book of the Law shall not depart out of your mouth, but you shall meditate on it day and night, that you may be careful to do according to all that is written in it.' Clearly, this passage reflects a tradition that sees Moses as the source for an authoritative book of the Law—a memory that fits well with Exod. 24.4; Num. 33.2; and Deut. 31.9.

After the slaughter at Ai and the hanging of its king, Joshua constructs an altar on Mount Ebal, as 'written in the book of the Law of Moses' (Josh. 8.30-31; cf. Deut. 27.4-5). Afterward, he inscribes upon the stones 'a copy of this Law' (v. 32). Even more remarkable are the claims in the subsequent verses (vv. 34-35): 'he read all the words of the Law. There was not a word of all that Moses commanded which Joshua did not read before all the assembly.' Thus, an attentive reader of Exodus–Joshua discovers that the Law had been recorded accurately, at least by Moses and Joshua.

In Josh. 22.1-6, Joshua praises and blesses the Reubenites, the Gadites, and the half-tribe of Manasseh for observing the commandments of Moses. In his farewell address, Joshua urges all the Israelites to be faithful in doing 'all that is written in the book of the Law of Moses' (23.6).

The book of Joshua concludes with the report that Joshua enacted a covenant with the people and 'made statutes and ordinances for them at Shechem'. It even adds that he recorded these words in the book of the Law of God (24.25-26). While Joshua admonishes the Israelites to adhere to the Law of Moses, vv. 25-26 lead one to believe that he, too, had received and recorded divine law. Thus, it is too simple to identify the Law of Moses with the entire Pentateuch or one or more of its sources.

Beginning with the book of Judges the reader hears repeatedly that the people of Israel did what was evil in the eyes of the Lord. According to Judg. 20.27, some people were faithful to the Lord by inquiring of his word at Bethel, where the ark rested at that time. One naturally assumes that the Law could have been found in the ark, but this is not explicitly stated, and one has the impression that Bethel was the site of a divine oracle—not necessarily the home of a written law.

1 Samuel–2 Chronicles

Throughout 1–2 Samuel, God continues to speak directly to particular individuals (e.g., Samuel), but there is no reference to the Law of Moses. Instead, a certain emphasis is placed on the location of the ark of the covenant (1 Sam. 4.11–6.14; 2 Sam. 6.2; cf. 15.24), which, tradition claims, held the Law (1 Kgs 8.2).

David's hymn in 2 Sam. 22.23 claims that he followed the Lord's ordinances and statutes. Although practically any reader might infer that this verse refers to the Law of Moses from Sinai, this is by no means certain. Indeed, 1 Sam. 30.25 shows how historical exigencies, in this case the division of the booty between the warriors and those who stayed behind after the slaughter of the Amalekites, required *ad hoc* legal rulings: David orders that the booty should be shared equally between the two parties. There is no attempt to connect this decision with Sinai: 'And from that day forward he [David] made it a statute and an ordinance for Israel to this day.'

In 1 Kgs 2.13, King David charges his son Solomon to obey what was 'written in the Law of Moses', and 3.3 says that Solomon walked in the 'statutes of David his father; only he sacrificed and burnt incense at the high places' (cf. 3.14). According to 6.11-12, in the context of the construction of the Temple, God urges Solomon to follow his statutes, ordinances, and commandments, which were first spoken to David (cf. 9.4-6; 11.10-11, 33, 38). 1 Kgs 8.56 indicates that the call to obedience refers indirectly to God's promise to Moses—in the Law.

Jeroboam shows his disdain for and independence of the Law (although this is not stated explicitly) by setting up two golden calves, one in Bethel and the other in Dan, and appointing a non-traditional feast on the fifteenth day of the eighth month (1 Kgs 12.28-33).

The introduction of Jehoash, whose obedience was secured by his having been instructed by Jehoiada the priest (2 Kgs 12.1-8), establishes a stark contrast to the actions of Jeroboam. The dominant figure in the subsequent section is obviously the priest, who places an innovative money chest at the entrance of the house of the Lord (12.9-16). The writer makes no attempt to declare this *ad hoc* action as consistent with the Law of Moses.

After the capture of Samaria and the exile, Israel and Judaea are admonished to turn from their recalcitrant ways and to follow 'all the Law which I [God] commanded your fathers, and which I sent to you by my servants the prophets' (2 Kgs 17.13; cf. vv. 15-16, 19, 34, 37). It became apparent that the promulgation of the Law represented a historical process that involved not only Moses but subsequent prophets as well.

As evidence of the importance of the Law in this narrative context, the writer reports that after the king of Assyria had settled peoples from the east in Samaria, it was brought to his attention that these peoples knew nothing about the 'law of the god of the land' (2 Kgs 17.26). The foreign king shows that he is even wiser than the former unfaithful inhabitants of this region by ordering one of the exiled priests to return and teach them the Law (vv. 27-28).

A pretext for the widespread disobedience in the north and the south is given in 2 Kings 22–23, which relates the discovery of the book of the Law in the Temple. 2 Kgs 23.21-23 adds the detail that the Passover had not been observed properly from the time of the judges until that of Josiah. Only in 23.25 is the reader told that the book was none other than the Law of Moses and that no king before or after matched the faithfulness of Josiah. That would seem to include even the ideal king David.

Contrary to 2 Samuel 6, 1 Chron. 15.15 claims that the Levites 'carried the ark on their shoulders with poles, as Moses had commanded according to the word of the Lord'. Such a command, however, is not preserved in the Pentateuch. David also orders the Levites to organize the musical worship (v. 16), designates the Levites to minister before the ark (16.4-6), and appoints Zadok as priest at Gibeon, presumably 'according to all that is written in the Law of the Lord' (16.39-40). 1 Chron. 21.29-31 informs the reader that the tabernacle made by Moses in the wilderness was now located at Gibeon.

As in 1 Kings, Chronicles reports that David urged Solomon to obey 'the statutes and the ordinances which the Lord commanded Moses for Israel' (1 Chron. 22.12-13), although David himself is credited with organizing the Levites (v. 6; cf. 24-32) and the Aaronites (24.4). Moreover, 1 Chron. 28.11 informs the reader that David presented to Solomon a plan for the construction of the Temple, its appurtenances, and the divisions of the priests and the Levites for service in the Temple. Verse 19 adds, 'All this he made clear by the writing from the hand of the Lord concerning it, all the work to be done according to the plan.' In this case, the Law of Moses plays no authoritative role, but David claims to have the plan from God.

In 2 Chron. 8.12-13, one learns that Solomon offers the burnt offerings according to the commandment of Moses for all the holy days of the year. As for the assignments of the priests and Levites, he follows the ruling of his father David (v. 15).

Although Rehoboam and all Israel forsook the Law of the Lord (2 Chron. 12.1), Asa returned to the pattern of faithfulness set by David and Solomon, even commanding Judaea to keep the Law and the commandments (1 Chron. 14.4). In 15.1-3, a certain Azariah, the son of Oded, informs Asa that Israel had existed for a long time 'without the true God, and without a teaching priest, and without law...' Although 2 Kings 22–23 attributes Israel and Judah's sinful ways to their unfamiliarity with the Law that had been concealed in the Temple, 2 Chron. 15.1-3 finds an additional cause in Israel's lack of a priestly teacher.

As with Asa before him, Jehoshaphat obeys the commandments (2 Chron. 17.3-5). And in his third year, he sends out princes, Levites, and a few priests to instruct Judah in the book of the Law of the Lord (vv. 7-9; cf. Deut. 17.18-20). Moreover, he establishes Levites to judge the people, requiring the former to be wise in the letter and the spirit of the Law (2 Chron. 19.8-11).[5]

In 2 Chron. 25.4, one reads that when Amaziah became king, he killed those servants responsible for assassinating Joash (= Jehoash), his father, but—consistent with what is written in the Law in the book of Moses—not their children. This seems to be based on Deut. 24.16, which apparently undermines group responsibility for a crime.[6]

Hezekiah is portrayed in 2 Chronicles 29 as a latter-day King David. He is credited with cleaning and sanctifying the Temple, and— as with David and Solomon before him—he stations the Levites according to the commandments of David, Gad, and Nathan (cf. 2 Chron. 31.2). Thus, *ad hoc* legal decisions are not only attributed to the ideal ruler but even to court prophets (v. 25). Under Hezekiah's rule the number of still unsanctified priests made it necessary for the Levites to flay the burnt offerings (v. 34). More startling than this, however, Hezekiah decided to introduce a Passover in the second month so that the priests would have more time to sanctify themselves (30.1-5). This is clearly a violation of the Law, but Hezekiah justifies it on the basis that the Passover, traditionally held in the first month, had not been observed by great numbers of people (v. 5). Verse 16 notes that the priests and Levites observed this postponed Passover according to the Law of Moses, the man of God. This Passover is presented as the most joyous celebration in Jerusalem since the time of Solomon (v. 26).

Consistent with this ideal presentation of Hezekiah, Josiah, his great-grandson, is known for his faithfulness and the discovery of the book of the Law given through Moses in the Temple (2 Chron. 34.14). It is difficult, however, to attribute Judea's sinfulness to the loss of the Law, since a tradition of teaching priests, Levites, and princes presumably existed from the time of Jehoshaphat (35.3; cf. 17.7-9). At least, one might argue, Josiah's Passover was observed correctly on the fourteenth day of the first month (35.1). The king commands the Levites to follow the Temple service established by David and Solomon, but the slaughter of the Passover lamb should be done according to the 'word of the Lord by Moses' (35.6). The burnt

---

5. Weingreen, *From Bible to Mishna*, pp. 23-24, 67.

6. Cf. M.P. Graham, 'Aspects of the Structure and Rhetoric of 2 Chronicles 25', in the present volume.

offerings were handled according to the written prescription in the book of Moses (v. 12). According to 35.18, Josiah's Passover surpassed all other Passovers (even those of Hezekiah, Solomon, and David!) since the time of Samuel the prophet.

Ezra–Nehemiah and Other Sources

Ezra 3.2 reports that Jeshua son of Jozadak and Zerubbabel erected an altar for burnt offerings in Jerusalem according to the Law of Moses, the man of God. Then the feast of booths was observed as written (v. 4). This altar is first mentioned in Exod. 20.24-25 and 27.1-8, and the feast of booths is described in Lev. 23.33, 42 and Num. 29.12-28. But the specific term, *succoth*, is found only in Leviticus 23, and the details for each day of the festival are recorded only in Numbers 29, where the expression 'according to the ordinance' is used repeatedly (vv. 6, 18, 21, 24, 27, 30, 33, 37). Thus, pentateuchal influence is evident.

Ezra 6.18 reports that the service of the priests and the Levites was established as 'it is written in the book of Moses'.[7] Not only does this prescription not exist in the Pentateuch, but several other narrative passages attribute this action to King David.

In Ezra 7.6-12, the scribe skilled in the Law of Moses (i.e., Ezra) is introduced. His chief concerns were the study, practice, and teaching of the Law in Israel (cf. vv. 25-26; 2 Kgs 17.26).

In Neh. 1.17, Nehemiah confesses that the Judeans had not kept the commandments given to Moses and paraphrases—if that is the correct characterization—Deut. 30.1-5 (Neh. 1.8-9).

A new authoritative archival document, 'the genealogy', is first mentioned in Ezra 2.63-64. If the family name of a claimant to priestly lineage could not be found in this list, that person would be branded as unclean and forbidden 'to partake of the most holy food, until there should be a priest to consult the Urim and Thummim' (Neh. 7.64-65; cf. Lev. 2.3, 7, 21-26). Neh. 7.5 calls this document 'the book of the genealogy of those who came up first'. Nowhere does the Pentateuch says that the priesthood is based on the consultation of a written genealogy, even if this may seem implicit in the laws about the Aaronite priesthood. In Lev. 22.3, rules of exclusion from

7. Houtman, 'Ezra and the Law', p. 105; J.R. Shaver, *Torah and the Chronicler's History Work* (BJS, 196; Atlanta: Scholars Press, 1989), p. 118.

offering to the Lord because of uncleanness are recorded. Consistent with this law, Ezra, who makes a distinction between priests and Levites, expects the priests to be Aaronites. Num. 3.10, 16.40, and 18.7 clearly mandate the Aaronite priesthood.[8] The reference to the Urim and the Thummim (Neh. 7.64-65) may be an allusion to Exod. 28.30, which notes that they are preserved in Aaron's breastpiece. The reference to the priest who is able to consult the Urim and Thummim echoes the language of Deut. 33.8, which says of Levi, 'Give to Levi your Thummim and your Urim to your godly one'. Thus, the genealogy has indirect sanction in the Pentateuch, even if no one is ever commanded to draw up a genealogy.

As in Ezra 3.4, the first festival to be observed in Nehemiah 8 is the feast of booths.[9] Ezra brings the book of the Law of Moses to the assembly at the Water Gate and reads aloud to the masses (vv. 1, 3, 5). Several Levites assist Ezra by reading and giving the sense of the Law (Neh. 8.7-9). On the second day the priests, Levites, and heads of the fathers' houses came to Ezra to study the Law (v. 13). They seem to be surprised that the feast of booths is to be observed in the seventh month (vv. 14-15) or that such a feast was even commanded. For seven days Ezra read from the book of the Law of God (v. 18).

Exceeding even the claims about Josiah's Passover in 2 Chron. 35.18, Neh. 8.17 claims that Ezra's first feast of booths could only be compared with that in the time of Joshua son of Nun. Verse 15 deals with the collection of branches 'as it is written', though the apparent legal precedent for this ruling (Lev. 23.40) referred to branches and fruits. Nehemiah 8 says nothing about the bringing of fruits.[10]

Neh. 9.13 refers to the divine giving of the Law to Moses on Sinai. The covenant sealed in 10.29 is based on God's Law given to Moses. In Neh. 10.32, both buying and selling is prohibited on the sabbath.[11] Selling had already been construed as work in Amos 8.5 (cf. Jer 17.21), and now it is extended to purchasing from sabbath violators. Neh. 13.15-22 enumerates cases under the rubrics of transporting and merchandizing, obvious violations of the sabbath. In pentateuchal law, plowing and harvesting (Exod. 34.21), kindling fires

8. Cf. Mal. 2.4, 23-24.
9. Houtman, 'Ezra and the Law', p. 108; Shaver, *Torah*, pp. 101-102.
10. Houtman, 'Ezra and the Law', p. 105; Shaver, *Torah*, pp. 101-104.
11. D.J.A. Clines, 'Nehemiah 10 as an Example of Early Jewish Biblical Exegesis', *JSOT* 21 (1981), pp. 114-15; Houtman, 'Ezra and the Law', p. 105.

in the home (Exod. 35.3), and work per se (Exod. 20.10) is forbidden.

The Damascus Document preserves an even more far-reaching list of prohibitions: no unnecessary talking, no lending, no talking about possessions, profit, work, no field work, no walking beyond 1000 cubits, no eating of foods not prepared beforehand or what dies in the field, no drinking outside the camp except when one bathes, no filling of vessels with water, no dispatching of servants, no wearing of filthy clothing, no chasing of an animal beyond 2000 cubits [round-trip], no hitting with the fist, no transporting objects out of and into one's house or booth, no opening of a vessel whose lid is stuck, no carrying of medicines, no lifting of a stone or earth in the home, no carrying of a child, no wrathful words or actions against one's servant or day-laborer, no assisting the birth of animals, no lifting animals out of a cistern or a ditch, no lodging near the *goyim*, no lifting a human out of a water reservoir or a latrine except with a ladder or a rope, no sacrificing except the sabbath-sacrifice, no sending of unclean persons to the altar, and no entering a house of worship unclean (9.14–12.1).

Nehemiah (10.35) also refers to the execution of the wood festival as written in the Law.[12] Specific instructions for this festival are lacking in the Pentateuch, but are detailed in the Temple Scroll (cols. 23-24). Similarly, 10.36 refers to the bringing of the first-fruits of the herds, the flocks, the trees, wine, and oil. Although pentateuchal law has no explicit formulations for wine and oil festivals, many biblical passages do speak of grain, wine, and oil. Again, the Temple Scroll fills the gap by preserving legislation for harvest festivals that were at least implicit in the Pentateuch (cols. 19, 11-23).[13]

Nehemiah (13.1-3) reports that the Judeans suddenly learn that they are forbidden to marry Ammonites and Moabites, who are not permitted to enter the assembly of God (cf. vv. 23-27).[14] The traditional source for this prescription is Deut. 23.3-5 with its reference to the Balaam story (Numbers 22–23) and the mistreatment of the Israelites by the Ammonites and Moabites. Neh. 10.31, which forbids intermarriage with the people of the land, has its basis in

12. Clines, 'Nehemiah 10', p. 112; Houtman, 'Ezra and the Law', p. 106; Shaver, *Torah*, pp. 88-89, 127.

13. Clines, 'Nehemiah 10', pp. 112-13; Houtman, 'Ezra and the Law', p. 106; Shaver, *Torah*, pp. 89, 126.

14. Clines, 'Nehemiah 10', pp. 115-16; Houtman, 'Ezra and the Law', p. 106.

Deut. 23.3-5 or 7.3. This theme stands at the beginning of the extant version of the Temple Scroll (col. 2) as well.

A final example should suffice to illustrate how the Law of Moses was understood at the close of the biblical period. In several of the Dead Sea Scrolls, the Law is treated as the ultimate authority (CD 5.8, 21; 8.14; 15.2, 8-9, 12; 16.1-2; 1QS 1.3; 5.8; 8.15, 22; 4Q513 frag. 4 1.5). CD 5.8 revealed a simple method whereby the intended meaning of a law may begin, but does not end, with its linguistic formulation. This passage quotes Lev. 18.13: 'Moses said—the sister of your mother you should not approach, for she is a blood relative of your sister. And the law concerning blood pollution was written for men, but applies equally to women.' This passage illustrates quite directly how one ancient interpreter of Moses was able to use a simple analogy to unpack the letter of the Law and permit its application to related cases and categories.

Concluding Observations

The 'Law of Moses' gradually became an authoritative and convenient rubric under which to subsume a plethora of laws, in fact, several legal collections deriving from diverse historical situations. According to the schematized history presented in the Hebrew Bible, the association of the Law with Moses extends from Sinai to Ezra, Nehemiah, the Dead Sea Scrolls, and beyond. Nevertheless, additional legislation or procedural instruction is claimed for several other historical figures. Joshua seems to have written down some of his own ordinances and commandments. David gave an executive order for the division of war booty, was credited with establishing Levitical worship, and even passed on a plan for the Temple to his son Solomon. On the negative side, Jeroboam set up golden calves and appointed a feast. Jehoiada, the priest who instructed King Jehoash, had a money chest erected in the Temple. Jehoshaphat sent out princes, Levites, and priests to teach the Law and to judge legal cases. Hezekiah, a thoroughly positive figure, instituted a non-traditional Passover in the second month. Ezra and Nehemiah appealed to the authority of genealogies in order to establish an acceptable priesthood. Nehemiah also extended the prohibition against selling on the sabbath to purchasing. The Damascus Document preserved an even lengthier list of prohibitions. Nehemiah also referred to a wood festival, as well as wine and oil festivals, which were unmentioned in the Pentateuch but detailed in the Temple Scroll. Finally, the Damascus Document showed how incest laws written with primary reference to men could be extended to apply to women.

The Law of Moses, therefore, appeared in many forms to assist newly emerging communities in dealing with continually evolving conflicts and situations. Whether one believes that this Law can be traced back to Sinai or to the time of David, Hezekiah, or Josiah, it is undeniable that Israelite-Judean laws were passed, combined, and created by analogy or by necessity with or without precedent. This is one of the most important conclusions to be drawn from a reading of Exodus through Nehemiah with an eye on the ancient meaning of the Law of Moses.

BAAL IN ISRAEL

The Contribution of Some Place Names and Personal Names to an Understanding of Early Israelite Religion*

J. Andrew Dearman

Introduction

Prior to the discovery of the Ug[aritic] texts it was sometimes thought that there were various and quite separate gods called Baal. This idea was encouraged by the presence in the Old Testament of various compound place names involving Baal, e.g. Baal-peor, Baal-hermon, Baal-meon, Baal-hazor, Baal-gad, etc. However, with the discovery of the Ug[aritic] texts it became clear that there was one great Canaanite storm-and-fertility deity Baal-Hadad of cosmic stature, so that we must assume that these Old Testament allusions refer to particular local manifestations of this one god.[1]

As this recently published statement makes clear, a paradigm shift took place in the interpretation of *ba'al* terminology in the Hebrew Bible as a result of the discovery of the texts at *Ras Shamra* (ancient Ugarit). An older scholarly consensus, that the term *ba'al* was primarily an appellative (= a common noun) used for a variety of local *numina*, tribal deities, and other 'foreign' gods,[2] changed to a new consensus with the realization that the Ugaritic storm god Ba'al (Hadad) was no mere local deity but a cosmic Lord, and that a south Canaanite form of his presence might lie behind the Ba'al who

---

* It is a pleasure to dedicate this essay to Professor John H. Hayes, whose fine scholarship and wise counsel are widely known and greatly admired.

1. J. Day, 'Baal (Deity)', *ABD* 1 (1992), p. 547. See also J.C. de Moor and M.J. Mulder in their entry, '*b'l*', *TDOT*, II (1975), pp. 181-200.

2. See A.S. Peake, 'Baal', *Dictionary of the Bible* 1 (1911), pp. 209-11; and W.W. Baudissin, 'Baal und Bel', in *RE* 2 (1896–1913), pp. 323-40; and his posthumously published *Kyrios als Gottesname im Judentum und seine Stelle in der Religionsgeschichte* (Giessen: A. Töpelmann, 1929), III, pp. 35-44.

was YHWH's rival for Israel's allegiance.[3]

Any consideration of the topic 'Ba'al in Israel' faces a formidable series of interlocking issues and a mass of secondary studies. In what follows, I take up the subject from the limited vantage point of two related sets of data, namely the Ba'al place names in the Hebrew Bible and some personal names from the period of Saul and David. As I hope to show, I do not think these data support the consensus summarized by Day. Specifically, I propose that: (1) components of the older viewpoint still have merit for the topic at hand; (2) the Ba'al place names do reflect the veneration of more than one *ba'al* deity in south Canaan;[4] (3) one or more of the sites preserves the appellative *ba'al* as a reference to YHWH; and (4) although it is a plausible hypothesis, there is no clear evidence that any of the Ba'al place names reflects a pre-Yahwistic cult of Ba'al among early Israelite clans.

The older viewpoint interpreted the Ba'al place names as representing the essence of baalistic religion. According to Peake,

> 'There was originally no supreme deity called Baal. . . there was only the Baal (or Baals) of particular places distinct from each other. The worship probably arose in connexion with agriculture. The local Baals fertilized each his own district by his streams and springs, and hence they were the owners of these naturally fertile spots.'[5]

Since Peake regarded the term *ba'al* as an appellative for Canaanite deities, he even described its occasional ascription to YHWH in early

3. Those who question the current consensus include H. Spieckermann, *Juda unter Assur in der Sargonidenzeit* (FRLANT, 129; Göttingen: Vandenhoeck & Ruprecht, 1982), pp. 200-25; and H. Niehr, *Der Höchste Gott. Alttestamentlicher JHWH-Glaube im Kontext syrisch-kanaanäischer Religion des 1. Jahrtausends v. Chr.* (BZAW, 190; Berlin: de Gruyter, 1990), esp. pp. 1-14.

4. '*Habba'al* [in the Hebrew Bible] cannot be regarded as an appellative of different Canaanite gods, but only as the name of a specific god with which Israel came into contact from the period of the settlement to the exile' (so Mulder, '*b'l*', p. 193); 'Baal, or, more fully, Baal Hadad, was a Canaanite weather and fertility god whose cult was extremely widespread throughout the entire Levant. By itself, *ba'al* means "lord", and the term can refer to other gods, but when used without qualification it almost invariably refers to Hadad' (quoted from W.J. Fulco, 'Baal', *EncRel* 2 [1986], p. 31). S. Olyan concludes similarly: 'most scholars, however, believe that the Baal of the Hebrew Bible is usually if not always the storm god Hadad' (*Asherah and the Cult of Yahweh in Israel* [SBLMS, 34; Atlanta: Scholars Press, 1988], p. 62).

5. Peake, 'Baal', p. 210.

Israel as 'perfectly innocent', something the nomadic Israelites had picked up from the inhabitants of Canaan upon their settlement in the land.[6]

The work of Eissfeldt plays a pivotal role in this discussion, considering the fact that his long scholarly career placed him in the camp of both the old consensus and its revision. Furthermore, his caution in adopting a new perspective seems commendable in hindsight. In his first published essay on the subject (1914), he described the *bĕ'ālîm* as the divinities of the Canaanite agricultural sphere, closely bound with the characteristics of the natural world, so that in a sense they are nature itself.[7] Israel encountered the *bĕ'ālîm* only upon its settlement in the land, where a process of blending (*Verschmelzung*) the conceptions of Yahweh (the fierce deity of Sinai) and Baalism began. But in 1939, under the influence of the Ugaritic discoveries and the increasing evidence for the veneration of Ba'al Shamayim in much of Iron Age Canaan, Eissfeldt reconsidered the references to the *bĕ'ālîm* in the Hebrew Bible.[8] In several, he proposed that the terms *bĕ'ālîm/habba'al* were used in a general polemical fashion to describe many of the cultic practices opposed by the writers. Behind other references (e.g., to the Phoenician deity opposed by Elijah), however, he cautiously proposed the deity Ba'al Shamayim. Eissfeldt preferred not to commit himself on a precise identity of Ba'al Shamayim, whether, for example, this deity could be identified with Hadad or traced back into Bronze Age sources; nevertheless, he did propose that in several instances *habba'al* in the Hebrew Bible referred to this cosmic deity who was YHWH's rival.

To his credit, Eissfeldt recognized that names combining a form of *ba'al* with a *Bestimmungswort* (e.g., the deity Ba'al Zebub or the toponym Ba'al Hermon) were difficult for his thesis. So he cautiously proposed that some of the names indicated local representations of a

6. Peake, 'Baal', p. 210.
7. 'Jahve und Baal', in R. Sellheim and F. Maass (eds.), *Kleine Schriften* (Tübingen: Mohr, 1962), I, pp. 1-12.
8. 'Ba'alšamēm und Jahwe', in R. Sellheim and F. Maass (eds.), *Kleine Schriften* (Tübingen: Mohr, 1962), II, pp. 171-98, esp. pp. 183-86. Cf. Albright's endorsement in his *Archaeology and the Religion of Israel* (Baltimore: Johns Hopkins University Press, 2nd edn, 1946), pp. 116-17, 156-57, although he believed that the *ba'al* opposed by Elijah was Melqart. 'The Canaanite Baals were all high gods in their own right. The *ba'al* par excellence, undoubtedly intended whenever the singular noun "Baal" is mentioned, was the storm-god' (p. 116).

great deity (i.e., Ba'al Shamayim). Wisely, however, he conceded that these names with a *Bestimmungswort* could also reflect the veneration of different gods (mountain deities or local, nature deities), as commonly interpreted by the older scholars. Nevertheless, even if they did indicate different deities, they did not number more than a dozen or so, and they were not decisive evidence against his claim that by the time of Elijah, Ba'al Shamayim was YHWH's chief rival in pre-exilic Israel.[9]

In their more recent works, Day, de Moor, and Mulder were less cautious about a common appellative usage of the term *ba'al* in the Hebrew Bible when referring to deities.[10] And thus it is not surprising that they ignored Eissfeldt's caution concerning the evidence of the Ba'al place names. Mulder even claimed that the Ba'al place names as a whole are of little value (*in religionsgeschichtliche Hinsicht*) except to illustrate how broadly based was the Baal cult in southern Canaan.[11] This is an unsatisfactory claim because it essentially dismisses the evidence which is most difficult for his conclusions about Ba'al in Israel. One can agree perhaps with the latter part of his claim—that the term *ba'al* was broadly used in southern Canaan—but only if 'Baal cult' is defined more broadly than the veneration of a single Canaanite deity.

---

9. See the dissertation by one of Eissfeldt's last students, R. Hillmann, 'Wasser und Berg. Kosmische Verbindungslinien zwischen dem kanaanäischen Wettergott und Jahwe' (PhD dissertation, Halle, 1965).

10. 'When *b'l* is not used in an absolute sense, but is connected with a genitive that defines it more precisely, it is frequently hard to decide whether *b'l* should be understood as a proper name or as an appellative honorific title of another god. The former should not be dismissed too hastily, because other divine names were also frequently connected with genitives. Thus it is just as legitimate to translate *b'l-x* "Baal of X" as it is to translate it "lord of x". Furthermore, it has been convincingly demonstrated that *b'l* followed by a genitive frequently means the storm god Baal' (de Moor, '*b'l*', p. 184).

Although one can agree with much of this reconstruction, the question regarding the Ba'al place names is still whether one is always dealing with the same deity in the construction *ba'al-x*, albeit in local manifestation, or whether indeed there was a variety of *bĕ'ālîm* behind the toponyms. It is possible to use the appellative *ba'al* in the sense 'the deity *ba'al* at place x', when there is another 'deity *ba'al* at place y', and in both cases, the deities may have another name (e.g., Hadad, Kemosh, YHWH).

11. Mulder, '*b'l*', pp. 194-95. Mulder does claim (p. 194) that Ba'al Peor, Ba'al Berith, and Ba'al Zebub [zebul] are all titles of the god Ba'al. None of the other Ba'al place names are examined in any detail.

Ba'al Place Names in the Hebrew Bible

The number of Ba'al place names in the Hebrew Bible is not large.[12] Some examples are the following: *b'l gd*,[13] *b'l hmwn*,[14] *b'l hswr*,[15] *hr b'l hrmwn*,[16] *[byt] b'l m'wn*,[17] *[byt] b'l p'wr*,[18] *[hr] b'l prsym*,[19] *b'l spwn*,[20] *b'l šlšh*,[21] *b'l tmr*,[22] *b'ly yhwdh*,[23] *b'lh*,[24]

---

12. W. Borée, *Die alten Ortsnamen Palästinas* (Leipzig: E. Pfeiffer, 1930), pp. 95-97. The list differs marginally from that of Borée. See also B.S.J. Isserlin, 'Israelite and Pre-Israelite Place-Names in Palestine: A Historical and Geographical Sketch', *PEQ* 89 (1957), pp. 133-44; A.F. Rainey, 'The Toponymics of Ancient Israel', *BASOR* 231 (1978), pp. 1-17, esp. pp. 3-4.

13. Josh. 11.17; 12.7; 13.5. The site is located at the northernmost extension of the Israelite inheritance according to these texts.

14. Song 8.11. Cf. *KAI* 24.

15. 2 Sam. 13.23.

16. Judg. 3.3; 1 Chron. 5.23.

17. Num. 32.38; Josh. 13.17; Jer. 48.23; Ezek. 25.9; 1 Chron. 5.9; cf. the Mesha Inscription, ll. 9 and 30.

18. Num. 25.18 (3, 5); 31.16; Deut. 3.29; 4.46; 34.6; Josh. 13.20; Hos. 9.10.

19. 2 Sam. 5.20; 1 Chron. 14.11; cf. Isa. 28.21.

20. Exod. 14.2, 9; Num. 33.7. This site is located on the coast of Egypt. Cf. O. Eissfeldt, *Baal Zaphon, Zeus Kasios und der Durchzug der Israeliten durchs Meer* (Halle: Niemeyer, 1932), and W.F. Albright, 'Baal-Zephon', in W. Baumgartner *et al.* (eds.), *Festschrift Alfred Bertholet zum 80. Geburtstag* (Tübingen: Mohr, 1950), pp. 1-14.

21. 2 Kgs 4.42. LXX presupposes *byt*.

22. Judg. 20.33.

23. 2 Sam. 6.2 (MT). Borée (*Ortsnamen*, p. 96) reads *b'lh* on the basis of Josh. 15.9. The MT of 6.2 is likely corrupt. The concluding yod of *b'ly* may be the result of dittography, in which case the reading would be Ba'al Judah, or the phrase reflects a syntactical corruption and actually refers to the lords or leaders of Judah. See J. Blenkinsopp, 'Kiriath-jearim and the Ark', *JBL* 88 (1969), pp. 143-56.

24. Josh. 15.9 (cf. v. 29), where the site = Qiryat Ye'arim. Cf. also Josh. 15.60 (= *qryt b'l*); 18.24; 1 Chron. 13.6. M. Noth (*Josua* [HAT, 7; Tübingen: Mohr, 2nd edn, 1953], pp. 89-90, 110) proposed that the equation of Ba'alah with Qiryat Ye'arim was editorial and not geographically correct. Qiryat Ye'arim was an old site in its own right, and the name Qiryat Ba'al in 15.60 and 18.14 shows another development where the names of two sites are mixed. Perhaps Ba'alah is the name of the nearby cultic site associated with the settlement. See the discussion below and further references in nn. 54 and 57.

hr hb'lh,[25] *b'lt*,[26] *b'lt b'r*,[27] *b'lwt*,[28] *bmwt b'l*,[29] and *gwr b'l*.[30] Most are located in the central and northern hill country of Cisjordan, but they are not limited to one geographical area. With one exception (2 Sam. 5.20, see below), the Hebrew Bible preserves no etiology for any of their names. The majority of these toponyms also have the theophoric term *ba'al* in the construct state, signifying originally the Ba'al *of* or *at* the geographic site. As is well-known, the grammatical construction *ba'al-x* is often used to designate a deity in the ancient Near East.[31] These Ba'al place names, therefore, are a subset of a larger linguistic and cultural pattern, where different grammatical constructions are used for deities that combine a divine name or theophoric element with a geographical reference.[32]

The list of Ba'al place names in Palestine might be expanded modestly with extra-biblical references such as *ba'ali-rasi*, if this Canaanite toponym from the annals of Shalmaneser III is the Mt Carmel of the biblical narrative,[33] and *b'l m'wn*, if this reference

25. Josh. 15.11.

26. Josh. 19.44.

27. Josh. 19.8; cf. 1 Chron. 4.33 (= *b'l*).

28. Josh. 15.24. Cf. Josh. 15.9.

29. Josh. 13.17. Line 27 of the Mesha Inscription has a *bt bmt*, which is likely the same place.

30. The MT is likely a corruption. Cf. BHS footnotes.

31. E.g., *b'lt gbl*, *KAI* 4.3-4; *b'l ṣdn*, *KAI* 14.18; *b'l lbnn*, *KAI* 31.1; *b'l ḥmn*, *KAI* 61.3-4. In the Hebrew Bible Ba'al Peor is both a place name (Hos. 9.10) and the name of a deity (Num. 25.3, 5).

32. For further discussion see M. Barré, *The God-List in the Treaty Between Hannibal and Philip V of Macedonia: A Study in Light of the Ancient Near Eastern Treaty Tradition* (Baltimore: Johns Hopkins University Press, 1983), p. 186 n. 472; P.K. McCarter, 'Aspects of the Religion of the Israelite Monarchy: Biblical and Epigraphic Data', in P.D. Miller, P.D. Hanson, and S.D. McBride (eds.), *Ancient Israelite Religion: Essays in Honor of Frank Moore Cross* (Philadelphia: Fortress Press, 1987), pp. 137-43. See, e.g., l. 1 of the Aramaic portion of the T. Fakhariyeh inscription, which refers to Hadad of Sikan (*hdd skn*). Line 16 has a variant construction, 'Hadad who dwells in Sikan' (*hdd ysb skn*), as well as the description of Hadad as the 'Lord [of the] Habur' (*mr' ḥbwr*). The Aramaic term Lord (*mr'*) in this construction is an appellative referring to Hadad, and the construction *mr'-x* is a synonym of *b'l-x*. Cf. the use of *mr'* for Melqart in *KAI* 47.1.

33. E. Michel, 'Die Assur-Texte Salmanassars III (858-824)', *WO* 2 (1954), pp. 38-39; Y. Aharoni, 'Mount Carmel as Border', in A. Kuschke and E. Kutsch (eds.), *Archäologie und Altes Testament* (Tübingen: Mohr, 1970), pp. 1-7; and

from the Samaria Ostraca refers to a site near Samaria rather than the better known Transjordanian site.[34] Two of the Ba'al place names in the Hebrew Bible (Ba'al Me'on and Bamoth Ba'al) can be compared with similar place names in Transjordan from the Mesha Inscription, which preserves some variations in their spellings.[35] Geographical identification, however, is less important for the topic at hand than the theophoric element in the toponyms. The Ba'al place names have the theophoric element *ba'al* in masculine (twelve singular and one plural)[36] and feminine (four singular and one plural) forms, and one has the definite article (Josh. 15.11). These toponyms vary from other uses of the divine name/appellative *ba'al* in the Hebrew Bible. Apart from the Ba'al place names, the Hebrew Bible uses only the masculine singular and plural forms in reference to deities. And also in these other references, the masculine singular form in the MT always has the definite article.

The obvious question about the Ba'al place names is: to whom do the various forms of the theophoric element *ba'al* refer? One naturally assumes the toponyms with the feminine theophoric element refer to goddess veneration (e.g., Hathor, Anat, Asherah, Astarte).[37] And this is the best conclusion, even though it is made more difficult by the fact that the feminine appellative/name occurs elsewhere in the Hebrew Bible neither with reference to a goddess nor as a theophoric element in Hebrew personal names from extra-biblical sources.[38] Whatever

S. Aḥituv, *Canaanite Toponyms in Ancient Egyptian Documents* (Jerusalem: Magnes, 1984), pp. 124-25.

34. Ostraca 27.3. Probably the term refers to the Ba'al Me'on of Num. 32.39 and of the Mesha Inscription, l. 9.

35. On the place names in the Mesha Inscription, cf. J.A. Dearman, 'Historical Reconstruction and the Mesha Inscription', in J.A. Dearman (ed.), *Studies in the Mesha Inscription and Moab* (ABS, 2; Atlanta: Scholars Press, 1989), pp. 170-96.

36. For the masculine plural form, see n. 23 above. The plural form is likely a textual corruption.

37. See *KAI* 4.3-4, where the chief goddess of Byblos is called *b'lt gbl*.

38. It is possible but unlikely that the feminine forms in the Ba'al place names, *b'lh/t*, represent a hypocoristicon by analogy with personal names. The masculine personal names *b'l* (12.2) and *b'l'* (1.7; 3.3; 27.3; 28.3; 31.3) in the Samaria Ostraca are likely abbreviations; cf. A. Lemaire, *Inscriptions hebraïques 1. Les ostraca* (LAPO, 9; Paris: Cerf, 1977), p. 50. See also the reference in n. 57 below to the place name Ba'alah and the possible explanation of its name as a reflection of the feminine gender of the city (*'yr* or *qryh*).

obscurities remain about the identity of the goddesses, the date of the toponyms, or the relationships between the toponyms and the Israelite settlement, the feminine theophoric element strongly implies that more than one deity stands behind the Ba'al place names. It is an indication of the strong presuppositions of de Moor and Mulder about the character of the *ba'al* terminology in the Hebrew Bible that neither one discusses these Ba'al place names with the feminine theophoric element.

The toponym Ba'al Gad is another example from the Ba'al place names which is difficult to reconcile with the newer viewpoint. The name could refer to a deity named Gad, venerated as a Ba'al figure at the site, or to a deity as the Lord (i.e., owner/possessor) of 'good luck', or less probably to a deity of a site named Gad. The use of the name Ba'al Gad as a toponym, then, is probably a secondary development. Perhaps the closest parallels are to the deities Ba'al Ḥamon, Ba'al Zebub (Zebul), and the obscure Ba'al Malage, since none of them are toponyms (see below). It is a leap of faith, however, to identify the deity venerated at Ba'al Gad with the cosmic storm god.

The prevailing scholarly view that the Ba'al place names 'are named after the local manifestation of Ba'al'[39] actually has much to commend it, as long as it is also conceded that there can be more than one divine Lord or Owner behind the theophoric element.[40] The older view had a double weakness in that: (1) the *bě'ālîm* of Canaan were interpreted only as local *numina*, and (2) a nomadic Israel encountered the *bě'ālîm* only when settling in the land. The variety of Canaanite religiosity could well support local deities as well as more than one 'high god', and the Ba'al place names probably preserve references to both categories of deities. And whether the tribes known as Israel were indigenous to Canaan (as is commonly claimed today), or whether a strong component was pastoral and had roots outside the agricultural zones, it is most unlikely that Israel's first exposure to *ba'al* deities came in the settlement period. Still, the greatest difficulty in assessing the Ba'al place names comes in the paucity of evidence preserved about them in the Hebrew Bible. These toponyms are prime examples of why scholars must be careful about controlling assumptions and their influence in assessing obscure features of the text.

Stated somewhat differently, there is no persuasive evidence that the

39. So Rainey, 'Toponymics', p. 6.
40. See n. 10 above.

Ba'al place names reflect regional characteristics of a single *ba'al* deity, or, as some interpreters put it, 'the storm god'. The problem for the 'local manifestation' theory is not the lack of evidence but that it exists in such variety. In addition to the Ugaritic texts, Egyptian texts, and biblical materials,[41] there are hundreds of relevant Iron Age Phoenician and Punic inscriptions. In the Iron Age four different *bĕ'ālîm* (Ba'al Shamayim, Ba'al Ṣaphon, Ba'al Ḥamon, and Melqart = the Ba'al of Tyre) reached international stature, not to mention the numerous deity names and toponyms preserved only once in extant sources.[42] Should not the variety of Iron Age *bĕ'ālîm* have some counterparts in the Middle Bronze Age and Late Bronze Age? Unfortunately, only one of the four international *bĕ'ālîm*, Ba'al Ṣaphon, is known from Late Bronze Age texts by this particular name, and he illustrates the difficulty of interpretation. At Ugarit the name Ba'al Ṣaphon refers to Hadad and his mountain home (*Jebel el 'Akra*); yet for Tyre of the seventh century, Ba'al Ṣaphon is but one of the three *ba'al* deities listed as Tyrian gods.[43] The problem of

41. For early uses of the term *b'l*, see G. Pettinato, 'Pre-Ugaritic Documentation of Ba'al', in G. Rendsburg *et al.* (eds.), *The Bible World: Essays in Honor of Cyrus H. Gordon* (New York: Ktav, 1980), pp. 203-10; H.-P. Müller, 'Religionsgeschichtliche Beobachtungen zu den Texten von Ebla', *ZDPV* 96 (1980), pp. 15-18. For Ugarit, see A.S. Kapelrud, *Baal in the Ras Shamra Texts* (Copenhagen: G.E.C. Gad, 1952); P.J. van Zijl, *Baal: A Study of Texts in Connexion with Baal in the Ugaritic Epics* (AOAT, 10; Neukirchen–Vluyn: Neukirchener Verlag, 1972). For Egypt, see R. Stadelmann, *Syrisch-palästinensische Gottheiten in Ägypten* (PÄ, 5; Leiden: Brill, 1967), pp. 27-47. The bibliography for the biblical materials is enormous. Perhaps the best introduction to the issues remains that of F.M. Cross, *Canaanite Myth and Hebrew Epic* (Cambridge, MA: Harvard University Press, 1973), pp. 1-215.

42. For bibliography and discussion, see P. Xella, 'Le polythéisme phénicien', in C. Bonnet, E. Lipiński, and P. Marchetti (eds.), *Religio Phoenicia* (Studia Phoenicia, 4; Namur: Société des études classiques, 1986), pp. 29-39; R. Clifford, 'Phoenician Religion', *BASOR* 279 (1990), pp. 55-64; H. Niehr, *Der Höchste Gott*, pp. 17-68.

43. See R. Borger, *Die Inschriften Asarhaddons, Königs von Assyrien* (AFO.B, 9; Graz: R. Borger, 1956), para. 69, IV. Ba'al Shamayim, Ba'al Malage, and Melqart are also listed. For other references to Ba'al Ṣaphon, see R. Clifford, *The Cosmic Mountain in Canaan and in the Old Testament* (HSM, 4; Cambridge, MA: Harvard University Press, 1971), pp. 58-79; *KAI* 50.3; 69.1; and P. Bordreuil, 'Attestations inedites de Melqart, Baal Hamon et Baal Saphon a Tyr', in C. Bonnet, E. Lipiński, and P. Marchetti (eds.), *Religio Phoenicia* (Studia Phoenicia, 4; Namur:

identifying the *bĕ'ālîm* comes in the (necessary) scholarly quest for lines of coherence among different texts and related material cultures, but it is difficult to explain the variety of *bĕ'ālîm* in the Iron Age on the assumption that there was only one cosmic Ba'al in Canaan.

In investigating the Ba'al place names, scholars are forced to depend on divine names formulated in the construction *ba'al-x* for comparative analysis. Although these names demonstrate convincingly that certain *bĕ'ālîm* were venerated far beyond their homeland, they remain only partial parallels to the phenomenon of Ba'al place names in the Hebrew Bible. To cite again the example of Ba'al Ṣaphon, this deity was worshiped around the Mediterranean basin; but evidence for his veneration is certain only if the precise construction *b'l ṣpn* appears in references to a deity or as a place name. The cult of Ba'al Ṣaphon does not necessarily assist in the interpretation of the toponyms Ba'al Gad, Ba'al Hazor, etc., whose names may refer to other deities. There is also the question of the identity of Ba'al Ṣaphon in the Iron Age. Should one assume that Hadad stands behind the 'name', as was the case earlier at Ugarit, or has the identity of the deity in question split off from the Bronze Age equation with Hadad?

Related to the question of identifying the Canaanite *bĕ'ālîm* is the question of dating the Ba'al place names. Surprisingly, there is no textual evidence for these toponyms before the Iron Age. None is named in the Amarna archives or in other Egyptian references to Canaanite toponyms.[44] One cannot make strong arguments from silence about the significance of this fact, but one might also conclude that at least *some* of the Ba'al place names are dated no earlier than the end of the Late Bronze Age or the early Iron Age. And thus the

Société des études classiques, 1986), pp. 82-86.

44. There are, however, personal names with the theophoric element *ba'al* in the Amarna archives, e.g., Ba'al-meḥir, EA 245.44; 257.3; 258.2; 259.2; Sipṭi-ba'lu, EA 330.3; 331.4; 332.3. Note also the plural form Ba'alūma, EA 162.76. W. Moran (*The Amarna Letters* [Baltimore: Johns Hopkins University Press, 1992], p. 386) proposes that the theophoric element *b'l* is an 'appellative of Haddu'. One must be cautious in drawing this conclusion in the case of every personal name. The theophoric element *ba'al* and the proper name Hadad cannot always be equated in the Amarna period and almost certainly not in the Hebrew Bible, where the *name* Hadad has been pushed to the margins. See the cautions offered by K. Koch, 'Zur Entstehung der Ba'al-Verehrung', in E. Otto (ed.), *Studien zur alttestamentlichen und altorientalischen Religionsgeschichte* (Göttingen: Vandenhoeck & Ruprecht, 1988), pp. 189-205, esp. p. 197.

name of some of the Ba'al place names may go back to early Israelite
clans. As Rainey observed cautiously,

> That such [place] names occur only in Iron Age documents. . . may
> possibly be taken as evidence for some early, non-Yahwistic elements in
> the tribal groups that came to make up Israel. It is also possible that Ba'al,
> or the name Ba'al at least, may have achieved popularity at local shrines
> only toward the end of the Late Bronze Age or the beginning of the Iron
> Age. Such a development cannot be traced since the local documentation
> is inadequate.[45]

The Ba'al place names, therefore, offer difficulties for any view
that interprets them as a homogeneous unit. They may share little
more than a common theophoric element, although it stands to reason
that some sites (perhaps even the majority) preserve a reference to a
great storm and fertility deity. Clearly, however, the appellative
ba'al-x applies to a variety of deities in Iron Age II, and there is no
compelling reason to assume that the masculine singular form *ba'al* in
the Ba'al place names all refer to the same deity in a slightly earlier
period in south Canaan, any more than the feminine theophoric
element must always refer to the same goddess. In most cases one
simply cannot know whether one of the Ba'al place names represents a
local deity of considerable antiquity, a storm god *par excellence* of
south Canaan, the personal deity of a family or clan which settled an
area, a specialist deity (e.g., healing, incantations, oracles) of a
regional shrine, Israel's deity YHWH, or even some combination of
these options.

The Examples of Ba'al Perazim and Ba'al(ê/ah)-Judah

Rosen has proposed recently that the toponym Ba'ălê Judah (MT *b'ly
yhwdh*) in 2 Sam. 6.2 represents 'a pre-Yahwistic cultic centre of the
Judah clan', similar in some respects to other clan shrines such as
Ba'al Perazim, Ba'al Hazor, and Ba'al Shalishah.[46] He bases his

---

45. Rainey, 'Toponymics', p. 4. Borée (*Ortsnamen*, p. 96) stated categorically
that 'we find none of these names in pre-Israelite sources', but he did not connect
them with the Israelite settlement. Isserlin ('Place Names', p. 135) did not connect
any of the Ba'al place names with Israel either, stating categorically that 'ba'al-x is
not a typically Israelite name'.

46. S.A. Rosen, 'Early Israelite Cultic Centres in the Hill Country', *VT* 38
(1988), pp. 114-17. 'The original saga of the tribe of Judah carries a strong

conclusion on two points: (1) that textual evidence for toponyms with the theophoric element *ba'al* in southern Canaan does not appear before the Iron Age, and (2) that many of these toponyms are located within the geographical boundaries of the Israelite settlement.[47] Rosen agrees with B. Mazar, Rainey, and others that 'at an early period and among certain groups of the intruders [including some of the Israelite clans], Ba'al was an important deity or deity appellative'.[48] In this conclusion Rosen approximates the older scholarly viewpoint, with the term *ba'al* applicable to a variety of deities. His primary contribution to the older view is the link between Israelite settlement in Canaan and the names of a few Ba'al place names.

Generally speaking, Rosen's conclusions are persuasive; however, one of them—that the two toponyms Ba'al(ê) Judah and Ba'al Perazim were pre-Yahwistic cultic centers for Judean clans—deserves reevaluation. He never shows why the use of the term *ba'al* by 'Israelites' implies that these clans were pre-Yahwistic.[49] The older scholars understood that the appellative *ba'al* could be used for YHWH as well as for Hadad or other deities, so that there is nothing in the use of the term itself that implies a form of Israelite worship that is pre-Yahwistic. Moreover, in the case of Ba'al Perazim, the Hebrew Bible provides limited evidence that the theophoric element *ba'al* is indeed an appellative for YHWH.

Ba'al Perazim
Rosen proposes that the name reflects the cultic center of the Perez clan.[50] Perhaps he is correct. He fails, however, to discuss the

Canaanite (Ba'alist, non-Yahwist) flavour' (p. 116). Rainey ('Toponymics', p. 4) also suggested the possibility of 'non-Yahwistic elements' in Israel as responsible for some of the Ba'al place names.

47. See the works of Borée, Isserlin, and Rainey in n. 45 above.

48. B. Mazar, 'The Early Israelite Settlement in the Hill Country', in S. Ahituv and B.A. Levine (eds.), *The Early Biblical Period. Historical Studies* (Jerusalem: Israel Exploration Society, 1988), pp. 35-48, esp. pp. 47-48.

49. For a similar assumption about early Israelite clans, see the proposal by R. Wenning and E. Zenger that a Late Bronze Age II/Iron Age I cultic site with bull iconography is an example of a pre-Yahwistic Israelite settlement, in 'Ein bäuerliches Baal-Heiligtum im samarischen Gebirge aus der Zeit der Anfänge Israels', *ZDPV* 102 (1986), pp. 75-86. There is nothing about the site—bull iconography or otherwise—that requires it to be pre-Yahwistic.

50. As Rosen acknowledges, this is a proposal of B. Mazar ('Israelite

etiological report in 2 Sam. 5.20 that David named the site in honor of YHWH (not Perez) after the defeat of the Philistines.[51] YHWH had 'broken through' (*prṣ*) the enemies and gained the victory.[52] In fact, Ba'al Perazim is the only Ba'al toponym in the Hebrew Bible with an etiological explanation of its name, and the account clearly presupposes that the term *ba'al* refers to YHWH, the Lord or Master (the Ba'al) who had gained the victory for Israel.

Of course, etiological reports need not reflect historical reality, but it is surprising how often commentators pass over the claim of the text itself without further comment—perhaps simply assuming that the etiology is inaccurate. For example, the claim of 2 Sam. 5.20 may be interpreted similarly to the accounts of sanctuary founding and altar building in the ancestral stories in Genesis. The old sanctuaries at Shechem (Gen. 12.6-7), Bethel (Gen. 12.8; 28.10-22), and Hebron (Gen. 13.18), along with their pre-Yahwistic religion, are integrated into Yahwism through these accounts of their founding by Abraham or Jacob. So by analogy, an older site such as Ba'al Perazim and its cult could have been claimed by a Judean clan. But there are no such examples in the Genesis ancestral accounts for Ba'al place names, and one should be cautious in assuming that 2 Sam. 5.20 represents such a case. A straightforward reading of 2 Sam. 5.20 indicates that the toponym Ba'al Perazim reflects an early form of Judean Yahwism, and while that claim itself may not be historically correct, there is no compelling evidence either for the contrary view that the name and its divine referent are 'pre-' or 'non-Yahwistic'.

Settlement', pp. 47-48; for a proposal that Giloh is the location of Ba'al Perazim, see p. 48).

51. The narrator already refers to Ba'al Perazim in 2 Sam. 5.20a before David names the site, but this is to make clear to the reader where the Israelites were located before engaging the Philistines in battle. It should be added that not all references to this site of battle with the Philistines use the name Ba'al Perazim. Isa. 28.21 refers to the militant activity of YHWH at 'Mount Perazim'. Also, other possible references to 'Mount Perazim' can be found in Josh. 15.8; 18.16; and 2 Sam. 23.13.

52. Cf. C.L. Seow, *Myth, Drama, and the Politics of David's Dance* (HSM, 44; Atlanta: Scholars Press, 1989), pp. 80-90, for a thorough investigation of v. 20 and its implications for the ark narratives in 2 Sam. 5–6. The parallel verse in 1 Chron. 14.11 has David say, 'God (*'ĕlōhîm*) has broken through my enemies.'

Ba'alê Judah (2 Sam. 6.2)

The site is also known as Qiryat Ye'arim (1 Sam. 7.1-2) and apparently by other names as well. These names include Ba'alah (Josh. 15.9), Qiryat Ba'al (Josh. 18.14), and possibly Mount Ba'alah (Josh. 15.11) or even the 'fields of the forest' (*šĕdê yā'ar*; Ps. 132.6). Joshua 15.9 (cf. 1 Chron. 13.6) and 18.14 respectively equate the site Ba'alah/Qiryat Ba'al with Qiryat Ye'arim.[53] Discerning the original name of the site is quite complicated, since it may have had more than one name among the Canaanite population groups. Rosen suggests that the 'local name' of the site was Ba'al Judah, which is possible, as are the names Ba'alah and Qiryat Ba'al. It is likely that the names of two different but closely related sites are preserved in these references.[54]

Whatever the name(s) of the Ba'al toponym in question, one should not overlook the significance of the (older) alternative name, Qiryat Ye'arim, which is used in 1 Sam. 6.21–7.2 (cf. Josh. 15.9; 17.14) as the resting place of the ark of the covenant. Qiryat Ye'arim is probably a pre-Israelite name of the site,[55] which became known subsequently among certain Israelites as the 'settlement of the Lord' (= Qiryat Ba'al) as a result of the ark's presence in the settlement. According to 1 Sam. 7.2, the ark was at the site for twenty years. The name change would explain why the site, previously referred to as Qiryat Ye'arim in 1 Sam. 7.1-2, is subsequently known as Ba'al(ê) Judah in 2 Sam. 6.2 or Qiryat Ba'al. The Hebrew Bible contains two partial analogies to this proposed name change for Qiryat Ye'arim: (1) Qiryat Sepher becomes Debir (Josh. 15.15; Judg. 1.11; cf. Josh. 15.49 [LXX]), and (2) Qiryat Arba becomes Hebron (Gen. 23.2; Josh. 14.15; 15.54; 20.7; Judg. 1.10).

A recent treatment of the site and its names by Seow assumes a historical background essentially opposite to that just proposed.[56] He suggests that the toponym Ba'alah/Qiryat Ba'al represents a

---

53. The expanded text of 4QSam[a] reads, *b'lh hy' qry[t y'rym 'šr] lyhwh*. The *lyhwh* is certainly a mistake for *lyhwdh*. See E.C. Ulrich, *The Qumran Text of Samuel and Josephus* (HSM, 19; Missoula, MT: Scholars Press, 1978), pp. 194-99.

54. Mazar ('Israelite Settlement', p. 39 n. 15) believes that the village was originally Hivite and proposes that the sanctuary of the settlement was on the nearby hill of *Deir el 'Azhar*. Perhaps the name of the latter was Ba'alah.

55. This is, in fact, the claim of Josh. 9.17. With the presence of the Yahwistic ark, the site's name changes under the influence of the nearby sanctuary (Ba'alah?) to Qiryat Ba'al or Ba'al Judah.

56. Seow, *Myth*, pp. 55-76.

pre-Israelite, pre-Yahwistic sanctuary where the myths of the storm god Ba'al were preserved. In his view, since the ark of the covenant resided there for several years, Ba'alah is the place where the mythological motifs of the storm god were adopted and subsequently transformed in early Yahwism. His proposal is plausible, but it is another theory based on the assumptions that (1) the names Ba'alah/Qiryat Ba'al are older than the Israelite settlement, and (2) the theophoric element in the toponym is a reference to the storm god Ba'al (Hadad). He also explains the feminine theophoric element *ba'ălāh* as a reflection of the city (which is feminine in gender) and not of the deity worshiped there, since the storm god in Canaan is typically masculine.[57] In the case of this particular toponym, the evidence is ambiguous for his interpretation and capable of supporting a quite different reconstruction.

To conclude, there is no convincing evidence for the view that Qiryat Ye'arim/Qiryat Ba'al or Ba'al Perazim were pre-Yahwistic cult centers used by Israelite or Judean clans. The relatively meager evidence in the biblical texts cited above points instead to the conclusion that the theophoric element *ba'al* in the two toponyms refers to YHWH, and not as an Israelite fertility deity but as a divine warrior associated with the ark of the covenant. It could still be the case that the appellative in these two Ba'al place names did not originally refer to YHWH and that early Israelite clans adopted the two sites and appropriated their names, but this conclusion can be based only on broad assumptions concerning the respective roles of Ba'al and Yahweh, not on the evidence of the biblical text itself.

Personal Names Formed with Ba'al from the Period of Saul and David

The study of personal names with theophoric elements and their implications for Israelite religion has received careful attention in recent years.[58] There are cultural links between divine names and

---

57. Seow (*Myth*, p. 76) proposes that the name Ba'alah is not a reference to goddess veneration at the site (which the feminine form suggests) but that the feminine form reflects the gender of *qiryah* or *'ir*.

58. J. Tigay, *You Shall Have No Other Gods: Israelite Religion in Light of Hebrew Inscriptions* (HSS, 31; Atlanta: Scholars Press, 1986); J. Fowler, *Theophoric Personal Names in Ancient Hebrew. A Comparative Study* (JSOTSup,

toponyms, and perhaps there is an analogy to be drawn between certain personal names and the Ba'al place names. For the period of Saul and David, there are a few individuals whose names contain the theophoric element *ba'al*, which have been polemically altered in the process of transmission in the Deuteronomistic History. The Chronicler preserves the names with the original theophoric element. They deserve brief consideration.[59]

'Ishba'al (*'yšb'l*), the son of Saul (1 Chron. 8.33, 9.39), is called Ishbosheth in 2 Sam. 2.8, a polemical scribal alteration substituting the term *bšt* ('shame') for the theophoric element *ba'al*.[60] One of the lists of Saul's sons (1 Sam. 14.49) preserves the names Jonathan, Ishvi, and Malchishua—but not Ishba'al—leading some interpreters to identify Ishvi with Ishba'al. The name Ishvi (*yšwy*) is possibly a corruption of the name *yšyw* or *yšyhw*, meaning 'YHWH exists' or 'man of YHWH' as presupposed by the LXX (and more particularly the Lucianic recension which reads *Iessiou*). If the names Ishba'al and Ishyah(u) refer to the same son of Saul, this would demonstrate explicitly the substitution of the appellative *ba'al* for YHWH.[61]

Meribba'al (*mryb b'l*), the son of Jonathan (1 Chron. 8.34; 9.40), is called Mephibosheth (*mpybš*), meaning 'from the mouth of shame' in 2 Sam. 4.4. According to 2 Sam. 21.8, Saul too had a son named Mephibosheth by his concubine Rizpah. The name of Saul's son may be a variant picked up from the name of Jonathan's son in the course of scribal transmission, but it is also possible that Saul had a son

49; Sheffield: JSOT Press, 1988); J.C. de Moor, *The Rise of Yahwism. The Roots of Israelite Monotheism* (BETL, 91; Leuven: Leuven University Press, 1990), pp. 10-41. A foundational study is that of M. Noth, *Die Israelitischen Personennamen im Rahmen der gemeinsemitischen Namengebung* (Stuttgart: Kolhammer, 1927).

59. The commentaries by P.K. McCarter (*I–II Samuel* [AB, 8-9; Garden City, NY: Doubleday, 1980, 1984]) contain discussions of the first four names with extensive references to variant readings among the versions.

60. For the possible renderings of Ishba'al—man of Ba'al, Ba'al exists, gift of Ba'al—see McCarter, *II Samuel*, pp. 82, 85-87.

61. So S.R. Driver, *Notes on the Hebrew Text of the Books of Samuel* (Oxford: Clarendon Press, 2nd edn, 1913), pp. 120-21; Mazar, 'Israelite Settlement', p. 48 and n. 39. Through textual reconstruction Mazar proposes other personal names with theophoric *ba'al*; in the same volume see 'The Military Elite of King David', p. 91 n. 20; and 'King David's Scribe and the High Officialdom of the United Monarchy of Israel', p. 135 n. 41.

Meppiba'al (*mpyb'l*), whose altered name Mephibosheth was the same as the altered name of Meribba'al.[62]

Be'alyada (*b'lyd'*), the son of David (1 Chron. 14.7), is also called named 'Elyada' (*'lyd'*), 'God knows' in 2 Sam. 5.16. Since David is treated more sympathetically than the Saulides by those making alterations, a theologically acceptable term was substituted for *ba'al*. Perhaps there is a parallel with the references to the Shechemite deity Ba'al Berith, also known as 'El Berith (cf. Judg. 8.33; 9.4, 27, 46).

Be'alyah (*b'lyh*), a servant of David (1 Chron. 12.6), whose name means 'YHWH is Lord or Owner', is not preserved in a 'corrected' version in 2 Samuel. One should compare the personal name *yhwb'l* from an unpublished find,[63] and the similar name of David's son Adonijah (*'dnyh*).

In light of the previous discussion concerning the Ba'al place names, there are essentially two conclusions that one can draw from these personal names employing the theophoric element *ba'al*. Either Saul and David worshiped a deity or deities known as Ba'al in addition to their veneration of YHWH,[64] or the theophoric element in these names was originally an appellative for YHWH and was understood as such by many in Yahwistic circles during the early Iron Age before the great conflict with Phoenician culture and religion in the ninth century. Saul and David are represented both in the Deuteronomistic History and in Chronicles as worshipers of YHWH, with Saul as disobedient to the instruction of YHWH, and David, with some exceptions, as obedient to YHWH's instruction. In terms of a state theology, both apparently were Yahwists, and the significance of these personal names seems to be that the theophoric element *ba'al* is an appellative for YHWH, as were *'ādôn* (Adonijah) and *melek* (Malchishua).[65]

The figure of Saul in the Deuteronomistic History is persuasive

62. So McCarter, *II Samuel*, pp. 124-25. The name Meribba'al also occurs in the Samaria Ostraca (2.7).

63. See N. Avigad, 'Hebrew Seals and Sealings and Their Significance for Biblical Research', in J.A. Emerton (ed.), *Congress Volume: Jerusalem, 1986* (VTSup, 40; Leiden: Brill, 1988), pp. 8-9.

64. So Noth, *Personennamen*, pp. 119-22. See also H.O. Thompson, *MEKAL, the God of Beth-Shan* (Leiden: Brill, 1970), pp. 172-79, who implausibly suggests that Michal, Saul's daughter, is named for *mkl*, the *ba'al* of Beth Shan. It is more likely that her name is a hypocoristicon meaning, 'who is like god?'.

65. Noth (*Personennamen*, p. 121) denies an analogy with these names, but in my opinion, on insufficient grounds.

evidence for this conclusion. No matter how his character is vilified or used as a foil for the person of David, he is not accused of the worship of Ba'al or any other deities besides YHWH. It is recorded that he consulted a medium, but he is described as unfaithful to YHWH, not as a polytheist. How easy it would have been for the compiler(s) of the Deuteronomistic History to describe Saul in terms similar to those used of Jeroboam, Ahab, Ahaz, and Manasseh. That they did not depict him as such suggests that in matters of state theology, Saul was a loyal Yahwist. Of course, it is possible that Saul and David acknowledged a series of minor deities arranged under the aegis of YHWH, the state deity, but these personal names with the theophoric element *ba'al* are not convincing evidence for this viewpoint.

Conclusion

The results of the preceding study agree at several points with the conclusions drawn by the older consensus. Nevertheless, there are two points at which the results of the present study differ with the older consensus. First, the older viewpoint was hesitant to relate any of the Ba'al place names to the emergence of Israel (since the clans and tribes were regarded as nomadic in background, and it was assumed they encountered the term *ba'al* only in the agricultural regions of Canaan). A basic Canaanite identity of early Israel is generally assumed among current scholars, whether or not there was a pastoral and/or a semi-nomadic substratum among the clans. Second, the older viewpoint did not equate the *bĕ'ālîm* represented at the sites with any cosmic or high deities. In the intervening decades a large percentage of primary texts have come to light in which the interpretation of some of the *bĕ'ālîm* as high gods seems assured. It seems wrong, however, to assume with a number of current scholars that the Ba'al place names simply reflect a local manifestation of the cosmic storm god or that these sites are all pre-Israelite (or pre-Yahwistic). As Eissfeldt proposed years ago, one must go on a case-by-case basis. Most likely, the Ba'al place names reflect a mixture of local and high god cults. A few may be Israelite and even refer to Yahweh with the appellative *ba'al*.

Put succinctly, the data examined in this study suggest that in South Canaan of the early Iron Age more than one deity could be designated by the appellative *baʻal*, including YHWH. Use of the appellative assumes diversity in application (among Israelites too), and it does not preclude religious or cultural conflict among various Canaanite subgroups (e.g., Israelite clans and their neighbors) who shared the practice. With the international spread of Phoenician culture and religion beginning in the tenth/ninth centuries—what might be described as part of the greatest 'missionary movement' of the Iron Age—conflict in Israel developed, and the subsequent use of the appellative for YHWH was discouraged or discontinued by the circles responsible for the Hebrew Bible.

W.F. ALBRIGHT AND THE QUESTION OF EARLY HEBREW POETRY

Yehoshua Gitay

Introduction

This paper focuses on the question of the co-existence of different stylistic media within the same biblical discourse. This combination of styles contradicts the unity of the biblical narrative, according to the diachronic-historical school, since the point of departure for this approach is the thesis that a literary work is unified both thematically and stylistically. Consequently, the appearance of prose and poetry together within a single biblical discourse suggests that two independent compositions have been combined.[1] Accordingly, biblical research during Albright's era focused on the pivotal question of chronology, utilizing the stylistic categories of prose and poetry as a historical criterion. However, since the historical data are not immediately available, scholars developed models that were supposed to provide—each from its specific point of view—the mechanism for dating the various styles and their respective authors. Albright himself was deeply involved in this historical-literary research, and his own stylistic-chronological model has affected biblical scholarship for more than two generations. Drawing on the growing interest in stylistic and literary matters and my own involvement in rhetorical study, this paper will examine Albright's stylistic-chronological model in accordance with the current directions of biblical literary research.

---

1.   A. Alt's statement (*Essays on Old Testament History and Religion* [Oxford: Basil Blackwell, 1966], p. 87) is characteristic:

> It depends on the observation that in each individual literary form . . . the ideas it contains are always connected with certain fixed forms of expression. This characteristic connection is not imposed arbitrarily on the material by the literary redactors . . . The inseparable connection between form and content goes back behind the written records to the period of popular oral composition and tradition, where each form of expression was appropriate to some particular circumstance.

Albright's Analysis

Almost all the literary cultures of the ancient Near East, including that of Greece, exhibit a common literary phenomenon, that is to say, epical or mythical literary compositions delivered in verse. Curiously enough, the Pentateuch, which appears to be the Hebrew literary analogy to the surrounding poetical works, is a prose narrative designed as a comprehensive historical discourse. Nonetheless, many scholars claim that Hebrew composition was originally cast in poetic form and so resembled the contemporary literature of Israel's neighbors. It was only later that this example of early Hebrew poetry took shape as prose.[2] Albright himself shared this view regarding the existence of an early stratum of Hebrew verse, although he was well aware of a major problem concerning the rediscovery of the early Hebrew verse: this literature no longer exists as a self-contained poetic narrative.

There is, therefore, a methodological problem: How should one define and then describe the non-extant literature? Here Albright the archaeologist is at work, and just as Albright the archaeologist desired to uncover the unseen, so Albright the biblical researcher sought to recover the missing Hebrew poetry. In order to achieve his historical-literary goal, Albright applied a proven archaeological tool—the comparative analogical method. Here the findings reveal that a sporadic phenomenon of local physical artifacts (i.e., pottery) hardly exists. The physical artifacts exhibit common cultural features that are widespread via international trade routes. Non-local pottery functions as the foundation of a global chronological order. The following is a demonstration of Albright's methodology of dating:

> One of the best-known pottery types of our age [Middle Bronze Age–Late Bronze Age] is the so-called Tell el-Yahudiyeh jug, a one-handled, pear-shaped . . . vase with a button base and a double handle. . . These small vases were used for perfume, and they became diffused very widely through trade channels. Hence they have long been employed by archaeologists as criteria of Hyksos date. . . [3]

2. For the literature, see E.L. Greenstein, 'The Formation of the Biblical Narrative Corpus', *AJSR* 15 (1990), p. 158 n. 27.

3. See W.F. Albright, *The Archaeology of Palestine* (Baltimore: Penguin Books, rev. edn, 1960), pp. 93-95.

The fragmentary local finding is, in the end, a part of a total phenomenon. Similarly, Albright concludes that the existence of isolated verses within the biblical narrative (e.g., Gen. 7.11b; 9.6; Num. 12.6-8) is not a unique phenomenon but a sample of a wider literary creation. That is to say, a specific literary form (poetry) that appears in one culture is apparently paralleled in several surrounding cultures. Form, whether it is that of a physical object or a genre of literature, is a general literary phenomenon that could not leave ancient Israel unaffected.

Since his objective literary target does not exist any more as a piece of literature, Albright is occupied with the method of his inquiry. How does he replace the phenomenological study of pottery with poetry? Albright conceptualizes the particular and introduces the concept of the scientific model that extrapolates on the basis of a miniature sample of a particular phenomenon that has been found. Albright explains,

> In the study of biblical tradition, historical analogy plays a particularly important role, for the Bible is not itself primarily an historical record. . . In order to understand the biblical tradition historically, historical analogy must be employed.[4]

Albright's task is, therefore, to find the 'miniature sample', that is, the single Hebrew verse within the prose narrative, and then to apply to the Hebrew verse the 'large scale', the existing literary phenomenon. The following is a demonstration of Albright's translation of a particular verse surrounded by the pentateuchal prose narrative:

> Hear now the words of [Yahweh]!
> In a vision I will make myself known to him,
> In a dream I will speak with him.
> Not so is my servant Moses;
> Of all My household he is most faithful.
> Mouth to mouth will I speak to him;
> [Not] in a vision and not in riddles,
> But the image of Yahweh shall he see (Num. 12.6-8).[5]

---

4.   See W.F. Albright, *Archaeology, Historical Analogy and Early Biblical Tradition* (Rockwell Lecture Series; Baton Rouge: Louisiana State University Press, 1966), p. 11.

5.   See W.F. Albright, *Yahweh and the Gods of Canaan* (Jordan Lectures in Comparative Religion, 7; London: Athlone Press, 1968), p. 37.

This verse is a sample, the remnant of a larger literary phenomenon. Albright concludes,

> The archaism is clear from the stylistic resemblances (including some repetition) to passages in the Ugaritic Baal Epic. For instance, in both we find successive three-beat cola beginning with 'In a dream. . . In a vision. . . ' The important point is that here we can draw on an archaic verse account for a view of the relation of God to the prophets and Moses which antedates our extant prose tradition.[6]

Albright presents his method, insisting that historical questions regarding the biblical material must be explored thoroughly. However, since the Bible itself cannot furnish the chronological-literary categories, Albright claims, the indications of the missing information must be sought in external evidence.

By establishing the external—rather than the internal—model as the tool for reconstructing the historical development of Hebrew literature, Albright stands in opposition to Wellhausen. The former attacks Wellhausen's internal model, which is based on literary-stylistic considerations of the biblical text. Wellhausen, for example, assigns a late date to the verses of wisdom literature, since they present a sophisticated and monotheistic view of universalism. Albright argues,

> [Wellhausen's] 'Hegelian' insistence that prophecy came before codified religious law led him to date most prophetic verse before *torah*. On the other hand, his unilinear system of religious evolution (which is partially Hegelian) resulted in his dating non-prophetic verse (Psalms, Wisdom literature) in the Persian and Greek periods. . . chiefly because of the 'advanced' concepts which were characteristic of it. . . [7]

Wellhausen's presupposition, argues Albright, is based on philosophical considerations; the Hegelian concept of gradual development, which dictates his dating, is wrong, claims the archaeologist. For Albright the comparative factual data are the only criteria for determining the date of the text.

In short, Albright's interest, especially in his later writings, is historical-chronological.[8] Hence, for him it is most important to

---

6. Albright, *Yahweh*, p. 38.
7. Albright, *Yahweh*, p. 1.
8. Attention should be given to the fact that Albright, especially in his later writings, does not develop a sense of ancient Hebrew epic. (Cf. C. Conroy,

isolate the literary strata that constitute the complex and varied biblical materials, while his own interest (based on the analogical material) concentrates on the first literary phase: early Hebrew verse. And how should we explain the appearance of the isolated verses within the prose narrative? Albright has the answer: the early united monarchy under the Davidic kingship nationalized the ancient epic, providing a historical narrative that is not a literary creation in itself but a prose paraphrase of the poetical material, the so-called J document.[9] Here the influence of Gunkel upon Albright cannot be ignored. Gunkel claimed that the establishment of the monarchy was also the cause of the emergence of historical writing in ancient Israel and that the literary medium of historical writing was prose![10]

Albright's thesis of an early Hebrew poetical stratum behind J has been sharply criticized in recent literature by Van Seters, who claims that J is a literary composition in itself, that is, the work of a single author and not the literary paraphrase of a poetic version.[11] Interestingly enough, Van Seters's method of argumentation is similar to Albright's own use of the principle of analogy. As was the case with his predecessor, Van Seters is not interested in internal analysis of the biblical literature. He rather searches for comparative material that suits his case for dating J to the exilic period.[12] His analogical material is found in the early Greek historiographical writing that would have been contemporary with the composition of J at this time.[13] Relying on research into the art of historiographical writing in

'Hebrew Epic', *Bib* 61 [1980], p. 11.) He was not occupied, as was his contemporary U. Cassuto, with the reconstruction of specific motifs of the almost lost Hebrew epic (for a summary of Cassuto's work, see Conroy, 'Epic', pp. 9-11; for Cassuto's reconstructions of certain epical tales, see his *The Goddess Anath* [Jerusalem: Magnes, 1971] [Hebrew] and his *Biblical and Oriental Studies* [Jerusalem: Magnes, 1973–75], I, pp. 7-16; II, pp. 16-59, 69-109).

9. See Albright, *Yahweh*, pp. 26, 30.

10. Cf. H. Gunkel, *The Legends of Genesis* (New York: Schocken Books, 1964), pp. 1, 137, and Albright's remarks in his introduction to this volume (p. viii).

11. See his treatment of the subject in his book, *In Search of History* (New Haven: Yale University Press, 1983) and his programmatic statements on pp. 8, 16-17.

12. Van Seters, *In Search*; and cf. his earlier work, *Abraham in History and Tradition* (New Haven: Yale University Press, 1975).

13. See Van Seters, *In Search*, esp. pp. 8-54, 209-48.

ancient Greece, Van Seters applies almost mechanically the conclusions of this research to the J material. Just as a Greek author would compose a historiographic work that included various literary genres, so J may be regarded as the composition of one author, a coherent literary creation that incorporates a variety of literary types and genres.[14]

Even though Van Seters's conclusion regarding the unity of J as a literary creation appears valid, the methodology and argumentation used in his attempt to refute Albright's thesis of early Hebrew poetry are not persuasive. Van Seters's argument presupposes literary dependence. For him it is self-evident that if a Greek composition is a single literary work, then similar works in Hebrew from the same time are by necessity unified literary creations as well. Van Seters uses Albright's concept of a literary model, but there is a meaningful difference between these two models: while Albright employs the analogical model in order to establish the existence of literature that no longer exists, Van Seters's literature (the J narrative) is extant. Therefore, Van Seters has demonstrated the possibility of his thesis but not its certainty. In order to establish the validity of his thesis literarily a structural-rhetorical analysis of the literature in question is required.

Current Literary-Stylistic Analysis

The question at hand is how Albright's historical-literary model relates to the current literary-stylistic studies of biblical narrative. The fundamental literary question is: What is the literary-rhetorical function of the use of prose and poetry in one literary unit? This literary question is pragmatic rather than structural, that is, the question is not *how* this specific literary phenomenon has been created, but *why* two different styles have been employed alongside one another.

A pragmatic analysis of this issue sheds fresh light on the function of each style and reveals that each is a literary vehicle with its own

14. Van Seters, *In Search*. Incidentally, in light of this conclusion, one must be surprised that Van Seters continues to maintain the documentary hypothesis, while arguing for a single composition that includes a variety of literary genres (we must admit, however, that he does not recognize the existence of E as a source). See his *Abraham* and his conclusion to *In Search* (pp. 309-12).

sphere of use. While prose is the objective language of administrative records, historical accounts, and law, poetry is the subjective medium of wishes, prayers, praises, and hymns. To substitute one literary form for another is unknown, since the style—prose or poetry—is fixed for each literary genre. Indeed, ancient literature furnishes us with numerous examples that delineate clearly the limits for the use of each genre.

In the case of Ramses II's military campaign to Kadesh on the Orontes, for example, there are two separate and lengthy accounts: the bulletin (or the record) and the poem. Lichtheim suggests that both derive from the same author, though each serves a different purpose: the prose relates the pertinent facts, in particular the humiliation of the Egyptian king by the Hittites, while the poem emphasizes the heroic role of the king.[15]

A close analysis of the biblical literature shows that a similar literary analysis may be applied to it as well. The Bible provides a number of examples in which the same topic—even the same event—is depicted once in prose and again in verse. In the case of Judges 4 and 5, the sensational defeat of Sisera, the Canaanite general, is reported. Judges 4 records the events in their historical sequence. The report is brief and factual. The preface introduces Deborah and identifies her person, position, and function (vv. 4-5). Similarly, the poem (ch. 5) introduces the hero and his function (v. 4), but it speaks about God rather than a human hero. The poem proceeds to describe the reaction of nature—earth, heaven, and mountain—to God's dramatic appearance (vv. 4-5), reports the dangerous situation (vv. 6-7), and graphically contrasts the tribes that took part in the war with those that refused to participate (vv. 14-18). It describes the natural forces that defeated the enemy (vv. 20-21) and gives a vivid, satirical description of Sisera's mother worrying about her son (vv. 28-30). The focus of the poem is on the suprahistorical aspects of the battle and so describes in detail God's appearance and the interference of nature on behalf of Israel. The narrative, on the other hand, laconically notes that God destroyed the enemy, 'and the Lord routed Sisera and all the chariots and all his army before Barak at the edge of the sword' (4.15). The foci of the two stylistic media differ, both with regard to the aims of their respective descriptions and with regard to

15. For the texts and commentary, see M. Lichtheim, *Ancient Egyptian Literature* (Berkeley: University of California Press, 1976), II, pp. 57-71.

their different treatments of themes. The reader, therefore, encounters in these two compositions different languages—the one of poetry and the other of prose.[16]

It should come as no surprise then for a biblical book such as Deuteronomy, the book of history and law, to appear in prose, while Jacob's blessing toward the end of the book (chs. 32–33) is in verse, the internal language of religious imagination.

Similarly, it is not incidental that the book of Deuteronomy, which is written mainly in prose, has a chronological parallel composed in verse, that is, the speeches of the prophet/poet Jeremiah. Obviously, the differences in style—prose versus poetry—do not project in this case two different historical periods. The stylistic medium was chosen deliberately by the prophet/poet in order to present effectively the divine announcement as a visionary plea, enriched with emotional appeal. The Deuteronomist, on the other hand, delivers speeches that rehearse the facts of history and transmit authoritative law.

Nonetheless, the appearance of the two styles within the book of Deuteronomy points out the stylistic poetics of the book: each theme or subject-matter is delivered in its own stylistic medium and together they comprise an entire literary discourse. A similar stylistic phenomenon appears in Jeremiah. Jer. 14.1–15.9, for example, constitutes one literary unit, composed mainly in poetry or rhythmical prose.[17] However, 15.3-4 is a passage that outlines the sins of Manasseh in prose. Stylistically, the prophetic speech distinguishes between the cause and the effect. The latter is described in colorful language, while the former is noted briefly in plain language, even in formulaic style. This arrangement suggests that the prophet's rhetorical focus was on the feature that required persuasion, that is, the effect or the punishment, which the people refused to accept. To this end, the prophet utilized the language of emotional appeal, vivid imagination and figuration. The cause—the sin—was familiar, and so

---

16. For a further discussion regarding the use of poetry and prose as two distinct literary media, see Y. Gitay, 'Oratorical Rhetoric', *Amsterdamse Cahiers* 10 (1989), pp. 72-83; and D.N. Freedman, 'Pottery, Poetry and Prophecy', *JBL* 96 (1977), pp. 5-26 (= his *Pottery, Poetry, and Prophecy* [Winona Lake, IL: Eisenbrauns, 1980], pp. 1-22).

17. For this division of the prophetic unit, see W.L. Holladay, *Jeremiah 1* (Hermeneia; Philadelphia: Fortress Press, 1986), pp. 414-44.

the language of historical fact, prose, was employed.[18]

The mixture of genres in a single discourse was clearly regarded as a useful rhetorical device in antiquity. The ancient Greek orators, seeking to appeal to their audiences, inserted verses at the climaxes of their prose speeches in order to strengthen the impact of the latter.[19] Is the Hebrew prose narrative that includes verse (such as Num. 12.6-8)[20] an artificial and hence meaningless text because it combines different styles? The literary response will take into account the nature and function of the biblical narrative: a dynamic text sensitively designed to affect its listeners/readers. What is the impact of Num. 12.6-8? It reveals God's unusual announcement to Miriam and Aaron, Moses' sister and brother who rebelled against his authority. The verses state the unique and unparalleled relationship between Moses and God. How, one asks, will the narrative address this critical issue of God's most intimate relationship with his servant Moses? By continuing to employ the ordinary language of prose? Form is an important facet of all communication, and this extraordinary situation cannot be recited in ordinary prose. Verse, however, provides the appropriate expression for this outstanding situation.[21]

Summary

In conclusion, Albright is concerned with the early history of Hebrew literature. He seeks to present the historical facts, and since the full data are no longer available, he provides an external analogical model that enables him to reconstruct the form of the non-extant literature. Albright's hypothesis about this early Hebrew poetry remains, in the end, unproven. That is to say, if we assume—on the basis of literary-historical comparisons—that ancient Hebrew literature was part of the

---

18. For a detailed study of Jeremiah's art of speech, see Y. Gitay, 'Rhetorical Criticism and the Prophetic Discourse', in D.F. Watson (ed.), *Persuasive Artistry* (JSNTSup, 50; Sheffield: JSOT Press, 1991), pp. 13-24.

19. See Aristotle, *Rhetoric*, 1404a.

20. Cited above as Albright's example of early verse.

21. Cf. F.M. Cross's remark, 'It is not impossible that the epic cycle in Israel was composed in a style in which prose narrative dominated but at climactic moments utilized poetic composition' ('The Epic Traditions of Early Israel: Epic Narrative and the Reconstruction of Early Israelite Institutions', in R.E. Friedman [ed.], *The Poet and the Historian* [HSS, 26; Chico, CA: Scholars Press, 1983], p. 20).

larger corpus of ancient Near Eastern literature, then we might share Albright's premise that there was a poetic precursor for the prose narrative. However, the assumption that isolated poetic sections within the pentateuchal narrative are the remnant of an earlier poetic stratum ignores the rhetorical dimension of the biblical narrative as a dynamic literary discourse.[22]

There is a rhetorical function of verse within prose narrative, and typically it concludes or summarizes specific messages. Thus, for example, Gen. 9.5 conveys the most important announcement regarding the prohibition of killing human beings. The style is prose, but due to the significance of the ban, the content is repeated in altered form:

> *špk dm h'dm*
> *b'dm dmw yšpk*
> *ky bslm 'lhym*
> *'śh 't-h'dm*
> Whoever *sheds* the blood of a HUMAN,
> by a HUMAN shall that person's blood *be shed*;
> for in God's image
> [God] made HUMANKIND (Gen. 9.6).

The style is repetitive and employs the device of chiasm, key words, and sound effects that create together an announcement in verse that is vivid, striking, and memorable.[23]

Albright focuses entirely on the external form of the text, but then ignores the insights that it provides into the meaning of the composition. Verse is not merely an external form; it is also a mirror of content. Consequently, poetry is the traditional language of myth and epic. The fact that the Pentateuch is mainly prose conveys in itself an important religious message. Prose is the language of history, the opposite of myth. This observation is expressed by Talmon as follows:

---

22. Attention should be given to Greenstein's observation, 'The alleged remnants of verse. . . may represent nothing more than stylistic features that had been normalized within the Hebrew prose discourse' ('Formation', p. 161).

23. For a convenient summary of the characteristics of biblical prosody, see W.T.W. Cloete, *Versification and Syntax in Jeremiah 2-25* (SBLDS, 117; Atlanta: Scholars Press, 1989), pp. 4-6. For the rhythmic structure of Gen. 9.6, see C. Westermann, *Genesis 1-11: A Commentary* (Continental Commentaries; Minneapolis: Augsburg, 1984), p. 467.

> The phenomenon [prose] is too striking to be coincidental. . . the ancient
> Hebrew writers purposefully nurtured and developed prose narration to
> take the place of the epic genre, which by its content was intimately bound
> up with the world of paganism. . . [24]

Hebrew writing thus functions ideologically: ancient composers used
its purposeful style to advance the biblical message of monotheistic
religion.

24. See S. Talmon, 'The "Comparative Method" in Biblical Interpretation—
Principles and Problems', in J.A. Emerton *et al.* (eds.), *Congress Volume:
Göttingen, 1977* (VTSup, 29; Leiden: Brill, 1978), p. 354.

THE LOCATION OF THE BROOK OF EGYPT

Paul K. Hooker

The majority of references to the 'Brook of Egypt' appear in two contexts. First, Assyrian historical inscriptions use the term in descriptions of royal activity in southern Palestine. Secondly, various texts in the Hebrew Bible employ the term to designate the boundary between the territory of Judah and either the domains of the pharaohs or a sort of 'no man's land' between Judah and Egypt. The purpose of this discussion is to review the Assyrian inscriptional evidence concerning the location of the Brook of Egypt. It will be argued herein that the designation 'Brook of Egypt', in earlier Assyrian inscriptions, was associated with the Wadi Besor, but that as Assyrian interests in southwestern Palestine grew, it became associated with Wadi el-'Arish, some 35 km further down the Mediterranean coast toward Egypt.

The term 'Brook of Egypt' (*naḥal [mât]muṣur*) in Akkadian usage was a designation of political geography, employed for the northeasternmost extent of Egyptian territory when seen from an outside, northern perspective.[1] It is not found in Egyptian literature, and references to it in the biblical tradition do not contain any identifiable geographic feature that conclusively determines its

---

1. N. Na'aman, *Borders and Districts in Biblical Historiography* (Jerusalem Biblical Studies, 4; Jerusalem: Simor, 1986), p. 246. Na'aman makes a similar suggestion regarding the use of the name 'Brook of Egypt': 'It was the river demarcating the border with Egypt from the point of view of the people living north-east of it.' From an Egyptian point of view, on the other hand, 'the Eastern Canal [of the Nile] with the frontier fortress at Sile, demarcated the eastern boundary of Egypt, while the Sinai Peninsula was considered part of Asia' (p. 241). The latter observation is significant because it would mean that a southwestward change in Assyrian territorial claims in the region would not necessarily involve infringement upon land claimed by Egypt, and it would therefore not necessarily evoke any hostile reaction on the part of the latter state.

location. To the contrary, there are several bodies of water between Gaza and the Nile—including the eastern branches of the Nile itself—which might legitimately lay claim to the title 'Brook of Egypt'.

Most scholars have identified the Brook of Egypt with Wadi el-'Arish in the Sinai, approximately one third of the distance from Gaza to Pelusium along the southeastern Mediterranean.[2] Some years ago, however, Na'aman challenged that consensus by arguing that the Brook of Egypt ought to be identified with Wadi Besor, immediately to the south of Gaza.[3] His suggestions were soon countered by Rainey in one of a series of articles on toponymic problems in Palestine, in which Rainey defended Wadi el-'Arish as the location of the Brook of Egypt.[4] Both Na'aman and Rainey based their cases in large measure on Assyrian inscriptions in which the Brook of Egypt figures prominently.

Assyrian Inscriptional References to the Brook of Egypt

An examination of the Assyrian inscriptional evidence should begin with the reign of Tiglath-pileser III (745–727 BCE), the first Assyrian monarch to campaign as far south as Gaza. The text ND 400 details the king's response to the revolt of Hanun of Gaza, in the course of which, Tiglath-pileser claims,

> *am-nu ṣa-lam šarru-ti-ia ina (al) na-ḫal-mu-ṣur a-ni* . . .
> A stela of my royal person [I set up] in the city of
> the Brook of Egypt. . . [5]

---

2. See, e.g., H.G. May (ed.), *The Oxford Bible Atlas* (London: Oxford University Press, 2nd edn, 1962), pp. 58-59 (map), where Wadi el-'Arish is labelled 'Brook of Egypt'.

3. N. Na'aman, 'The Brook of Egypt and Assyrian Policy on the Border of Egypt', *TA* 6 (1979), pp. 68-90; and 'The Shihor of Egypt and the Shur that is before Egypt', *TA* 7 (1980), pp. 95-109.

4. A.F. Rainey, 'Toponymic Problems (cont'd.)', *TA* 9 (1982), pp. 130-35, esp. pp 131-32.

5. D.J. Wiseman, 'Two Historical Inscriptions from Nimrud', *Iraq* 13 (1951), p. 23. See also H. Tadmor, 'Philistia Under Assyrian Rule', *BA* 19 (1966), pp. 88-89. Na'aman ('The Brook of Egypt', p. 131) argues that the determinative URU which precedes *naḫal muṣur* in this text should be understood in a 'more generalized sense' than Wiseman and others have understood it. Na'aman would translate simply, 'I [erected] my royal stele at the Brook of Egypt'.

Unfortunately, 'the city of the Brook of Egypt' is not associated in this text with any identifiable landmark. Tadmor and others who have commented on this passage have assumed that the Brook of Egypt is to be identified with Wadi el-'Arish,[6] but this identification cannot be established on the basis of this text.

Na'aman argues that the text, to the extent that it supports any identification at all, supports Wadi Besor as a better candidate for the Brook of Egypt than Wadi el-'Arish. He buttresses his assertion with two points. First, the reference to the Brook of Egypt comes in association with Tiglath-pileser's actions at Gaza, and since Wadi Besor is substantially closer to Gaza than Wadi el-'Arish, Besor is more likely the Brook of Egypt. Secondly, ND 400 makes reference to the *mu'nayya*, 'whose seat is below [i.e., south of] Egypt'. Na'aman identifies the *mu'nayya* with the Meunim of 1 Chron. 4.41, and he adduces 1 Chron. 4.39-41 in support of his argument that the Meunites/*mu'nayya* were, at least until the days of Hezekiah, situated at the entrance of Gedor:

> They [the sons of Simeon] journeyed to the entrance of Gedor, to the east side of the valley, to seek pasture for their flocks. . . for the former inhabitants belonged to Ham. These, registered by name, came in the days of Hezekiah, king of Judah, and destroyed their tents and the Meunim who were found there. . .

Na'aman reasons that the Meunites were situated south of Wadi Besor in the region of Gaza and that 'this is probably the same area that Tiglath-pileser reached and where he forced the tribes to pay him tribute'.[7]

6. So Tadmor, 'Philistia Under Assyrian Rule', pp. 88-89.

7. Na'aman, 'The Brook of Egypt', p. 70. Na'aman reads 1 Chron. 4.39 with LXX 'Gerara' (instead of MT's 'Gedor') and understands the region under consideration in 1 Chron. 4.39-44 to be the area immediately around Gaza and the Wadi esh-Shari'a/Nahal Gerar. Tadmor ('Philistia Under Assyrian Rule', p. 89) assigns the area 'south of Eg[ypt]', where the text locates the *mu'nayya* to 'south or southeast of el-'Arish', but without explanation as to how he arrived at this identification. See also I. Eph'al, *The Ancient Arabs: Nomads on the Border of the Fertile Crescent, 9th–5th Centuries BC* (Leiden: Brill, 1982), pp. 219-20. All three of these scholars agree that the *mu'nayya* of ND 400 should be understood as the Meunim of the biblical tradition. However, E.A. Knauf ('Mu'näer und Mëuniter', *WO* 16 [1985], pp. 114-15; and *idem*, 'Meunim', *ABD* 4 [1992], pp. 801-802) has differed, arguing that an identification between the 'Meunim' of 1 Chron. 4.41 and the *mu'nayya* of ND 400 is 'impossible'. In addition, S. Vargon ('Gedud: A Place-

While it must be admitted that ND 400 provides, at best, ambiguous evidence concerning the location of the Brook of Egypt, it seems to provide more support for Wadi Besor than for Wadi el-'Arish. Other evidence can be adduced, as well. Wadi Besor has along its banks the remains of several MB IIB forts, which might logically have served as border stations guarding the southernmost entrance into Canaan during the Bronze Age. Thus we have evidence that, for at least some time, Wadi Besor had served as a natural and political boundary, one which might readily have been recognized by the initial Assyrian expeditions into the area. Na'aman further points to the fact that within the biblical tradition, the southern boundary of Canaan ran along a line between Gaza and the southern end of the Dead Sea, or along a line roughly described by the path of Wadi Besor.[8] Taken together, all of this suggests that Tiglath-pileser simply acknowledged the existing boundary between Palestine and Egypt as Wadi Besor and designated that wadi as the 'Brook of Egypt' in his inscriptions.

Sargon II's first Palestinian excursion (720) involved, among other things, suppressing a second revolt by Hanun of Gaza, during the course of which the latter received aid from Egypt. Sargon claims to have pressed the campaign into the Sinai, defeating the Egyptian force and sacking the town of Raphia.[9] Although Raphia's location between el-'Arish and Besor is well established, the fact that it is between the two, rather than on one or the other, renders this reference less than conclusive.

The same must be said of Sargon's reference to the Brook of Egypt in VA 8424.[10]

ša pat-ti ^{âl}na-ḫal m[u-ṣur....] ša šùl-mu ^{d}šamši^{ši} ú-šá-a[ṣ-bit]...ameÌ$_{na-}$si-ku ša ^{âl}la-ba-an. . .

which is on the border of the Brook of E[gypt. . .] toward the sunset I stationed [my army?]. . . the sheikh of Laban. . .

name in the Shephelah of Judah', *VT* 52 [1992], pp. 557-64) has recently suggested that 'Gedor' in 1 Chron. 4.39 should be read 'Gedud', which he then identifies with Tell-Judeideh in the Judean Shephelah.

8.　Na'aman, 'The Brook of Egypt', pp. 75-76.

9.　For the inscription, see A.G. Lie, *The Inscriptions of Sargon II, King of Assyria* (Paris: Librairie Orientaliste Paul Geuthner, 1929), pp. 8-9. English translation: *ANET*, p. 285.

10.　E.F. Weidner, 'Šilkan(ḫe)ni, König von Muṣri, ein Zeitgenosse Sargons II', *AfO* 14 (1941–44), pp. 41-45.

Sargon's inscription locates something, presumably a town, on/in the region of the Brook of Egypt, though the specific geographic name is missing. Nothing else in the text gives any information useful to the puzzle.

One Sargonic text, however, which does not seem to have figured prominently in the discussion of this issue is ND 3411, first published by Gadd in 1954. It is a broken section of a cylinder that bears part of an inscription that refers in abbreviated fashion to a long list of Sargon's military exploits, territorial conquests, and other feats. The cylinder mentions the Brook of Egypt in l. 11, where *naḫal (mat)muṣur* appears as part of a list of the boundary extremities of Sargon's domains. Six lines later and as a prelude to the description of the capture of Hanun of Gaza in 720, the text claims,

> . . . *i-na (alu)ra-pi-ḫi taḫtu (mat)mu-uṣ-ri iš-ku-nu-ma*. . .
> . . . at the city of Rapihu [Raphia] he made havoc of the land of
> Egypt. . .[11]

The implication of the text is clear: at least in 720 and at the time of the initial Philistine campaign, Raphia was regarded as a city within the land of Egypt, so that Sargon's depredations there are described as creating 'havoc *of the land of Egypt*'. As we have already observed, Raphia was located between Wadi Besor and Wadi el-'Arish. If Raphia is in the land of Egypt, the conclusion is inevitable that the 'Brook of Egypt'—Sargon's term connoting the political and geographical boundary between his domain and the northernmost extent of Egyptian land—lies to the northeast of Raphia. From this text, one must conclude that the term 'Brook of Egypt' is associated with the Wadi Besor through at least the early days of the reign of Sargon.[12]

The next major references to the Brook of Egypt come from the inscriptions of Esarhaddon. The first is Nineveh A, III, ll. 39-42, which Borger renders:

11. C.J. Gadd, 'Inscribed Prisms of Sargon II from Nimrud', *Iraq* 16 (1954), pp. 198-201.

12. The actual date of ND 3411 can be no earlier than 714, since the text refers to the death of Rusa, the king of Urartu. Sargon's decisive victory over Urartu, as a result of which (Sargon claimed) Rusa committed suicide, took place in 714. The phraseology used in describing earlier events, however, was in all probability already fixed. Thus, Raphia is placed 'in the land of Egypt', because the earliest versions of Sargon's descriptions of those events surrounding the 720 campaign assumed that the Brook of Egypt was Wadi Besor.

^{uru}Ar-za-a šá pa-a-ṭi na-ḫal mât Mu-ṣur (ri) áš-lu-lam-ma ^IA-su-ḫi-
li šarra-šu bi-re-tú ad-di-ma a-na mât Aš-šur^{ki} ú-ra-a ina ṭi-ḫi abul qabal
âli šá ^(uru)Ni-na-a^(ki) it-ti a-si kalbi u šaḫî (ŠAḪ) ú-še-šib-šu-nu-ti ka-
mi-iš.[13]

Arza, which is in the region of the Brook of Egypt, I plundered; its king,
Asuhili, I threw in irons and led him to Assyria. Beside a gate in the midst
of Nineveh I left him bound with a bear, a dog, and a pig.

This text appears to give another clue to the location of the Brook of
Egypt: the name of a specific city in its immediate vicinity. However,
Arza cannot be located with any certainty. Na'aman has attempted to
show that it should be identified with 'Yurza', which is mentioned in
the Shishak city-lists and in second-millennium texts from the reign of
Thutmose III. In order to make this case, Na'aman argues for the
linguistic similarity between the two names.[14] However, the best that
Na'aman can show is that 'Arza' might possibly be a shortened form
of 'Yurza', and he concedes that a more likely foreshortening would
have been 'Urza' rather than 'Arza'. It is altogether possible that
Yurza and Arza are not to be identified, and thus we cannot draw any
significant conclusions from Nineveh A, III.

The other text from Esarhaddon is, however, more helpful.
Borger's Fragment F, obverse, ll.16-17 reads, in part:

. . . *30 bêru qaq-qar ul-tú* ^{uru}Ap-qu šá pa-ṭi mât Sa-me-n[a x?] a-di
^{uru}Ra-pi-ḫi a-na i-te-e na-ḫal mât Mu-ṣur. . .[15]

. . . 30 *bêru* from Aphek, which is on the border of Samen[a] (Samaria?)
to Raphia, as far as the Brook of Egypt. . .

The text gives a spatial reference for the Brook of Egypt, which is
connected to the widely accepted location of Raphia, some seventeen
km southwest of Gaza, between Wadi Besor and Wadi el-'Arish. The
key to the reference is the phrase *ana itê*. By Na'aman's reasoning, the
phrase should be read 'beyond the border' or 'across the border', thus
emphasizing that Raphia lies to the southwest of the Brook of Egypt.

The phrase *ana itê* also appears in the inscriptions of Sargon II, in
the description of the flight of Yamani of Ashdod into Egypt in 712.
In the previous year, after overthrowing the pro-Assyrian king,
Ashdod crowned Yamani and began withholding tribute from Sargon

13. R. Borger, *Die Inschriften Asarhaddons, Königs von Assyrien* (*AfO.B*, 9;
Graz: R. Borger, 1956), p. 50.
14. Na'aman, 'The Brook of Egypt', pp. 72-75.
15. Borger, *Die Inschriften Asarhaddons*, p. 112.

II. When it became clear that the Assyrians were preparing to respond militarily to his revolt, Yamani contacted a Pir'u of Egypt seeking aid and perhaps shelter in the event that the situation in Ashdod became untenable for him. In 712, the situation did in fact become untenable, and Yamani fled Ashdod for Egypt. But in the interim between Yamani's initial contact with the Pir'u and his flight from Sargon, political circumstances in Egypt had changed. Shabako, the Ethiopian king, had completed the consolidation of his power in Upper Egypt in early 712 and was preparing to invade Lower Egypt and assume control of the Nile Delta. The Nile princes of Sais and Bubastis were no longer the dominant powers in the region, Bubastis having collapsed into merely local authority and Sais having largely withdrawn into the west following the campaign of Piye.[16] Thus, as Spalinger has pointed out, 'Yamani did not meet the Pir'u of Egypt whom he had contacted less than a year earlier. He simply went south, into Upper Egypt, and finally met the king of Kush.'[17]

This is the context for the phrase in question. It reads:

ana itê māt Muṣri ša paṭ māt Meluḫḫa innabitma[18]

Na'aman's interpretation of the Sargon text and its implication for translating the Esarhaddon text is this:

Subsequently, Yamani was detained by the Nubian ruler and extradited to Assyria. It is thus clear that Yamani crossed through Egypt and reached Nubia in his attempt to gain support there. Accordingly, only the translation 'across the Egyptian border' or 'to the (very end) of the Egyptian border' for the phrase *ana itê māt Muṣri* would suit the context

16. See K.A. Kitchen, *The Third Intermediate Period in Egypt (1100–650 BC)* (Warminster: Aris & Phillips, 1973), pp. 363-72; and A.J. Spalinger, 'The Military Background of the Campaign of Piye (Piankhy)', *Studien zur altägyptischen Kultur* 7 (1979), pp. 273-301, esp. pp. 285-86 and 293-95.

17. A.J. Spalinger, 'The Year 712 BC and its Implications for Egyptian History', *JARCE* 10 (1973), p. 97. See also D.B. Redford, 'Sais and the Kushite Invasions of the Eighth Century BC', *JARCE* 22 (1985), pp. 5-15, esp. pp. 6-7, for further discussion of this point and a refinement of the date for Shabako's conquest of the north.

18. So Na'aman, 'The Brook of Egypt', p. 73, with discussion of the text following. The text itself was published by H. Winckler, *Die Keilschrifttexte Sargons nach den Papierabklatschen und Originalen* (Leipzig: E. Pfeiffer, 1889), I-II, pl. 26, no. 56, ll.100-101. For English translation, see *ANET*, p. 286, or Luckenbill, *ARAB*, II, § 62.

of the passage. ['He (Yamani) fled beyond the Egyptian border, which is
at the border-region of Nubia, and his (hiding) place could not be
detected.'] Hence the above-cited passage from the annals of Esarhaddon
is to be translated: 'A distance of thirty *bêru* from the town of Aphek
(situated) on the border-region of Samaria as far as Raphia beyond the
border of the Brook of Egypt.'[19]

Na'aman's translation of the Sargon text, however, is problematic. In
712, Yamani would not have fled 'beyond' the Egyptian border to
reach the 'border-region of Ethiopia'. That borderline would have
been contiguous with the border-region of Ethiopia, and thus the
phrase should be translated:

> (he fled) as far as the border of Egypt, which is the border-region of
> Ethiopia.

It is clear, as Rainey has pointed out, that Yamani 'did not have to go
to Nubia itself to seek political asylum with the Cushite king', and thus
'in neither [the Sargon nor the Esarhaddon] passages can *ana itê* mean
"across"'.[20] Applied to the Esarhaddon text, this rendering eliminates
Na'aman's reading 'beyond the Brook of Egypt' and leaves us with a
different picture of the relationship between Raphia and the Brook of
Egypt:

> *ultú* ^uru^*Apqu. . . adi* ^uru^*Rapihi ana itê nahal mât Muṣur. . .*
> from Aphek. . . to Raphia, as far as the border of the Brook of
> Egypt. . .

On the basis of this translation, it would seem clear that for
Esarhaddon the Brook of Egypt lies to the *south* of Raphia, rather
than to the northeast as in Sargon's ND 3411. This impression is
strengthened by the sense of Esarhaddon's inscription as a whole. The
passage is a description of Esarhaddon's tenth campaign, during which

19. Na'aman, 'The Brook of Egypt', pp. 73-74.
20. Rainey ('Toponymic Problems', p. 131) translates, 'He (Yamani) fled to the
border of Egypt, up to the border region of Nubia'. Spalinger ('The Year 712 BC',
p. 97) renders the same phrase, '[He fled to] the border of Egypt, which is (at) the
border of Ethiopia.' It is also possible that the relative clause *ša pāt meluhha* modifies
not *itu* (border) but *muṣri* (Egpyt), in which case the phrase could be translated: '(he
fled) as far as the border of Egypt, which is the territory of Ethiopia.' See
Oppenheim's translation in *ANET*, pp. 285-86. Rainey is certainly correct in his
assessment of the *CAD* translation of *ana itê* as across in this passage as
'unfortunate'. Elsewhere in *CAD*, the phrase is never so translated.

the king boasts that he and his army marched some 'thirty double hours' between Aphek and Raphia, without finding water from any source except wells. The feat is made more impressive if Esarhaddon must travel on beyond even Raphia 'as far as the Brook of Egypt' to find flowing water, whereas the impression is somewhat diminished if the Brook of Egypt is encountered before reaching Raphia. It therefore seems consistent with the aims of the language and the propaganda of Esarhaddon's inscription to identify the Brook of Egypt with Wadi el-'Arish, rather than Wadi Besor.

We arrive at the following assessment of the Assyrian inscriptional evidence. On the basis of ND 400 from the reign of Tiglath-pileser III and especially from ND 3411 from the reign of Sargon II, it would seem that, at least through the early years of the reign of Sargon II, the Brook of Egypt is best understood as Wadi Besor. Wadi Besor is close to Gaza, the southwesternmost extent of Tiglath-pileser's 734 campaign. Gaza is the southern end of Canaan, and the presence of MB IIB forts along the bank of Besor lends additional credence to the notion that, in still more ancient times, a political boundary between the territories of Canaan and Egypt coincided with the natural boundary of the wadi. It would seem likely that Tiglath-pileser III merely accepted this division of property, calling a halt both to his 734 campaign and Assyrian territorial claims at the 'Brook of Egypt', that is, the Wadi Besor. Sargon's early traditions clearly support this state of affairs by referring to Raphia as a location within the land of Egypt. However, it seems clear from the inscriptions of Esarhaddon, especially from Fragment F, that Esarhaddon conceived of the boundary between Palestine and Egypt to be Wadi el-'Arish, beyond Raphia, and not Wadi Besor.

We are thus led to the conclusion that the Assyrian view of the northernmost extent of the territory controlled by Egypt changed and that the designation 'Brook of Egypt' was moved from Wadi Besor to Wadi el-'Arish sometime between the early stages of the reign of Sargon II and the middle of the reign of Esarhaddon. The question naturally arises: What political circumstances would have given rise to the need for such a shift?

Assyrian kings pressed their claims for dominance in Palestine on two important occasions during this period. The better documented of the two is Sennacherib's invasion of Palestine in 701, during the course of which he encountered an Egypto-Ethiopian force at Eltekeh.

Sennacherib's main concern, however, seems to have been suppressing the western revolt, for all accounts indicate that as soon as Hezekiah was pacified, Sennacherib returned to Nineveh to deal with upheaval in other parts of the empire. No evidence suggests that Sennacherib attempted to alter his territorial claims vis-à-vis Egypt.

The other occasion is Sargon's 720 campaign, mentioned above. One of the results of that campaign appears to have been the inauguration of a new Assyro-Egyptian trade relationship. The case for this relationship and its beginnings in Sargon's 720 campaign is built upon Calah Prism fragment D, in which Sargon claims to have 'opened the sealed *karu* of Egypt and made Egyptians and Assyrians trade together'.[21] The establishment of this relationship provides an excellent context within which to understand the shift in Assyrian identification of the Brook of Egypt from Wadi Besor to Wadi el-'Arish.[22]

Trade routes between Egypt and Assyria would of necessity have passed along the Sinai coast of the Mediterranean between the Nile River and the Philistine cities of Gaza, Ashkelon, and Ashdod, before turning inland through the Jezreel Valley, past Megiddo, and on north toward the Euphrates. The security of those routes, and especially of that portion passing through the Sinai and into the southern region of Philistia, would have been of paramount concern to the Assyrians. Caravans moving through this sparsely inhabited region would have been particularly vulnerable to bands of marauders. In addition, the security of the routes would also have been affected by local political upheaval. One method of insuring security would have been to establish large garrisons of Assyrian troops throughout the area. As a reading of Assyrian history of the late eighth century shows, however, the demands on Sargon's military were overwhelming, and few if any

21. First publication of Nimrud Prism Fragment D is by C.J. Gadd, 'Inscribed Prisms of Sargon II from Nimrud', *Iraq* 16 (1954), pp. 179-80. See H. Tadmor, 'The Campaigns of Sargon II of Assur: A Chronological-Historical Study', *JCS* 12 (1958), p. 34, for the best transliteration and translation of the text.

22. See J.H. Hayes and S.A. Irvine, *Isaiah, The Eighth Century Prophet: His Times and His Preaching* (Nashville: Abingdon, 1987), p. 31; and J.H. Hayes and P.K. Hooker, *A New Chronology for the Kings of Israel and Judah and Its Implications for Biblical History and Literature* (Atlanta: John Knox, 1988), p. 73. A fuller treatment of this subject appears in my 'The Kingdom of Hezekiah: Judah in the Geo-political Context of the Late Eighth Century BCE' (PhD dissertation, Emory University, 1993), pp. 87-121.

troops could have been spared to serve guard duty in the Sinai desert, particularly if other means could have been found to achieve the same ends.

The other method available to Sargon was to 'hire' protection by charging a dependable vassal people or client king with the responsibility for securing the trade routes through his region. The Assyrians used this method several times with substantial success. Throughout Syria, after the provincialization of Damascus in 732, the Assyrians established under the control of local authorities a series of caravanserais, checkpoints, and way stations along the main trade routes.[23] Only two years earlier, at the conclusion of his 734 campaign against Philistia, Tiglath-pileser III appointed Idibi'lu, an Arab leader in the northern Sinai, to oversee the border of Egpyt.[24] Sargon replaced the rebellious Azuri of Ashdod with Azuri's more tractable brother, Ahimiti, in the years prior to the Ashdod revolt in 712.[25] In each case, the method had the obvious advantage of requiring few, if any, Assyrian troops, and it also served as a reward to the client or vassal for past loyalty or an incentive for future obedience. In addition, it enhanced the prestige of the client or vassal, at least by making him an official in the Assyrian government, and quite possibly by expanding the vassal's territorial holdings.

Sargon would most likely have used this latter method, turning to Hezekiah as a client upon whom he could depend to protect the Egyptian trade routes along the marauder-plagued Sinai coast and through the troubled areas of Philistia. The Assyrian king would have given to Hezekiah the responsibility for securing the Sinai trade route between Wadi el-'Arish and Wadi Besor. This would have provided Sargon with an economical solution to the problem of controlling the desolate region of the northern Sinai. In exchange for assuming

23. Eph'al (*The Ancient Arabs*, pp. 94-99) points to four letters discovered at Nimrud: ND 2644, ND 2381, ND 2437, and ABL 414. Each of these inscriptions describes matters pertaining to the oversight of way stations and sentry posts along the routes throughout southern Syria. In the first of these documents, the official who wrote the letter asks the king to grant a special royal appointment to 'Ba-di-'-ilu', along with permission to graze his flocks 'in the midst of the land' (ND 2644, ll. 6-8). In ABL 414, Bel-liqbi writes to the king of his plans to appoint several local officials to positions within the cities of Sibte and Sazana. These appointees will, claims Bel-liqbi, 'keep watch over the road stations'.

24. See *ANET*, pp. 282-83; and Eph'al, *The Ancient Arabs*, pp. 24-29, 93.

25. See *ANET*, pp. 285-87.

responsibility for protecting Assyro-Egyptian trade crossing the Sinai, Hezekiah would have been granted the right to claim the region between Gaza and Wadi el-'Arish as Judean territory. Sargon would thus have extended the domain of Judah—heretofore an ally in the region—from Wadi Besor to Wadi el-'Arish, renaming the latter the Brook of Egypt.[26]

Conclusions

In summary, it is suggested here that the Brook of Egypt is best viewed as a political designation for the boundary between Egypt and Palestine/Judah, a designation reflective primarily of Assyrian interests in the region. In their early contacts with southern Palestine, Assyrian kings essentially recognized as the 'Brook of Egypt' the existing and traditional boundary between the regions: Wadi Besor. Following Sargon's 720 campaign to Raphia, however, and especially as trade between Egypt and Assyria blossomed as a result of the establishment of relations between Sargon and the Nile Delta princes, the control and security of the region south of Gaza and the Wadi Besor became more important. It is reasonable to conclude, then, on the basis of Assyrian texts of the late eighth and early seventh centuries that the designation 'Brook of Egypt' ceased to be identified with Wadi Besor and became identified with Wadi el-'Arish.

26. Na'aman ('The Brook of Egypt', p. 80) suggests a similar shift in the identification of the Brook of Egypt but places the shift during the Persian period, resulting 'from the unification of Syria-Palestine and Egypt under the rule of the Persian empire, which increased the importance of the coastal region connecting these two political units'. As we have seen, the Esarhaddon text would indicate a much earlier shift than the Persian era. I would suggest, however, that the shift occurred for quite similar political and economic reasons.

DEFINING THE BOUNDARIES
A Cultic Interpretation of Numbers 34.1-12
and Ezekiel 47.13–48.1, 28

Kenneth D. Hutchens

Num. 34.1-12 and Ezek. 47.13–48.1, 28 contain descriptions of the
boundaries of the land to be allotted to Israel. It has proven difficult to
identify these closely related boundaries with either the area settled by
the Israelites or with the known political boundaries of Israel in any
historical period. A survey of their general lines illustrates this
problem. In the west the boundary is the Mediterranean Sea and
includes the coastal area inhabited traditionally by the Philistines and
the Phoenicians. The boundary is problematic due to the inclusion of
non-Israelite land. In the south the boundary runs from the
Mediterranean Sea along the 'Brook of Egypt' to the area of Kadesh-
Barnea and then to a point at the southern end of the Dead Sea. It
seems to correspond both to Israelite control and the southern
boundary of Judah given in Joshua 15. The eastern boundary,
however, creates problems. It is drawn along the Jordan River from
the Dead Sea to the Sea of Galilee and excludes traditionally Israelite
territory and claims in the Transjordan. Merely defining the extent of
the northern boundary—including the eastern boundary north of the
Sea of Galilee—has proven difficult. Scholars have been unable to
agree on the identity of the sites listed as points in this boundary. A
minimalist position draws the northern boundary from the Sea of
Galilee to the northeast then turning west and running slightly north
of Dan to the Mediterranean Sea in the area of Tyre. A maximalist
approach places the northern boundary east of Damascus and at the
northern end of the Beqaʻ Valley so that the territory included is most
of modern Lebanon and southern Syria.

Historical Approaches

A number of historical approaches to these boundaries have been attempted. Each seeks to explain the origin of the boundaries by tracing them to a historical or political boundary that corresponds in extent to those found in Numbers 34 and Ezekiel 47–48. These attempts can be divided into two broad approaches. One seeks a boundary from within the history of ancient Israel, and the second looks for a boundary outside of the history of Israel in the wider ancient Near Eastern context. This essay will examine both approaches in light of the literary and material evidence and suggest a new way of understanding the origin of the boundaries found in Numbers 34 and Ezekiel 47–48.

Both Elliger and Noth have argued that part of the boundaries found in Numbers 34 and Ezekiel 47–48 reflect borders from the history of Israel. The former takes the maximalist position on the northern boundary and traces it to the period of David.[1] Noth, in contrast, takes a minimalist position and connects the northern boundary to the tribe of Dan.[2] While compelling in reference to the northern boundary, such historical solutions fail to explain fully these boundary lists. Exclusion of the central Transjordanian territories, obviously included in the area of Israelite settlement and a part of David's Israel, is especially problematic for this approach. The location of the western boundary on the Mediterranean with the clear presence of both Philistines and Phoenicians in this area is also difficult to explain historically.

More holistic approaches to these boundaries have been offered from the broader context of the ancient Near East. The most widely accepted solution to the origin of these boundaries traces them to a Late Bronze Age Egyptian province of Canaan.[3] B. Mazar first identified the biblical boundaries of Canaan with the Egyptian

---

1. K. Elliger, 'Die Nordgrenze des Reiches David', *PJ* 32 (1936), pp. 34-73.
2. M. Noth, *Numbers: A Commentary* (OTL; Philadelphia: Westminster, 1968), pp. 248-51.
3. For a survey of the usage of the term 'Canaan' in Egyptian records, see M. Görg, 'Der Name "Kanaan" in ägyptischer Wiedergabe', *BN* 18 (1982), pp. 26-27; for its use in cuneiform texts, see M. Weippert, 'Kinaḫḫi', *BN* 27 (1985), pp. 18-21.

province of that name.[4] The reference to the 'land of Canaan' in Num. 34.2 served as a clue for Mazar in the identification of these boundaries as those of 'a fixed administrative-territorial formula originating at a time long before the Israelite conquest, when Canaan, Phoenicia, and southern Syria constituted an Egyptian province'.[5] Evidence for the existence of such a province is derived from a number of Late Bronze Age texts, most notably the mention of 'the provinces of Canaan' in the el-Amarna letters.[6] The boundaries of this province are said to have fluctuated during the Eighteenth Dynasty and into the Nineteenth Dynasty until they were stabilized as a result of the peace treaty between Ramesses II and the Hittites.[7]

Mazar's argument, however, requires that he not only prove the existence of an Egyptian province of Canaan but one which shares substantially the boundaries listed in Numbers 34 and Ezekiel 47–48. This proves a most difficult proposition. The treaty between Ramesses II of Egypt and the Hittite king Hattusilis, extant in both Egyptian and Hittite copies, contains no boundary demarcations at all.[8] So, for the boundaries of this province Mazar depends on a combination of Numbers 34, Josh. 1.4, Papyrus Anastasi III, and the identification of the Zedad of Num. 34.8 and Ezek. 47.15 with the village of Zaddad, located north of the Anti-Lebanon.[9]

It is circular, however, to use biblical texts to establish the extent of Egyptian control when arguing that the boundaries of an Egyptian province of Canaan correspond to the biblical boundaries. This leaves only the Egyptian evidence to validate Mazar's case. Yet no Late Bronze Age text defines the boundaries of Canaan. Mazar states that the boundaries are 'clearly defined' in Papyrus Anastasi III and

4. B. Maisler (subsequently, Mazar), 'Lebo-hamath and the Northern Boundary of Canaan', *BJPES* 12 (1945–46), pp. 91-102. Reprinted in S. Aḥituv and B.A. Levine (eds.), *The Early Biblical Period: Historical Studies* (Jerusalem: Israel Exploration Society, 1986), pp. 189-202.

5. Maisler, 'Lebo-Hamath', p. 192.

6. *EA* 36.15, cited in Maisler, 'Lebo-hamath', pp. 192-93. But note that W.L. Moran (*The Amarna Letters* [Baltimore: Johns Hopkins University Press, 1992], pp. 109-10) lists this letter, the only mention of Canaan as a province, as too fragmentary to translate and questions the reconstruction of *pi-ḥa-ti* ('provinces') and the reading of *ki-na-ḥi* ('Canaan').

7. Maisler, 'Lebo-hamath', p. 193.

8. *ANET*, pp. 199-203.

9. Maisler, 'Lebo-hamath', p. 193.

quotes, '"the land of Ḫurru from Sile up to Upi", i.e., from the border post of Sileh near Qantara up to the region of Damascus'.[10] Two objections to this argument arise. First, the phrase 'from Sile up to Upi' does not constitute a clearly defined boundary. Sile is a single point, while Upi is the region of southern Syria which included Damascus.[11] Presumably the Mediterranean served as a western limit to this area, but nothing is said of an eastern or northwestern boundary. Secondly, the phrase 'from Sile to Upi' does not correspond to the boundaries listed in Numbers 34 and Ezekiel 47–48. Sile is a site in the Nile Delta to the west of the Sinai peninsula.[12] The Brook of Egypt, which forms the southeastern boundary in Numbers and Ezekiel, is clearly on the eastern side of the Sinai peninsula. Finally, the lack of certainty in the placement of the northeastern biblical boundary makes it difficult to argue for or against its identification with Upi.

The lack of clearly defined boundaries for Late Bronze Age Canaan in Egyptian texts requires the use of incidental information to ascertain the extent of Egyptian control and administration. When approached this way, Egyptian control in Syria-Palestine differs from the biblical boundaries in the east, south, and possibly the north. First, the Jordan River forms the eastern boundary from the Sea of Galilee to the Dead Sea in Numbers 34 and Ezekiel 47–48. The Egyptian province of Canaan should, therefore, also lack central and southern Transjordanian holdings. As evidence to support this assertion, Mazar states that no town in the Gilead mountains is mentioned among the cities conquered by the Egyptians in the Eighteenth and Nineteenth Dynasties, although Ramesses II does mention Moab.[13]

There is evidence, however, that Egyptian presence and control extended east of the Jordan River. A case in point is the city of Peḥal, equated with Pella and located at Ṭabqat Faḥil. Peḥal appears in the Amarna texts in the same vassal relationship to Egypt as cities in the

10. Maisler, 'Lebo-hamath', p. 193.

11. For a discussion of the extent of Upi, see W.T. Pitard, *Ancient Damascus: A Historical Study of the Syrian City-State from Earliest Times until its Fall to the Assyrians in 732 B.C.E.* (Winona Lake, IN: Eisenbrauns, 1986), pp. 49–79.

12. Located at Tell Abu Seifeh. See Y. Aharoni, *The Land of the Bible: A Historical Geography* (Philadelphia: Westminster, rev. edn, 1979), p. 42.

13. Maisler, 'Lebo-hamath', p. 193 n. 18.

Cisjordan.[14] There are references to this locality in records from the reigns of Thutmosis III, Amenhotep III, Seti I, and Ramesses II.[15] For instance, a stele found at Beth-Shean commemorates the suppression by Seti I of a rebellion led by the cities of Hammath (located in the Beth-Shean valley) and Peḥal in the Transjordan.[16] There is no evidence to conclude that Egypt did not consider this city in the Transjordan as part of its Asian empire.[17] Furthermore, the close relationship between Pehal and the cities of Beth-Shean and Hammath in Cisjordan argues against any Egyptian administrative division based upon the Jordan River.

There is also growing evidence of Egyptian activity and influence in the southern Transjordan. Several toponyms from the great topographical list of Thutmosis III appear to come from this region.[18] In the years immediately before the Egyptian–Hittite treaty, Egyptian interest in the Transjordan appears to have increased. Ramesses II mentions in his Luxor reliefs a campaign in Moab, including the conquest of Botirat[19] and possibly Dibon.[20] The mention of Dibon in an Eighteenth Dynasty topographical list has been proposed and

14. *EA* 256.8, 13, 34. Both *EA* 255 and 256 are from Mut-Bahlu, the ruler of Piḥilu or Peḥal, who claims to be a loyal vassal of Egypt.

15. The texts are: Thutmosis III, *KRI* II.211, 215; Amenhotep III, R. Giveon, 'Toponyms Ouest-asiatiques Soleb', *VT* 14 (1964), pp. 239-55; Seti I, *KRI* I.29.54A, 32.49A and A2, 33.15, 34.13, 15; Ramesses II, *KRI* II.163.26, 215.11. See K.A. Kitchen, 'The Egyptian Evidence on Ancient Jordan', in P. Bienkowski (ed.), *Early Edom and Moab: The Beginning of the Iron Age in Southern Jordan* (SAM, 7; Sheffield: J.R. Collis, 1992), pp. 21-34.

16. *KRI* I.12.7-14; for a translation, see *ANET*, pp. 253-54.

17. See the possible reference to Peḥal in Papyrus Anastasi IV 16.11, copied in the reign of Seti II, in the context of preparing chariots for a visit of Pharoah, in R.A. Caminos, *Late-Egyptian Miscellanies* (London: Oxford University Press, 1954), pp. 198-219.

18. See D.B. Redford, 'A Bronze Age Itinerary in Transjordan (Nos. 89-101 of Thutmose III's List of Asiatic Toponyms)', *JSSEA* 12 (1982), pp. 55-74; Z.A. Kafafi, 'Egyptian Topographical Lists of the Late Bronze Age on Jordan (East Bank)', *BN* 29 (1985), pp. 17-21; and Kitchen, 'Evidence', pp. 23-25.

19. *KRI* II.179-183. Kitchen ('Evidence', pp. 27-28) locates this city at Raba Batora, fourteen miles south of the Arnon.

20. See J.A. Dearman, 'Historical Reconstruction and the Mesha' Inscription', in J.A. Dearman (ed.), *Studies in the Mesha Inscription and Moab* (ABS, 2; Atlanta: Scholars Press, 1989), p. 155; and Kitchen, 'Evidence', pp. 28-29.

disputed.[21] Egyptian artistic influence is tangible in the Transjordan,[22] and finally, it is becoming apparent that Glueck's Transjordanian occupational gap was overstated.[23] This activity, coupled with the literary evidence above, strongly suggests an Egyptian claim to the area. The Pharaohs were not hesitant to claim territory, and there is no evidence that they faced any determined competition for this region.[24]

In reference to the north, Mazar assumes that biblical Lebo-Hamath and Zedad are the 'northernmost points of the Land of Canaan along its border with the Hittite domain'.[25] He proceeds to locate these cities and indeed most of the points listed in the northern borders of both Numbers 34 and Ezekiel 47. He argues that *lbw'* cannot be the combination of a preposition and an infinitive meaning 'entrance' but must instead be a city in the region of Hamath. Mazar equates it with Lab'u in the records of Tiglath-Pileser III, Byzantine Libo, and Rbw' found in Egyptian texts, and he identifies it as Tell Labweh in the northern part of the Valley of Lebanon.[26] In fact, Mazar's location of Lebo-Hamath is based largely on conclusions drawn from his argument that the biblical boundaries are based on those of Egyptian Canaan. Finally, Mazar argues on the basis of Ezekiel 47–48 that Damascus or Upi was included in the land of Canaan, since the borders of that land reached to the borders of Hamath.

Mazar's argument depends upon locating the northern boundary found in Numbers 34 and Ezekiel 47–48 far enough north to include the territory that Egypt historically controlled in central Syria and Lebanon. There is little evidence, however, on which to fix any of the

21. Dearman, 'Reconstruction', p. 155; Kitchen, 'Evidence', pp. 28-29.

22. Kitchen ('Evidence', p. 29) discusses the Balu'a and Shihan stelae in this regard. See also M.-L. Mussell, 'The Seal Impression from Dhiban', in J.A. Dearman (ed.), *Studies in the Mesha Inscription* (ABS, 2; Atlanta: Scholars Press, 1989), pp. 247-51; and W.A. Ward, 'A Possible New Link between Egypt and Jordan During the Reign of Amenhotep III', *ADAJ* 18 (1973), pp. 45-46.

23. J.M. Miller, 'Early Monarchy in Moab?', in Bienkowski (ed.), *Early Edom and Moab*, pp. 77-91.

24. See B.J. Kemp, 'Imperialism and Empire in New Kingdom Egypt (c.1575–1087 BC)', in P.D.A. Garnsey and C.R. Whittaker (eds.), *Imperialism in the Ancient World: The Cambridge University Research Seminar in Ancient History* (London: Cambridge University Press, 1978), pp. 10-14.

25. Maisler, 'Lebo-hamath', p. 196.

26. Maisler, 'Lebo-hamath', pp. 199-201.

localities in the biblical northern boundary.[27] North argues convincingly on the basis of Hebrew grammar, the biblical texts, and the difficulties of the Egyptian records involved that Lebo-Hamath is not a city of Hamath but 'the entrance of Hamath'.[28] He draws the biblical northern boundary slightly to the north of Tel Dan and across the southern entrance into the Beqa' Valley, locating Lebo-Hamath at Marj 'Ayun.[29] If the argument for a minimal northern boundary proves correct, it undercuts Mazar's contention that the biblical boundaries originated in Late Bronze Age Egyptian Canaan. It is impossible to draw the boundaries of Egyptian control of Syria-Palestine that far south in Lebanon and Syria.[30] Finally, in the south Egyptian texts include Sinai in Canaan, while biblical texts exclude it.

While a growing number of scholars have followed Mazar, even refining his argument, none has been able to resolve the two main obstacles to the identification of Late Bronze Age Egyptian Canaan with Numbers 34 and Ezekiel 47–48.[31] First, Late Bronze Age texts leave Canaan ill-defined and provide no boundaries for it. Secondly, there is a substantial and growing body of evidence that Egypt's control extended beyond the boundaries that are outlined in the biblical texts. Mazar's approach is thus unable to solve the problem of the extent of the land in Num. 34.1-12 and Ezek. 47.13–48.1, 28.[32]

27. Both M. Noth ('Das Reich von Hamath als Grenznachbar des Reiches Israel', *PJ* 33 [1937], pp. 36-51) and R. North ('Phoenicia-Canaan Frontier of Lebô of Hama', *MUSJ* 46 [1970], pp. 71-103) agree that no point in the northern boundary can be fixed with certainty.

28. North, 'Frontier', pp. 71-103.

29. North, 'Frontier', pp. 97-102.

30. For a discussion of Egyptian control in Syria-Palestine, see D.B. Redford, *Egypt, Canaan and Israel in Ancient Times* (Princeton: Princeton University Press, 1992), pp. 125-91.

31. Those following Mazar include: R. de Vaux, 'Le Pays de Canaan', *JAOS* 88 (1968), pp. 23-30; Aharoni, *Land*, pp. 64-77; M. Weinfeld, *Deuteronomy 1–11* (AB, 5; New York: Doubleday, 1991), pp. 173-77; and Z. Kallai, 'The Boundaries of Canaan and the Land of Israel in the Bible', *ErIsr* 12 (1975) 27-34.

32. Against those who trace these texts to Late Bronze Age Egyptian Canaan, N.P. Lemche (*The Canaanites and their Land: The Tradition of the Canaanites* [JSOTSup, 110; Sheffield: JSOT Press, 1991], pp. 25-106) argues that: (1) in the second millenium 'Canaan' was a vague geographical area, defined only by the Mediterranean to the west and Egypt to the south, and (2) the use of 'Canaan' in the Bible is ideological, containing no reliable early information on the Canaanites or their land.

Tuell attempts to connect the boundaries found in Ezekiel 47–48 with the Persian period,[33] differentiating the boundaries found in Ezekiel from those found in Numbers 34 on the basis of orientation and content. He argues that the current version of Ezekiel 40–48 reflects the Persian period and that the boundaries found in Ezekiel 47–48—as their origin and detail in the north show—are the boundaries of the satrapy of Abar Nahara or 'across the River (Euphrates)'. A Judean claim to religious dominance throughout this province has led to this usage of Persian provincial boundaries. This creative attempt to explain the boundaries of Ezekiel 47–48 lacks documentary evidence and must be deemed a failure. In fact, nearly all the evidence for the extent of Abar Nahara shows a much larger area than that envisioned in Ezekiel 47–48.[34]

None of these historical approaches has been able to explain convincingly the extent of the land described in Numbers 34 and Ezekiel 47–48. A close comparison of Numbers 34 with Ezekiel 47–48 must precede any attempt at a solution to this problem.

The Relationship between Numbers 34 and Ezekiel 47–48

The relationship between Num. 34.1-12 and Ezek. 47.13–48.1, 28 has proven difficult to unravel. The boundaries described in these chapters share a number of points and appear to be closely related, especially in the north. These chapters also share some rare terminological combinations.[35] Yet when describing the actual boundaries of the land, Numbers 34 and Ezekiel 47–48 vary in terminology, syntax, and the localities listed. Auld reaches the conclusion shared by many that 'neither text depends on the other, but both on a common list of names'.[36]

---

33. S.S. Tuell, *The Law of the Temple in Ezekiel 40-48* (HSM, 49; Atlanta: Scholars Press, 1992), 153-73.

34. Tuell, *Law*, pp. 157-70. The problems caused by the evidence for the inclusion of the Transjordan, the Phoenician coast, most of Syria, and even Cyprus in Abar Nahara are readily apparent from Tuell's strained attempts to explain each.

35. These include the combination of *nhl* and *'rṣ* and the use of *npl* with *nhlh* in Num. 34.2 and Ezek. 47.14. See A.G. Auld, *Joshua, Moses and the Land: Tetrateuch-Pentateuch-Hexateuch in a Generation since 1938* (Edinburgh: T. & T. Clark, 1980), pp. 75-82.

36. Auld, *Joshua*, p. 76.

Little attempt has been made, however, to reconstruct a common list behind these texts. While possible developments in both Numbers 34 and Ezekiel 47–48 make tentative any attempt to reconstruct a *Vorlage*, a comparison of the agreements in these texts may at least provide an entry into the nature of a common list underlying both of these chapters.

The boundaries in Numbers and Ezekiel consist of a combination of natural features, cities, and political boundaries. Political boundaries, however, play only a small role in these texts. In fact, when Numbers 34 and Ezekiel 47–48 are compared, it is primarily natural features that they share:

Numbers	*North*	Ezekiel
34.7	Great Sea	47.15
34.8	entrance of Hamath	47.15-16 (G); 48.1
34.8	Zedad	47.15
34.9	Hazer-enon	47.17; 48.1
	East	
34.12	the Jordan	47.18
34.12	Salt Sea; Eastern Sea[37]	47.18
	South	
34.4	Kadesth-Barnea; waters of Meriboth-Kadesh[38]	47.19; 48.28
34.5	River of Egypt; the River	47.19; 48.28
34.5	the Sea; the Great Sea	47.19; 48.28
	West	
34.6	the Great Sea	47.20

The only exceptions to the use of natural features to define the boundary in this shared list are: (1) the cities of Zedad and Hazer-enon in the north and (2) in the south, the city Kadesh-Barnea in Numbers, where Ezekiel has a reference to the oasis there. At least one additional natural feature may have been part of the shared list. Num. 34.11 lists 'the shoulder of the sea of Chinnereth' as part of the eastern boundary. In Ezekiel political boundaries, which may have

---

37. While Numbers and Ezekiel may use different terminology, they refer to the same natural features, and in each case, the terminology found in Numbers agrees with Josh. 15.1-5.

38. These appear to be variant names for the city located at 'Ain el-Qudeirat. D.W. Manor, 'Kadesh-Barnea', *ABD* 4 (1992), pp. 1-3.

touched on the same point, are found in a corresponding position.[39] With this shared list of natural features and a few cities, it is possible to draw a reasonably clear boundary for the land. This leads to the conclusion that the common list behind Numbers 34 and Ezekiel 47–48 was one based largely upon natural features, the only exceptions being on the northern boundary, which lacks a clear natural demarcation corresponding to those of the west, east, and (to a lesser degree) the south.

This common list has been expanded and modified to reflect the terminology and understanding of the respective editors of both Numbers and Ezekiel.[40] In Ezekiel this modification included a closer definition of the northern boundary and the probable use of the boundaries of the Neo-Assyrian provinces of northern Transjordan.[41] Numbers has apparently updated the list in the south by means of the boundary of Judah found in Josh. 15.1-5, and in the north and northeast, on the basis of a boundary of Dan[42] or the United Monarchy.[43]

If a boundary based primarily on natural features underlies these texts, how is it to be explained? The area delimited by the Mediterranean Sea, the entrance to the Beqa' Valley, the Sea of Galilee, the Jordan River, the Dead Sea, the oasis of Kadesh-Barnea, and the 'Brook of Egypt'[44] still does not fully correspond to Egyptian control of Syria-Palestine, the Persian satrapy of Abar Nahara, or Israelite control in any period of history. In order to understand the extent of the boundaries found in Numbers 34 and Ezekiel 47–48, another factor must be considered, that is to say, religion.

39. Locating the exact boundaries of the Assyrian provinces in the Transjordan has proven problematic. See E.O. Forrer, *Die Provinzeinteilung des assyrischen Reiches* (Leipzig: J.C. Hinrichs, 1920), pp. 59-70.

40. Space limitations preclude a full examination of the various developments found in these texts.

41. De Vaux, 'Pays', p. 29.

42. M. Noth, *Das Buch Josua* (HAT, 7; Tübingen: Mohr, 1938), p. 92.

43. Elliger, 'Nordgrenze', pp. 71-73. Placing the border of the Davidic Empire on a maximalist line is problematic (see J.M. Miller and J.H. Hayes, *A History of Ancient Israel and Judah* [Philadelphia: Westminster, 1986], pp. 179-85).

44. Variously located at Wadi el-Arish or Wadi Besor. See M. Görg, 'Egypt, Brook of', *ABD* 2 (1992), p. 321; and P.K. Hooker, 'The Location of the Brook of Egypt', in the present volume.

A Cultic Approach

Boundaries—even those based on natural features—are human constructions, and as such they are influenced by political, social, and religious factors.[45] Therefore, any attempt to understand the biblical boundary lists should be sensitive to all these factors. Moreover, since the boundary descriptions in question are found in texts that are widely held to be Priestly in origin, one must inquire about the religious factors that may have been involved in their origin and function.[46] A clearer understanding of the boundaries delimited in Numbers 34 and Ezekiel 47–48 may depend on taking seriously the function of these boundaries in Israelite Priestly circles.

Several contextual issues suggest that the boundary lists in Numbers 34 and Ezekiel 47–48 were important for the ancient Yahwistic cult in Jerusalem. First, it is apparent from the Hebrew Bible that the status of the land had important implications for the cult in ancient Israel. Cultic distinctions in reference to the land are common in the Hebrew Bible and include: (1) references to the land of Israel as clean or required to be clean for proper worship (Josh. 22.19; 2 Kgs 5.17; Ps. 137.4); (2) references to foreign lands as unclean (Amos 7.17; Hos. 9.3); (3) references to the pollution/profanation of the land of Israel (Lev. 18.24-30; 20.22-24; Num. 35.33-34; Deut. 21.23; Jer. 2.7; 16.18; Ps. 106.34-39); and (4) references to the cleansing of the land of Israel (Ezek. 39.12, 14, 16; 2 Chron. 34.8). The clean land of Israel was distinguished from other, unclean lands, and the Priestly provenance of several of these texts suggests that such ideas would have been shared by the editors of Numbers 34 and Ezekiel 47–48.

Secondly, one's observance of the law in general, and of certain laws in particular, is related to one's presence in the land of Israel (e.g. Lev. 19.23; 23.10; 25.2; Num. 15.2, 18; Deut. 4.5, 14; 5.31; 6.1; 11.31-32; 12.1). Observance of the laws regarding purity and agricultural offerings intended for the priesthood and Temple may further presuppose a distinction between Israel and the surrounding lands. The divinely ordained boundaries in Numbers and Ezekiel may

---

45. See W. Norton, *Explorations in the Understanding of Landscape: A Cultural Geography* (New York: Greenwood, 1989).

46. Num. 34.1-12 is predominately connected to P, while Ezek. 47–48 is related to the prophet/priest Ezekiel or to Priestly editors of his book. See the commentaries.

be intended to make that distinction possible.

Thirdly, the question of the cultic status of the land, often only implicit in the Hebrew Bible, is made explicit in the discussions of the rabbis.[47] The Tannaim distinguish between the clean land of Israel and the unclean lands outside Israel. The uncleanness of these non-Israelite lands could potentially contaminate persons and objects (*m. Miq.* 8.1; *m. Ohol.* 2.3; 17.5; 18.6-7; *m. Toh.* 4.5; 5.1; *m. Naz.* 7.3; *t. Kelim B. Qam.* 1.5). Produce grown within the land of Israel, which is susceptible to tithes and offerings, is differentiated from that grown outside it (*t. Ter* 2.9; *t. Sheb.* 4.12; *t. Dem.* 1.4; *t. Kelim B. Qam.* 1.5). While these texts derive from the postbiblical period, they illustrate the practical implications inherent in the view of purity and the land found in the Hebrew Bible.

Fourthly, the immediate context of both Num. 34.1-12 and Ezek. 47.13–48.1, 28 argues for their function to define for cultic purposes the boundary between the clean land of Israel and the surrounding unclean lands. Both texts relay divine instructions for the boundaries of the land of Israel: Numbers 34 demarcates the Cisjordan lands, those seen as primary to the promise, before the original entry into the land, and Ezekiel 47–48 demarcates Israel's entire territory for the divinely engineered return from exile.

Contextual issues supporting the cultic function of these boundaries are clearest in Ezekiel, where the sanctuary is the centerpiece of the restored Israel outlined in Ezekiel 40–48. It serves as a locale for God's presence, and as such, its purity is strictly guarded by control of access, ritual, and ordinance. The land plays a role in the effort to control access to the Temple and reflect the order upon which the restored Temple is built. Holiness was most intense at the Temple but gradually diminished as one moved farther away, reaching the limit of purity at the carefully defined border of the land of Israel.[48] Outside the boundaries of Ezekiel 47–48 were the unclean lands of the nations.

Finally, the very nature of the boundaries in Numbers 34 and Ezekiel 47–48, especially their common points, argues for their

---

47. See R.S. Sarason, 'The Significance of the Land of Israel in the Mishnah', in L.A. Hoffman (ed.), *The Land of Israel: Jewish Perspectives* (University of Notre Dame Center for the Study of Judaism and Christianity in Antiquity, 6; Notre Dame: Notre Dame University Press, 1986), pp. 109-36.

48. See J.P. Brereton, 'Sacred Space', *EncRel* 13 (1987), pp. 526-35, for examples of similar phenomena from other cultures.

practicality as cultic boundaries. These boundaries depart from the known historical boundaries of Israel in at least two areas. First, they exclude the central and southern Transjordanian regions known to have been controlled by Israel at various times in its history.[49] Secondly, they include within the boundaries the coastal area, which was historically dominated by the Philistines and Phoenicians during Israel's period of statehood.[50] These departures have an important goal in common: to rescue the boundaries from the exigencies of history and tie them firmly to clearly observable and unchangeable natural features. In the east, the boundary would no longer shift with the fortunes of Israel's relations with the Transjordanian states but would be secured at the Jordan River. Similarly, the western boundary would be fixed at the Mediterranean coast.

Are the boundaries delineated in the north and south as clearly marked as those to the west and east? The combination of natural features, the effective limits of settlement, and historical factors produce a reasonably clear southern boundary. The northern boundary, however, is the most difficult to fix for several reasons. First, there is no natural frontier to the north of Israel that would correspond to the Mediterranean Sea or Jordan River. Lacking a clear natural marker to the north, one would expect the cultic boundary to be drawn along the same line as a historical boundary, perhaps with added precision by the inclusion of more boundary points. The northern boundary appears to do just that. It consists of a combination of cities, natural formations, and (in Ezekiel) political boundaries. Along these lines, the phrase *lbw' ḥmt* is best understood as the southern entrance into the Beqa' Valley, which forms such a natural marker.[51]

It is noted once in P and twice in Ezekiel that the priest must distinguish between the holy and the common, the unclean and the

49. The departure from the Jordan River valley north of the sea of Galilee may be due to topographical features or the use of a historical northern boundary. Note that the Mishnah grants Israelite-owned land in Syria clean status if it can be entered directly from the land of Israel (*m. Ohol.* 18.6-7).

50. For the complex relationship of Josh. 13–19 to the boundaries being considered in this paper, see Auld, *Joshua*, pp. 72-87.

51. See the usage of *lbw'* ('entrance') in Gen 35.16; 48.7; and 2 Chron. 26.8. The parade example for *lbw'* as 'entrance' is 2 Chron. 26.8, where Uzziah's fame is said to have spread *'d-lbw' mṣrym* ('as far as the entrance into Egypt'). North, 'Frontier', pp. 97-103.

clean (Lev. 10.10; Ezek. 22.26; 44.23), and Milgrom refers to boundary making as the 'the essence of the priestly function'.[52] As this role is dependent on the priest's ability to make such distinctions, the fixing of boundaries to natural features would have been an immense aid in the practical necessity of deciding whether an offering had come from clean or unclean land. It would have simplified decisions about personal impurity deriving from contact with unclean land.[53] While the price of such clearly defined natural boundaries is the exclusion of the Transjordan, Priestly traditions of apostasy and the danger of such arising in the Transjordan may have made such exclusion acceptable, if not desirable.[54]

Origin of the Boundaries

The boundary lists of Ezekiel 47–48 and Numbers 34 appear to have been shaped by religious and historical factors. How might such boundaries have originated?

The Late Bronze Age usage of 'Canaan' to refer to a vaguely defined area in Syria-Palestine under Egyptian control probably played a role in the biblical ideas of Canaan, as Num. 34.2 suggests. Late Bronze Age usage did not define biblical Canaan's boundaries but supplied a name for the land that Israel believed it had been promised. The Israelites themselves defined the boundaries of their land in ways related to the historical circumstances and particular purposes of the boundaries. One such way was by Israel's ability to control land. The northern and southern boundaries defined by Numbers 34 and Ezekiel 47–48 seem to correspond both to the limits of settlement and historical boundaries of ancient Israelite rule. Both the nature of these borders and the stability of the southern boundary probably contributed to this use of historical boundaries for cultic purposes. The historical western and eastern boundaries of Israel, however, proved too imprecise and variable for priestly distinctions about purity. At this point, religious concerns left historical considerations

52. J. Milgrom, *Leviticus 1-16* (AB, 3; New York: Doubleday, 1991), p. 615.

53. On *sancta* contagion and contamination, see Milgrom, *Leviticus*, pp. 443-56, 976-1000.

54. See D. Jobling, *The Sense of Biblical Narrative II* (JSOTSup, 39; Sheffield: JSOT Press, 1986), pp. 88-147. The relevant biblical texts include Num. 22–24; 32; and Josh. 22.

behind in order to obtain the precise boundaries that were readily available in the Mediterranean Sea and Jordan River. Ezekiel 40–48 was willing to give up totally Israel's claims to the central Transjordan because of the overriding concern for purity, and the redactors of Numbers 34 opted for a division of Israelite land that preserves a claim to the Transjordan, while placing it on a subordinate level to the Cisjordan.

Both Numbers 34 and Ezekiel 47–48 have been connected with Priestly circles[55]—usually those related to the Jerusalem Temple. This is the context in which one would expect a cultic boundary to originate. Priestly personnel were responsible for guarding the purity of the Temple and for ruling on the acceptability of offerings and the cultic status of individuals. Finally, the Temple aspired to be a pan-Israelite institution.

Dating these boundaries, like dating all Priestly materials, is notoriously difficult.[56] A cultic boundary is less likely to betray its date of origin than a political boundary. The construction of the Temple and the use of these texts in Numbers and Ezekiel provide outside termini for a date. The prerequisite idea—that lands outside of Israel are unclean—appears as early as the eighth century (cf. Amos 7.17 and Hos. 9.3). Within this time frame one can only speculate. Perhaps the most likely period for a definition of the cultic boundaries of Israel would have been in a time of increased emphasis upon the Jerusalemite Temple cult and the unity of all Israel. Although an earlier date is not ruled out, the late pre-exilic period fits these requirements well.[57] A Priestly demarcation of the clean land of Israel may have operated alongside, or even competed with, more political drawings of Israelite boundaries.

Conclusion

This paper has argued that religious factors played a key role in the definition of the boundaries of the land of Israel that are found in

55. See the commentaries.

56. See S.J. De Vries, 'A Review of Recent Research in the Tradition History of the Pentateuch', *SBLSP* (1987), pp. 459-502.

57. Josiah's period would have been especially conducive to such boundary making (2 Kgs 22–23). See Miller and Hayes, *History*, pp. 377-402; B. Oded, 'Judah and the Exile', in J.H. Hayes and J.M. Miller (eds.), *Israelite and Judaean History* (OTL; Philadelphia: Westminster, 1977), pp. 435-88.

Numbers 34 and Ezekiel 47–48. First, the Priestly task of deciding the purity of offerings and persons necessitated a clearly observable distinction between clean and unclean land. Secondly, a desire to safeguard the sanctity of the Temple and the divine presence in the Temple led to a careful definition of Israel's land. These cultic factors, combined with others from Israel's history, have contributed to the precise definition of Israel's land in Numbers 34 and Ezekiel 47–48.

WAS OMRI A PHOENICIAN?*

Jeffrey K. Kuan

Introduction

Although Omri was one of Israel's greatest kings, the earliest Israelite
monarch to be mentioned in ancient nonbiblical records, and the one
whose name became synonymous with the kingdom of Israel in
Assyrian inscriptions long after his reign,[1] very little is known about
his origin. In the accounts of all the Israelite kings, every king is
mentioned either with a patronym or a patronym and tribal origin.[2]
Jeroboam, for example, is identified as the son of Nebat, an
Ephraimite of Zeredah (1 Kgs 11.26), Baasha as the son of Ahijah, of
the house of Issachar (1 Kgs 15.27), Shallum as the son of Jabesh[3]
(2 Kgs 15.10), and Hoshea as the son of Elah (2 Kgs 15.30).
However, such information is lacking in the account of Omri. This led
Noth to suggest that the name Omri probably is not Israelite but of

---

*   I am most indebted to my teacher and friend, John H. Hayes, who pointed
me in the direction of the Phoenicians. It is thus with great pleasure that I dedicate
this article to him. I want to thank Theodore J. Lewis of the University of Georgia
for his constructive criticism in the preparation of this paper.
    1. In Sargon's inscriptions, e.g., Israel is referred to as 'Bit Humria' (*ARAB*,
II, §§80, 92, 99, 118).
    2. The only other exception is Zimri, who may not have been an Israelite (so
J.A. Soggin, *A History of Ancient Israel* [Philadelphia: Westminster, 1984],
p. 202). Tibni, the other contender for the Israelite throne at this period, is,
however, identified as 'the son of Ginath'.
    3. In this instance, 'Jabesh' is more probably a place name rather than a
patronym, which according to T.R. Hobbs is to be identified with Jabesh-gilead
(*2 Kings* [WBC, 13; Waco, TX: Word Books, 1985], p. 195). There is, however,
another Jabesh, which is clearly distinguished from Jabesh-gilead in 1 Sam. 31.11-
13.

Arabic origin.[4] It appears that, so far, only Gunneweg[5] and Soggin[6] have taken Noth's suggestion seriously. Other historians continue to speculate on Omri's supposed Israelite parentage, most linking him to the village of Jezreel of the tribe of Issachar.[7]

There are four clues in the biblical text that hint at Omri's non-Israelite origin. The first of these is the fact that the Hebrew Bible supplies no information about Omri's parentage or background. This lack of information cannot be simply dismissed as having no foundation in the sources.[8] It is uncertain whether such information ever existed in the official Israelite records for the Omride dynasty. If it did not, then the Omrides themselves may have been responsible for concealing that origin. If it did, then the Deuteronomistic History may have had great difficulty in seeing a foreigner, perhaps even a non-Yahwist, as king over Israel.

Secondly, that the Deuteronomistic History would have theological problems with a foreigner as king, especially a successful king, is evident in the Deuteronomistic prohibition (Deut. 17.15) of making a foreigner king. Noth is certainly right to suggest that this prohibition is probably occasioned by Omri.[9] If there had been no specific instance of foreigners ruling Israel, then it is unlikely that such a prohibition would have arisen.

Thirdly, Mic. 6.16 belongs to an oracle of judgment against Samaria and dates to the second half of the eighth century BCE.[10] The

---

4. M. Noth, *The History of Israel* (New York: Harper & Row, 2nd edn, 1960), p. 230 n. 1. See also J.A. Montgomery, who observes correctly that the lack of a patronym hints at Omri's non-Israelite origin, but it will be shown that he, like Noth, is wrong to link that origin with Arabia ('Arabic Names in I. and II. Kings', *The Moslem World* 31 [1941], pp. 266-67).

5. A.H.J. Gunneweg, *Geschichte Israels bis Bar Kochba* (Theologische Wissenschaft, 2; Stuttgart: Kohlhammer, 3rd edn, 1979), pp. 94-95.

6. Soggin, *History of Israel*, p. 203.

7. See, e.g., B.D. Napier, 'The Omrides of Jezreel', *VT* 9 (1959), pp. 366-78; B. Mazar, 'The House of Omri', in A. Ben-Tor *et al.* (eds.), *Yigael Yadin Memorial Volume* (ErIsr, 20; Jerusalem: Israel Exploration Society, 1989), pp. 215-19.

8. So H.J. Katzenstein, *The History of Tyre* (Jerusalem: Schocken Institute for Jewish Research of the Jewish Theological Seminary of America, 1973), p. 143 n. 74.

9. Noth, *History of Israel*, p. 230 n. 1.

10. C.S. Shaw, 'The Speeches of Micah: A Rhetorical-Historical Analysis' (PhD dissertation, Emory University, 1990), pp. 271-73, 284-86.

prophet indicts the people for following the *ḥuqqôt 'omrî* and all the *ma'ăśēh bêt-'aḥāb*. Most scholars suggest that the statutes of Omri and the deeds of Ahab refer to apostasy to Baal and idolatry.[11] It is more probable that such an attack of more than a century later against the Omride dynasty occurred, because the Omrides were foreigners and their national policies were influenced by their national origin.

Finally, 1 Kgs 16.21-22 relates the fact that Omri had to fight Tibni, the son of Ginath, for four years before he finally secured control over all Israel. The biblical account reports that a sizeable portion of Israel's population had sought to make Tibni king, while another group opted for Omri. Jones suggests the likelihood that Omri may have been the nominee of Canaanite elements, and Tibni of the Israelite population.[12] This would make sense—especially if Omri was a foreigner—and explain why he encountered such strong resistance in his attempt to assume the kingship. Although, according to the biblical records, no other usurpers of the throne of Israel (Baasha, Jehu, Shallum, Menahem, Pekah, and Hoshea) had to fight another contender before securing the throne, in all likelihood there was limited civil war.[13] In the case of Omri, however, it is clear that he fought a major, prolonged civil war to establish his control, and his struggles are given a specific time limit.

This paper will argue that if Omri's origin was not Israelite, it was in all probability Phoenician. The following will be used as evidence: (1) while the root *'mr* occurs only in the name Omri in the Hebrew Bible, it is common in Phoenician and Punic; (2) during the Omride rule, close political ties existed between Israel and Phoenicia, not least of which was the marriage of Ahab, the son of Omri, to Jezebel, the daughter of Ethbaal (Ittobaal), the king of Tyre and Sidon; (3) archaeological levels at key sites (Samaria, Megiddo, Hazor, and Dan)

---

11. So, for example, J.L. Mays, *Micah: A Commentary* (OTL; Philadelphia: Westminster, 1976), p. 148.

12. G.H. Jones, *1 and 2 Kings* (NCB; 2 vols.; Grand Rapids: Eerdmans, 1984), II, p. 295.

13. Two examples can be cited. The first is Jehu, who (in 841–840) had to use military force to secure the Israelite throne (839). This struggle may have lasted over a year. The second is Hoshea, who had probably been recognized as king over Israel by Tiglath-pileser III in 732–731, but who still had to fight the reigning monarch, Pekah, before he finally ascended the throne. See J.H. Hayes and P.K. Hooker, *A New Chronology for the Kings of Israel and Judah and its Implications for Biblical History and Literature* (Atlanta: John Knox, 1988), pp. 64-65.

reflect strong Phoenician influence; and (4) Ahab's patronage of the Baal cult culminated in the building of a temple to the deity in Samaria.

The Name Omri

The question of Omri's name has evoked discussion since the time of W.R. Smith[14] and Nöldeke.[15] These scholars were perhaps the earliest to relate the name to the Arabic root *'amara* ('to live'). Smith suggested that the verb also means to worship and that the name Omri probably means 'a worshipper of Yahweh'.[16] Nöldeke, however, disagreed and preferred to retain the meaning of 'live' or 'life', and Gray posited further that the name may be the hypocoristicon *'Omriyahu*, possibly '(The) life (which) Yahweh (has given)', or 'Pilgrim (at the shrine) of Yahweh'.[17]

Gray, in addition, suggests that the name Omri may have been a nickname, meaning 'the man of the sheaf',[18] cognate with the noun *'ōmer*, which is probably related to the Arabic noun *ḡumr*. Obviously, however, there is no certainty about the proto-semitic root from which Omri's name derived—whether * *'mr* or * *ḡmr*.

Noting the absence of the root *'mr* elsewhere in the Israelite onomastica,[19] Noth concluded that Omri may have been of Arab descent.[20] Layton supports this, adding that the root *'mr*—with the

---

14. W.R. Smith, *Kinship and Marriage in Early Arabia* (Boston: Beacon Press, 2nd edn, 1903), pp. 68-70.

15. T. Nöldeke, 'Review of *Kinship and Marriage in Early Arabia*, by W. Robertson Smith', *ZDMG* 40 (1886), p. 185.

16. Smith, *Kinship and Marriage*, p. 70.

17. J. Gray, *I & II Kings* (OTL; Philadelphia: Westminster, 2nd edn, 1970), p. 365.

18. Gray (*I & II Kings*, p. 365) notes that this is paralleled by the name 'Tibni', which means 'the man of straw', from the noun *teben*.

19. Scholars have already noted that the name *'amrām* is not derived from * *'mr* but is a verbal sentence composed of * *'am-* + *rām*. So G.B. Gray, *Studies in Hebrew Proper Names* (London: Adam & Charles Black, 1896), pp. 45, 47, 51; M. Noth, 'Gemeinsemitische Erscheinungen in der israelitischen Namengebung', *ZDMG* 81 (1927), p. 20 n. 2; p. 31 n. 1; *idem, Der israelitischen Personnamen im Rahmen der gemeinsemitischen Namengebung* (Stuttgart: Kohlhammer, 1928), p. 33; and recently, S.C. Layton, *Archaic Features of Canaanite Personal Names in the Hebrew Bible* (HSM, 47; Atlanta: Scholars Press, 1990), pp. 186-88.

20. Noth, 'Gemeinsemitische', p. 20 n. 2; *idem, History of Israel*, p. 230 n. 1;

possible exception of Omri's name—is totally absent in Northwest Semitic, and he concludes that the root is native to Arabic and not Northwest Semitic.[21] Such a conclusion, however, overlooks the earlier work of Benz on Phoenician and Punic personal names. The latter identifies at least four Phoenician-Punic names built on the root *'mr*, namely, *'mrn*, *'mr̄rn* or *'mr bn*, *'mrt*, and *hmr'*.[22] Although the root *'mr* does not occur in verbal forms in the Phoenician-Punic language (at least in the corpus of inscriptions discovered so far), it would be a mistake to dismiss it as not native to the language. Barr rightly notes that archaic vocabulary is often preserved precisely in names.[23] Moreover, if the element *ḫamr-* in Amorite personal names (e.g., *Ḫamrurapi*, *Ḫamru*, and *Ḫumrum*) is related to the root *'mr*,[24] then it undermines Noth and Layton's assumption that the root is native only to Arabic. Thus, the argument that Omri is of Arab descent based on such assumptions cannot be sustained.

Admittedly, the name Omri is borne not only by the Israelite king but also by three individuals mentioned in 1 Chronicles.[25] But is this enough to suggest that the name is Israelite in origin? The Chronicles lists in which the names appear are almost certainly exilic or postexilic and include names that appear almost exclusively in postexilic times and that are foreign in origin. Moreover the lists are so full of problems as to render their historical reliability suspect. In addition, precisely because of the achievements of Omri, the king of Israel, individuals may have been named after him later.

Because of the existence of the root *'mr* in other Phoenician-Punic names and the strong Phoenician connection of the Omrides (see below), it is certainly feasible to suggest that the name may be Phoenician in origin.

idem, *Israelitischen Personnamen*, pp. 63, 222 n. 7.

21. Layton, *Archaic Features*, p. 187 n. 168, p. 188.

22. F.L. Benz, *Personal Names in the Phoenician and Punic Inscriptions* (StP, 8; Rome: Biblical Institute, 1972), p. 380.

23. J. Barr, *Comparative Philology and the Text of the Old Testament* (Oxford: Clarendon Press, 1968), pp. 181-84.

24. So H.B. Huffmon, *Amorite Personal Names in the Mari Texts: A Structural and Lexical Study* (Baltimore: Johns Hopkins University Press, 1965), pp. 198-99.

25. 1 Chron. 7.8; 9.4; 27.18.

Israelite–Phoenician Relations

There is clear evidence that a strong relationship existed between the Omride dynasty and the Phoenicians, not least of which is the marriage of Ahab and Jezebel, the daughter of Ethbaal, king of the Sidonians (1 Kgs 16.31). Menander, according to Josephus, refers to Ethbaal both as 'the king of the Tyrians'[26] and as 'the king of Tyre and Sidon'.[27] Thus, in all probability, Tyre and Sidon at the time formed a political unit dominated by Tyre. This is supported also by contemporary Assyrian inscriptions that regularly mention Tyre and Sidon together—and in this sequence.[28] The dominance of one power over another in the same region or national state is also illustrated by the case of Israel. According to the Moabite Stone, it was Omri who conquered Moab, which remained a vassal state until the death of Ahab (2 Kgs 1.1; 3.4). While it is certain that the marriage of Athaliah (daughter of Omri or Ahab; cf. 2 Kgs 8.18, 26) to Jehoram sealed an alliance between Israel and Judah, it is plausible that the relationship was more than an alliance between equals—Israel may well have dominated affairs in Judah. It is clear that at a later time, Jehoshaphat, king of Judah, saw himself as subordinate to Ahab, king of Israel. 1 Kgs 22.45 notes that Jehoshaphat made peace (*wayyašlēm*) with the king of Israel.[29] This is supported by 1 Kgs 22.4, which has Jehoshaphat say to the king of Israel, 'I am as you are, my people as your people, my horses as your horses', thus indicating his subordinate status to the king of Israel. It is natural for two nations on the ascent to seek an alliance with one another. Though it is not possible to determine which party initiated the Phoenician–Israelite relationship, in all likelihood the initial impetus for such an alliance must have been commercial. In this way the alliance was not unlike the one that existed between Hiram of Tyre and Solomon (1 Kgs 9.26-28; 10.11, 22).[30] By establishing cooperative relations with Israel, Tyre could

26. *Ant.* 8.324.

27. *Ant.* 8.316-18.

28. Cf. *ANET*, pp. 280-81.

29. S. Parpola has recently pointed out that the Akkadian verb *salāmu*, equivalent to the Hebrew *šlm*, does not necessarily denote parity relations but 'could equally well connote "to seek detente" or "to surrender"' ('Neo-Assyrian Treaties from the Royal Archives of Nineveh', *JCS* 39 [1987], p. 182).

30. Cf. J.K. Kuan, 'Third Kingdoms 5:1 and the Israelite-Tyrian Relations

once again have access to the trade route across Israel to the Gulf of Aqabah, from which it could trade with the Arabian and African coasts.[31] Naturally, this alliance was commercially beneficial for both nations, and it certainly contributed greatly to the wealth of Israel and the Omride dynasty. The marriage of Jezebel, the daughter of Ethbaal, to Ahab, the son of Omri should be viewed as an action that stabilized this commercial-political relationship.

A further indication of the close alignment between Israel and Tyre, admittedly *ex silentio*, is derived from the events of the anti-Assyrian coalition that fought against Shalmaneser III on several occasions. Tyre, Sidon, and Byblos are missing from the list of nations and city-states that engaged Shalmaneser in the battle at Qarqar reported in the Monolith Inscription.[32] Oded has explained this as the Phoenician cities' inclination towards non-intervention in wars outside their territories.[33] However, at a time when Tyre and Sidon were so closely aligned with Israel, it is difficult to imagine that they would remain aloof from regional politics or follow a policy different from that of the other Syro-Palestinian states. If Tyre and Sidon had been pro-Assyrian and paid tribute in 853, this would probably have been recorded in Shalmaneser's inscriptions. There are three documentations of the tribute that Shalmaneser received from Tyre and Sidon, and all are reported in literary contexts noting that Assyria had to suppress opposition in the region. First, in the bronze reliefs from the Gates of Balâwât there are thirteen bands depicting the achievements of Shalmaneser III. In the upper relief of Band III, Tyre and Sidon are depicted as bringing tribute to Shalmaneser while he was on his first western campaign in 858–857. The accompanying inscription reads, *ma-da-tú šú GIŠeleppēti šá URUṣu-ra-a-a URUṣi-du-na-a-a am-ḫu-ur* ('The tribute of the ships of the Tyrians and Sidonians I

During the Reign of Solomon', *JSOT* 46 (1990), p. 39.

31. S. Yeivin has recognized the importance of the Aqabah–Israel–Phoenicia trade route as a viable competitor of the Egypt–Phoenicia trade route ('Did the Kingdom of Israel Have a Maritime Policy?', *JQR* 50 [1959–60], pp. 193-228). See also J.M. Miller, 'The Omride Dynasty in the Light of Recent Literary and Archaeological Research' (PhD dissertation, Emory University, 1964), pp. 195-96.

32. The text was first published by H.C. Rawlinson, *Cuneiform Inscriptions of Western Asia* (5 vols.; London: British Museum, 1861–1909), III, pls. 7 and 8. See *ARAB*, I, §611, and *ANET*, pp. 278-79, for English translations of the text.

33. B. Oded, 'The Phoenician Cities and the Assyrian Empire in the Time of Tiglath-pileser III', *ZDPV* 90 (1974), pp. 40-41.

received').[34] Secondly, in a fragment of an annalistic text (III R 5, 6),[35] Shalmaneser records the following in his eighteenth year (841–840): *ma-da-tu šá* ^{URU}*su-ra-a-a* ^{URU}*si-du-na-a-a šá* ^{I}*ia-ú-a mâr ḫu-um-ri-i am-ḫur* ('I received the tribute of the Tyrians and Sidonians, and of Jehu[36] the [Bīt]-Ḫumrite').[37] Thirdly, from the Black Obelisk

34. The first serious study of these materials was done in 1908 by A. Billerbeck and F. Delitzsch, 'Die Palasttore Salmanassars III. von Bālāwat', in *Beiträge zur Assyriologie semitischen Sprachwissenschaft* (Leipzig: Hinrichs, 1908), IV, pp. 1-144; pl. I-IV. L.W. King reproduced better pictures of the bands with his study in 1915 (*Bronze Reliefs from the Gates of Shalmaneser, King of Assyria B.C. 860-825* [London: British Museum, 1915]). A transliteration of the 'Gate Inscription' and the inscriptions on the bands may be found in E. Michel, 'Die Assur-Texte Salmanassars III. (858–824)', *WO* 2 (1954–59), pp. 408-15; *idem*, 'Die Assur-Texte Salmanassars III. (858–824)', *WO* 4 (1967–68), pp. 29-37. See also *ANEP*, nos. 356-58; *ANET*, p. 281.

It is not certain that the tribute represented Tyre's pro-Assyrian stance and acceptance of Assyrian hegemony. Katzenstein correctly points out that the Tyrian king is not depicted in the relief as leading the delegation of tribute-bearers but rather as remaining behind in his city (*History of Tyre*, p. 164 n. 187). A contrast may be made with the depiction on Band VI where Sangara king of Carchemish delivered the tribute in person (King, *Bronze Reliefs*, pl. XXXIV). Similarly, in the Black Obelisk, panel B, Jehu is represented as bowing before Shalmaneser when he offered his tribute (*ANEP*, no. 355). Therefore, it is likely that from the perspective of the Tyrians, this was not a political gesture but a commercial one.

35. Rawlinson, *Cuneiform Inscriptions of Western Asia*, III, pl. 5, no. 6. Cf. *ANET*, p. 280.

36. The identification of *Ia-ú-a* with Jehu has been widely accepted by scholars. P.K. McCarter ('"Yaw, Son of Omri": A Philological Note on Israelite Chronology', *BASOR* 216 [1974], pp. 5-7), however, suggests that *ia-ú-a* (or *ia-a-ú* in the Marble-Slab inscription) may only represent the divine name 'Yaw' and can be regarded as a hypocoristic form of *either* Joram or Jehu. He concludes that *ia-ú-a* is more likely Joram on the bases of the epithet *mār ḫumri* and the chronological problems of the reigns of Ahaziah and Joram. M. Weippert ('*Jau(a) mār Ḫumrî*—Joram oder Jehu von Israel?' *VT* 28 [1978], pp. 113-18) has challenged McCarter's argument and persuasively shown that *ia-ú-a* represents **Yah-hū'a*, i.e., Jehu.

37. According to H. Tadmor ('The Historical Inscriptions of Adad-nirari III', *Iraq* 35 [1973], p. 149), the phrase ^{I}*ia-ú-a mâr ḫu-um-ri-i* ought not be translated as 'Jehu son of Omri', but as 'Jehu, the king of Bit-Ḫumri'. He cites parallel usages from S. Parpola (*Neo-Assyrian Toponyms* [Neukirchen-Vluyn: Neukirchener Verlag, 1970], pp. 75-92) where 'the kings of Bit-(A)gusi, Bit-Adini, and Bit-Dakuri etc. are called *mār Agūsi*, *mār Adīni* and *mār Dakūri*'. Yet, *māru* is not used in Akkadian for 'king'. The phrase *DUMU* ^{URU}*GN* is, however, used to denote a citizen or native of a city or a country (*CAD* 10/1 [1977], pp. 315-16). Therefore, it

Shalmaneser again notes in his twenty-first year (838–837): *ma-da-tu šá* ^{KUR}*ṣu-ra-a-a* ^{KUR}*ṣi-du-na-a-a* ^{KUR}*gu-bal-a-a am-ḫur* ('The tribute of the land of the Tyrians, Sidonians, and Byblians, I received').[38] If Tyre and Sidon had paid tribute in 853, while the anti-Assyrian coalition (of which Ahab of Israel was a strong participant) was fighting Shalmaneser at Qarqar, this would in all likelihood have been recorded in the Assyrian inscriptions. Therefore, it is reasonable to assume that Tyre and Sidon were indeed involved in the anti-Assyrian coalition of 853. Moreover, Katzenstein suggests that Tyre and Sidon participated by contributing a large sum of money to the allies' war chest,[39] and it is conceivable that Ahab's excessively large military contingent was not an exaggeration[40] but included non-Israelites. Is it not possible that Phoenician participation in the coalition may have been more than monetary contribution? Because of their close alliance with Israel, Phoenician troops could have fought under Ahab's leadership, just as the troops of Moab, Judah, and Edom probably did.[41] The strong and cordial relations between the Omrides and the Phoenicians would be expected, if the Omrides themselves had Phoenician roots.

Archaeological Evidence

The close relationship between the Omrides and the Ethbaalites is reflected in the the strong Phoenician influence that is evident in the archaeological remains at several Israelite sites from the period. If Omri's origin was indeed Phoenician, the great Omride interest in Phoenician culture becomes understandable. One of the most important pieces of archaeological evidence related to this period is the distinctive Phoenician influence reflected in the architectural remains of key sites in the northern kingdom. Characteristic of the buildings and

is likely that *mâr ḫu-um-ri-i* is used as a synonym to the gentilics ^{URU}*ṣur-ra-a-a* and ^{URU}*ṣi-du-na-a-a*. Cf. J. Hughes, *Secrets of the Times: Myth and History in Biblical Chronology* (JSOTSup, 66; Sheffield: JSOT Press, 1990), p. 183 n. 55.

38. See E. Michel, 'Die Assur-Texte Salmanassars III. (858–824)', *WO* 2 (1954–59), p. 154; *ANET*, p. 280.

39. Katzenstein, *History of Tyre*, p. 169.

40. See, e.g., M. Elat, 'The Campaigns of Shalmaneser III against Aram and Israel', *IEJ* 25 (1975), pp. 25-35.

41. So J.M. Miller and J.H. Hayes, *A History of Ancient Israel and Judah* (Philadelphia: Westminster, 1986), p. 270.

defenses at Samaria (Strata I and II),[42] Hazor (Strata VIII and VII),[43] Megiddo (Stratum IVA),[44] and Dan (Stratum III)[45] are bossed masonry and well-hewn ashlar blocks. The bossed masonry was executed meticulously and used both for the foundations of buildings and for the outer defensive walls. Dressed stones were carefully fitted and joined together, and those that had chipped corners were patched with precision.[46] Crowfoot has shown that this type of masonry is certainly Phoenician, and it shows up not only in Ugarit but also in the harbor survey of Tyre.[47] Archaeologists are almost unanimous in identifying this type of masonry and construction technique as Phoenician.[48] According to Shiloh, however, since all the examples of ashlar masonry found outside Israel are later than the reigns of Solomon and Ahab, this type of stonework should be regarded as an original Israelite innovation.[49] A. Mazar points out that ashlar masonry was widespread not only in late Iron Age Phoenician architecture but also in the succeeding period in Phoenicia, Cyprus, and the Phoenician colonies in the Mediterranean. He notes in particular that the fact that its earliest known examples are Israelite may be due to the fact that

42. J.W. Crowfoot *et al.*, *Samaria-Sebaste I. The Buildings at Samaria* (London: Palestine Exploration Fund, 1942), pp. 9-11, 94-96.

43. Y. Yadin *et al.*, *Hazor I* (Jerusalem: Hebrew University Press, 1958), p. 30; *idem*, *Hazor II* (Jerusalem: Hebrew University Press, 1960), pp. 43-47.

44. R.S. Lamon and G.M. Shipton, *Megiddo I* (Chicago: University of Chicago Press, 1939), pp. 47-59. For the stratigraphy of Megiddo, see Y. Yadin, 'New Light on Solomon's Megiddo', *BA* 23 (1960), pp. 62-68.

45. A. Biran, 'Tell Dan Five Years Later', *BA* 43 (1980), pp. 172-77.

46. Cf. K.M. Kenyon, *Royal Cities of the Old Testament* (New York: Schocken Books, 1971), p. 76.

47. Crowfoot *et al.*, *Buildings at Samaria*, pp. 5-9. Cf. A. Poidebard, *Un grand port disparu Tyr* (Haut-commissariat de la République française en Syrie et au Liban, Service des antiquités, Bibliothéque archéologique et historique, 29; Paris: Librairie Orientaliste Paul Geuthner, 1939).

48. See the important studies by G. Van Beek and O. Van Beek, 'Canaanite-Phoenician Architecture: The Development and Distribution of Two Styles', in B. Mazar (ed.), *Y. Aharoni Memorial Volume* (ErIsr, 15; Jerusalem: Israel Exploration Society, 1981), pp. 70*-77*; pls. V-VII; I. Sharon, 'Phoenician and Greek Ashlar Construction Techniques at Tel Dor, Israel', *BASOR* 267 (1987), pp. 21-42. Cf. also A. Mazar, *Archaeology of the Land of the Bible, 10,000–586 B.C.E.* (ABRL; New York: Doubleday, 1990), pp. 471-75.

49. Y. Shiloh, *The Proto-Aeolic Capital and Israelite Ashlar Masonry* (Qedem, 11; Jerusalem: Hebrew University Press, 1979), pp. 82-87.

Israelite sites have been more extensively excavated than those in Phoenicia.[50]

In addition to ashlar masonry, Miller notes that the proto-Ionic capitals found at Samaria, Hazor, and Megiddo are further evidence of Phoenician influence,[51] and Mazar adds that the volutes decorating these capitals are a stylized form of the palmette, one of the best-known motifs in Canaanite and Phoenician art.[52] While no such capitals have been found in Phoenicia proper, Miller argues that their Phoenician character is confirmed by the fact that the Greeks of Cyprus and Ionia borrowed them from Phoenicia about the eighth century.[53] Although most scholars agree that these capitals are Phoenician in origin,[54] Shiloh notes the close connection between ashlar masonry and Proto-Aeolic capitals and challenges this assumption. He argues that no such capitals have been found on sites in Phoenicia proper and suggests instead that they were an Israelite innovation based on Phoenician wooden prototypes and should properly be called Israelite capitals.[55] Alternatively Mazar argues that the lack of evidence from Phoenicia cannot be taken as proof that such stone capitals were not in use there as early as the tenth century.[56]

In the debris of the royal quarter at Samaria, ivory deposits were also found.[57] While the majority of the ivory fragments were discovered in the contexts of later strata, a few showed up in Stratum II, which is assignable to Ahab. It is probable that some of the ivory that originated in the Ahab stratum continued to be reused in the later periods of Israelite history. The discovery of these ivory deposits reminds one of the reference to Ahab's house of ivory in 1 Kgs 22.39. A comparison with the ivory materials found later in Nimrud makes it

50. Mazar, *Archaeology*, p. 474.

51. Miller, 'Omride Dynasty', pp. 134-36.

52. Mazar, *Archaeology*, p. 475.

53. Mazar, *Archaeology*, p. 134. Cf. W.F. Albright, *The Archaeology of Palestine* (London: Penguin Books, 4th edn, 1960), p. 126.

54. See, e.g., Crowfoot *et al.*, *Buildings at Samaria*, pp. 14-15; Y. Aharoni, 'Beth-Haccherem', in D.W. Thomas (ed.), *Archaeology and Old Testament Study* (Oxford: Clarendon Press, 1967), p. 179; Mazar, *Archaeology*, pp. 474-75.

55. Shiloh, *Proto-Aeolic Capital*, pp. 88-91.

56. Mazar, *Archaeology*, p. 475.

57. J.W. Crowfoot and G.M. Crowfoot, *Samaria-Sebaste II. Early Ivories from Samaria* (London: Palestine Exploration Fund, 1938).

clear that the ivory carvings were used to adorn furniture.[58] The
Crowfoots concluded from their examination of the ivories that the
art represented by the Samarian finds was Phoenician.[59] The ivory
finds again illustrate the extent of the Phoenician influence that the
Omrides incorporated in their cultural expressions.

Before leaving the archaeological evidence, Israelite pottery should
be mentioned. Beautiful and delicate vessels known as Samaria ware
had been found in many places in Israel. Similar vessels have shown
up in excavations on the Phoenician coast.[60] Katzenstein is probably
right to suggest that these vessels should be called Phoenician ware.[61]

Notably, when the Omride dynasty came to an end, so too did the
Phoenician material culture in Israel. The excavators of Samaria
found a distinct break in the material culture between Strata I-II and
Stratum III, and Kenyon notes that while new buildings were added in
Stratum III, the style of the masonry, with roughly coarse blocks, is a
complete break from the Phoenician-style masonry of Periods I-II.[62]
Kenyon likewise observes that the pottery of Stratum III is distinct
from that of Strata I-II.[63] The ware is significantly coarser and dirtier
and more closely resembles that of Stratum IV than that of I-II. The
technique of burnishing is also considerably different. Thus, when
Jehu usurped the throne in Israel, the close relationship between Israel
and Phoenicia was terminated completely. Again, if the Omrides were
Phoenician in background and sympathy, it becomes more intelligible
why the eradication of the Omrides also terminated Phoenician
cultural influence.

58. M.E.L. Mallowan, *Nimrud and its Remains* (3 vols.; London: Collins,
1966), II, pp. 411-15. Cf. also R.D. Barnett, *Catalogue of the Nimrud Ivories with
Other Examples of Ancient Near Eastern Ivories in the British Museum* (London:
British Museum, 1957).

59. Crowfoot and Crowfoot, *Early Ivories*, pp. 49-53.

60. J. Du Plat Taylor, 'The Cypriot and Syrian Pottery from Al Mina, Syria',
Iraq 21 (1959), pp. 87-88.

61. Katzenstein, *History of Tyre*, p. 148.

62. Kenyon, *Royal Cities*, p. 90.

63. In J.W. Crowfoot *et al.*, *Samaria-Sebaste III. The Objects from Samaria*
(London: Palestine Exploration Fund, 1957), pp. 94-95.

Attitude towards Baalism

Finally, the Phoenician inclination of the Omrides is indicated in their policy toward Baalism. It is true that the biblical materials linking the Omrides to Baalism were written from a Yahwistic and pro-Judean perspective and that these materials were confined basically to the Elijah stories, which were probably included by a later prophetic circle. Yet because of the strong relationship that the Omrides had with the Phoenicians, Baalistic presence in Israel—particularly in the capital city of Samaria—cannot be ruled out. This may indeed be the only period in Israel's history that Baalism posed a threat to Yahwism.[64] In his introduction to Ahab, the Deuteronomistic History notes specifically that Ahab went and served Baal, and worshiped him. He erected an altar for Baal in the house of Baal, which he built in Samaria (1 Kgs 16.31bb-32). It is likely that Baalism was present because of the metropolitan nature of Samaria and the ecumenical politics in Syria-Palestine at that time. The Baal temple could have been built to accommodate the Phoenician segment of the population resident in Samaria for commercial or emissarial purposes. But if Omri himself had Phoenician roots, it may be that Omri and Ahab were polytheistic and quite accommodating to the Baal cult. Noteworthy also is the fact that the Omride princess, Athaliah, who later ruled over Judah, was associated with a Baal temple in Jerusalem (2 Kgs 11.18). When Jehoram became king of Israel, he destroyed the *maṣṣēbâ* (or more probably *maṣṣēbôt*, according to the LXX and Vulgate) of Baal in Samaria (2 Kgs 3.2). However, it is more likely that he was not able to stamp out Baal worship completely. The account of how Jehu purged Israel of Baalism (2 Kgs 10.18-28), though certainly propagandistic, may not be without a kernel of truth.

---

64. J.H. Hayes ('Hosea's Baals and Lovers: Religious or Political?', a paper delivered at the national meeting of the SBL, 1990) has argued that the references to Baals and lovers in the book of Hosea should not be understood as religious references but as partners in political relations. He further argues that if Baalism had been a problem in eighth-century Israelite society, it would hardly have escaped the attacks of contemporary prophets, such as Amos, Isaiah, and Micah. Moreover, there is complete silence concerning the problem of Baalism in the narrative accounts of the book of Kings for this period (see *Abstracts: American Academy of Religion [and] Society of Biblical Literature, 1990* [Atlanta: Scholars Press, 1990], pp. 372-73).

Conclusions

The thesis of this essay—that Omri was a Phoenician who became one of Israel's greatest kings—has been argued on the basis of four points: (1) Omri's name is possibly of Phoenician origin; (2) there were close commercial and political ties between the Omrides and Ethbaalites; (3) strong Phoenician influence is evident in the archaeological remains of the period; and (4) the Omrides tolerated—if not nurtured—the worship of Baal in Israel. If the argument has been established, then three historical implications follow.

First, what we have in Omri was a mercenary who rose in rank to become the *śar* of the army. When the nation was in turmoil following Zimri's revolt, Omri seized the throne with the help of his army and then struggled for the next four years to consolidate his power over Israel. His ethnicity may have alienated some factions of the populace, but that did not prevent him from finally assuming the kingship.

Secondly, this also suggests that the population of Israel was an ethnic mixture and raises the question of Israelite identity. In all likelihood, there was more racial and religious diversity in Israel than the biblical writers have conveyed, and an Israelite was one who owned land and paid taxes. In this context, the Deuteronomistic prohibition against making a non-ethnic person king reveals the Deuteronomistic historian's interest in keeping the throne in the hands of the ethnic Israelite populace.

Finally, the conclusion that Omri was a Phoenician also suggests that in ancient Israel and Judah the crown went to the leader with the strongest military support. David, for example, was clearly a military strongman and a mercenary who seized power following the king's death. As soon as he was able to exert control over the nation, David moved his royal capital to a new vicinity. In this regard, Omri's rise to the Israelite throne was not dissimilar. Evidently, this policy was continued in the northern kingdom of Israel, where a military strongman always took control of the nation when opportunities presented themselves.

WHEN ISRAEL WAS A CHILD
Ancient Near Eastern Adoption Formulas
and the Relationship between God and Israel

Janet L.R. Melnyk

Introduction

The biblical representation of God as a father has been one of the most popular images of God throughout history. At first glance, this kind of parental theology might seem to be a clear and simple understanding of how the Hebrew Bible portrays God's affiliation with Israel. Since the parent–child relationship is common to human experience, it is not surprising that the prophets and biblical writers appropriated such a familiar metaphor to describe God. However, a closer inspection of this usage reveals a slightly different sort of arrangement—that of adoption. Although actual cases of adoption appear infrequently in the Hebrew Bible, it is the thesis of this study that the institution of adoption was clearly in view as the biblical writers described God's relationship with Israel.

The biblical representations of Israel as God's child often use adoption clauses similar to those found in ancient Near Eastern texts. In addition, the stipulations of adoption—raising the child, providing an inheritance (usually land), and punishment for the rebellious child—can all be found in biblical texts that portray God's relationship with Israel. Before examining these specifics, however, it is necessary to look at how families and adoption were understood in ancient Near Eastern texts.

Family Identity and the Importance of Children

Of the three kinship levels known from the Hebrew Bible—the tribe (*šēbeṭ*), clan (*mišpāḥâ*), and family (*bêt-'āb*)—identity and responsibility are strongest in the family. Most characters are introduced with reference to their parents or children, usually a father or son (e.g., 'Achan son of Carmi, son of Zabdi, son of Zerah' [Josh. 7.1]). Women, however, are introduced as someone's mother or daughter or wife (e.g., 'Rebekah, who was born to Bethuel son of Milkah, the wife of Nahor, Abraham's brother' [Gen. 24.15]).

These familial designations serve to locate each person within the community, that is to say, both the individual and the community view personal identity as linked to family identity. In effect, adoption could literally transform the status of the adoptee. Not only would one's present condition change, but also one's future (because of an inheritance) and past (due to a new family history). Understanding the practice of adoption in this context will illuminate the significance of Israel's adoption by God. The biblical writers conceived Israel's identity as deriving from God, the father, which, in turn, distinguished Israel from neighboring peoples.[1]

The practice of adoption in ancient Israel and the Near East comes from an overwhelming concern to have children. In the Old Testament, children are considered to be gifts from God (Gen. 33.5; Ps. 113.9), and in Ps. 127.3, sons are called 'a heritage from the Lord', and children 'a reward'. Sons guaranteed the continuation of the family name into the next generation (Gen. 48.16) and augmented a father's house or family by bringing in wives and children. Daughters, on the other hand, would eventually marry and belong to their husbands' or fathers-in-law's families.

Children are also signs of prosperity. Zechariah envisions the messianic era when Yahweh returns to Zion as a time when 'the streets of the city shall be full of boys and girls playing in them' (8.5). Likewise, in a Phoenician inscription from Karatepe, King Azitawadda associates children with his city's good fortune, praying that it would be blessed 'with an abundance of children'. The presence of the children would guarantee not only prosperity, but also that 'the name of Azitawadda will endure forever like the name of the sun and moon'.[2] As one might expect, many Hebrew blessings express this same desire for offspring, and a large family was among the most desirable of all God's gifts. The blessing from Psalm 128 expresses a wish for the father's children to be as numerous as 'olive shoots around his table' and his wife 'like a fruitful vine' (v. 3). A large

1.   Cf. Isa. 63.19.
2.   *ANET*, p. 654.

family is also an important element in the covenant with Abraham (Gen. 15.5-6) and is included in the Sinai covenant among the blessings promised for obedience (Lev. 26.9; Deut. 28.4). The same concern for procreation appears in the marriage blessing for Rebekah ('May you, our sister, be the mother of thousands of ten thousands; and may your offspring take over the gates of their enemies' [Gen. 24.60]) and in Isaac's blessing of Jacob's search for a wife ('May El Shaddai bless you, make you fertile and multiply you; may you grow into a company of peoples' [Gen. 28.3]).

In contrast to these hopes for fertility, barrenness was regarded as tragic. In the event of childlessness (or more accurately, *son*lessness), a maidservant or concubine was often given to the husband for the purpose of childbearing. Gen. 30.1 reveals Rachel's determination for children when she threatens Jacob, 'Give me sons or I shall die!' After Jacob's exasperated response ('Am I God? Not!' [v. 2]), she proceeds to give her maid Bilhah to him as a surrogate (vv. 3-6). Not to be outdone, Leah follows suit and gives her own maid, Zilpah, to Jacob five verses and two sons (from Bilhah) later. According to Gen. 16.2 and 30.3, this procedure allows the wife to 'be built up' (*'ibbāneh mimmennâ*) or 'have children through' the maidservant.[3] The children are considered to be legitimate offspring of the husband and therefore heirs of his estate, however, only if the father (and sometimes the mother or other family members) claims the child as his own.

This practice of obtaining children through slaves or concubines was also customary in other ancient Near Eastern societies, as texts from Assyria, Egypt, Mari, and Nuzi indicate. A Neo-Assyrian document allows the husband to obtain a female slave if sons are not provided by the first wife,[4] and clauses from one Egyptian[5] and two Assyrian[6] marriage documents provide for a female slave if the wife cannot have children. Again, Nuzi adoption and marriage agreements allow the husband to take a slave wife or concubine if his first wife

---

3. It is interesting to note that it is Rachel and Leah who name the surrogate sons, not Bilhah and Zilpah.

4. A.K. Grayson and J. Van Seters, 'The Childless Wife in Assyria and the Stories of Genesis', *Or* 44 (1975), pp. 485-86.

5. J. Van Seters, 'The Problem of Childlessness in Near Eastern Law and the Patriarchs of Israel', *JBL* 87 (1968), pp. 405-406.

6. T. Frymer-Kensky, 'Patriarchal Family Relationships and Near Eastern Law', *BA* 44 (1981), p. 211.

does not bear children,[7] or in some cases if she bears only daughters.[8] In a Mari text, the governor of Mari marries the king's daughter, whose dowry includes a concubine, just in case she is barren.[9]

The inclusion of slave-wives, concubines, and their children within a household necessarily raised the question of legitimacy and inheritance. The possibility of adding many children to one's family would require some adjustments in inheritance policies. The Code of Hammurabi presupposes both the desire for children and the uncertainty of heirs. In laws 144-145, the wife is allowed to give a maidservant to her husband, or the husband may take a concubine and bring her into his house for the purpose of childbearing if the wife has not become pregnant.[10] The maidservant's children may be legally adopted by the father as stated in laws 170 and 171 only if the father chooses to do so and declares that they are his children.[11] According to law 171, however, the father is not required to adopt these children, and consequently he may be selective in his choice of heirs. Similarly, a Nuzi lawsuit declares that if the father has not specifically identified them as heirs, the sons of a concubine cannot inherit his property.[12]

The role of choice in adoption is also relevant to the consideration of God's relationship with Israel. Biblical writers contend that not only did Yahweh choose Israel (Deut. 7.7; 1 Chron. 16.13; Ps. 105.6; Isa. 41.8, 9; 43.20; 44.1; 45.4; 65.22), but Israel was selected from among all other peoples to be his children (Deut. 7.6; 14.2). In

7. E.A. Speiser, 'New Kirkuk Documents Relating to Family Laws', *AASOR* 10 (1930), p. 31, §2.17-21.

8. Speiser, 'New Kirkuk Documents', p. 59, §26.18-23.

9. G. Dossin (ed.), *Correspondance de Šamši-Addu et de ses fils* (ARM, 1,4; 2 vols.; Paris: Imprimerie Nationale, 1950-51), I, §46.50.

10. R.F. Harper, *The Code of Hammurabi, King of Babylon, About 2250 B.C.* (Chicago: University of Chicago Press, 2nd edn, 1904) p. 50. Also in G.R. Driver and J.C. Miles, *The Babylonian Laws* (Ancient Codes and Laws of the Near East; 2 vols.; Oxford: Clarendon Press, 1952-55), II, p. 57; and *ANET*, p. 172.

11. Harper, *Code of Hammurabi*, p. 60; *ANET*, p. 173.

12. Joint Expedition with the Iraq Museum at Nuzi, §666 and §671, as cited in L.J. Braaten, 'Parent-Child Imagery in Hosea' (PhD dissertation, Boston University, 1987), p. 87; and T.L. Thompson, *The Historicity of the Patriarchal Narratives: The Quest for the Historical Abraham* (BZAW, 133; Berlin: de Gruyter, 1972), p. 260.

addition, his *bḥyr*[13] ('chosen ones') are specifically designated to be his heirs (Ps. 33.12; 89.4; Isa. 65.9).

This concept of adoption as a selective process is described by a Babylonian document, in which the father adopts only one of his secondary wife's sons:

Šaḫira, [son of. . .] married Bēlessunu and Asatum. She bore his 5 children. Among the 5 children whom Asatum bore to Šaḫira, Šaḫira adopted (*[an]a mārūtīšu ilqe*) Iakūnum, his oldest son.[14]

This inscription uses the common adoption formula *ana mārūti leqû* (literally, 'to take into the status of sonship'), the same phrase used in the Code of Hammurabi (laws 185, 186, and 190) to designate the responsibilities of an adopted child and the adoptive father. In addition, the nominal forms *līqû* ('adoption'), *liqûtu* ('adopted child'), and *lēqû* ('adoptive father') are found in various Babylonian laws and in the Laws of Eshnunna.[15] The closest Hebrew equivalent to *ana mārūti leqû* is the phrase used in Esth. 2.7, when Mordecai takes the girl into his care after the deaths of her parents: *lĕqāḥāh mordŏkay lô lĕbat* ('Mordecai adopted her as his daughter').

Therefore, it appears that while adoption was practiced in the ancient Near East, not all children born to slave-wives or concubines were adopted. Similarly, biblical writers have indicated an awareness of—if not the actual practice of—adoption, and they have identified Israel as the one chosen by Yahweh from among all others. With these points established, we may now move to the specific act of adoption, the requirements and stipulations involved for the participating members, and the possible negation of prior adoptions.

Stipulations of Adoption

While the act of adoption may be expressed in several ways, each includes recognizable phrases that are characteristic of adoption agreements. These phrases require a statement that usually consists of

13. The noun *bḥyr*, translated as 'chosen' or 'elect', is used in the Hebrew Bible exclusively for those in relationship with Yahweh as 'Yahweh's chosen'. Cf. BDB, p. 104.

14. Driver and Miles, *The Babylonian Laws*, I, pp. 332-33.

15. H.F. Lutz, *Early Babylonian Letters from Larsa* (Yale Oriental Series; Babylonian Texts, 2; New Haven: Yale University Press, 1917), §50.6; and R. Yaron, *The Laws of Eshnunna* (Jerusalem: Magnes, 1969), pp. 106-108.

two parts: (1) the declaration of the new relationship between the adopted child and the adoptive parent, and (2) the description of the parties involved. The binding formula of the adoption in many cases is the declaration that describes the new relationship.

Claiming the Child as One's Own

Most of these pronouncements occur as variations of 'You are (s/he is) my child.' The Law of Hammurabi (§170.37-47) outlines the adoption process using this direct pronouncement as evidence of a legitimate adoption:

> If a man's first wife bore him sons and his female slave also bore him sons, and the father during his lifetime states to the sons whom the slave bore him, '*(You are) my sons!*' he will count them with the sons of his first wife.[16]

A biblical example of the pronouncement declaration is the statement, 'I will be a father to him and he will be a son to me' (2 Sam. 7.14; 1 Chron. 17.13; cf. 22.10; and 28.6). This is generally accepted as an adoption formula, since it states parental identity and is similar to other ancient Near Eastern adoptive formulas.[17] Although this straightforward statement may appear to be rather simplistic for a legal adoption agreement, it makes more sense when seen in the light of modern adoption practices. When the court is in session and the judge is preparing to legalize an adoption, it is the parents' acknowledgment of the child[18] as one of their own flesh and blood that is required before the state can recognize the adoption as official.[19] This is the single thread on which a legal adoption process hangs: the declaration of parental relationship. On the ninth of Tammuz, in the

16. Harper, *Code of Hammurabi*, p. 61; *ANET*, p. 173.

17. M. Weinfeld, 'The Covenant of Grant in the Old Testament and in the Ancient Near East', *JAOS* 90 (1970), p. 190.

18. And the child's acknowledgment of the parents when the child is old enough.

19. According to Adoption Case #852A from the District Court of Kiowa County, Kansas, the adoption of Tami Leigh Walters and Todd Eugene Walters was legitimated when the adoptive parents, Bruce and Lorraine Raber, declared their intent to 'properly support, rear and educate' the children as their own 'natural children', at which point the children were 'declared to have been adopted' and were 'renamed Tami Leigh Raber and Todd Eugene Raber. . . the children and heirs of Bruce and Lorraine Raber', 20 February, 1985.

thirty-second year of Nebuchadnezzar, an adoption agreement was signed that follows the same pattern:

> Innin-shum-ibni son of Nabu-ahhe-shullim came to Balta daughter of Nabu-ahhe-shullim, his sister, stating as follows: 'Give me your seventeen-day-old son Dannu-ahhe-ibni, that I might rear him, and he will be my son.' Balta acceded to him, and gave him her seventeen-day-old son Dannu-ahhe-ibni for adoption. He then inscribed him as next-(heir)-in-line to his own son Labashi.[20]

In each of the above illustrations, the declaration of sonship not only confirms the adoption, but provides the basis for the formulation of new familial ties. The parent–child relationship between Yahweh and Israel is portrayed in Exodus 4 with just such an adoption declaration. Verse 22 recounts, 'Thus says the Lord, *Israel is my first-born son*'.[21] The same identification of Israel as God's child is made in Hos. 11.1 ('When Israel was a child, I loved him, and out of Egypt *I called my son*'); Jer. 31.9 ('For *I am a father to Israel*, and *Ephraim is my first born*'); and rhetorically in Jer. 31.20 ('Is *Ephraim my dear son?* Is he *my child* of delight?').[22] Deut. 14.1 makes the claim directly to Israel: '*You are the sons* of the Lord your God'. A more complete account of Israel's adoption is reported in Jer. 3.19: 'I thought *I would set you among my sons*,[23] and give you a desirable land, the fairest heritage of all the nations; and I thought *you would call me, My Father*, and would not turn from following me'. S. Paul identifies the Hebrew phrase *'ăšîtēk babbānîm* in the above passage as the inter-dialectal semantic equivalent of the Akkadian *ana mārūti šakānu* ('to establish for the status of heir'), which is used in various Babylonian texts.[24] From these examples, it seems clear that the

---

20. *ANET*, p. 547. A later example of such an adoptive tie is found in an Aramaic papyrus, in which Uriah of Syene adopts Yeheniah with the declaration *bry yhwh* ('My son he will be'). E.G.H. Kraeling (ed.), *The Brooklyn Museum Aramaic Papyri* (Publications of the Department of Egyptian Art; New Haven: Yale University Press, 1953), p. 226, ll. 5 and 9.

21. Italics are mine.

22. Other third person references to the Hebrews as God's children/sons include: Exod. 4.23; Deut. 32.5; 32.19; Isa. 1.2, 4; 30.1, 9; 43.6; 45.10; Jer. 4.22; and Hos. 11.10.

23. The JPSV translates *w'nky 'mrty 'yk 'šytk bbnym* as 'I had resolved to adopt you as My child.'

24. S. Paul, 'Adoption Formulae: A Study of Cuneiform and Biblical Legal Clauses', *Maarav* 2/2 (1979-80), p. 184. See also W.F. Leemans, *Legal and*

biblical formulas used for God's relationship with Israel contain the same declarative statement as the ancient Near Eastern adoption texts. The next task is to determine whether the stipulations of adoption mentioned above—raising the child, providing an inheritance (usually land), and punishment for the rebellious child—are present in the biblical representations of God as Israel's father.

Raising the Child as One's Own

The first adoption proviso requires the father to bring up the adoptee as one of his own children. The adoption agreement for Dannu-ahhe-ibni, the seventeen-day-old baby mentioned earlier, includes a statement by his uncle, the adopter, declaring that he will raise the child and consider him his second son. This issue of caring for the adopted child becomes the critical factor in an Old Babylonian inheritance case. Shamash-Nasir, the adopted son of Awil-Nabium, is brought to trial by another son of Awil-Nabium, who claims that Shamash-Nasir was never adopted. Shamash-Nasir counters the accusation by declaring, 'Awil-Nabium (is) my father. While I was a small child he took me in adoption and *reared* me. I can produce witnesses.' The witnesses are produced and swear, 'Awil-Nabium took Shamash-Nasir in adoption as a small child, and *reared* him; we certify his being *reared*.' After hearing this, the judges 'thereupon reinstated Shamash-Nasir as the son of Awil-Nabium'. (Names of witnesses follow.)[25] From the legal terminology and the final decision of the judges, it is evident that because Awil-Nabium *raised* Shamash-Nasir, he was accorded the status of sonship.

Many biblical texts describe Yahweh's rearing Israel in a nurturing, parental manner. Notably, the perspective is often God's, as Scripture places the words in his mouth. 'Sons I have raised and brought them up', he declares in Isa. 1.2, and 'As one whom his mother comforts, so I will comfort you', he promises in Isa. 66.13. 'With weeping they will come', Yahweh predicts, 'and with consolations I will lead them back. I will let them walk by brooks of water, in a straight path in which they shall not stumble; for *I have become a father to Israel, and Ephraim is my first-born*' (Jer. 31.9). In these words Jeremiah portrays Israel as one who needs parental guidance and care, first

Economic Records from the Kingdom of Larsa (Studia ad tabulas cuneiformes collectas a F.M.Th. de Liagre Böhl pertinentia, SLB I,2; Leiden: Brill, 1954).
    25. *ANET*, pp. 544-45

implicitly—by suggesting that without Yahweh Israel will (again) stumble and thirst—and then explicitly stated in the conclusion by Yahweh's declaration.

Perhaps the finest presentation of Yahweh as Israel's parent is found in Hosea 11. Here God is represented as the perfect parent, adopting and rearing Israel, teaching and providing for him. Yahweh recollects how he loved his child and first called Israel 'my son' when he was in Egypt. This is the initial stage of God's relationship with Israel, his son. The reference to a specific time in history when Israel became Yahweh's son reinforces the interpretation of the relationship in terms of adoption. Yahweh then declares that he himself taught the child to walk and carried him in his arms—both metaphorical acts of child-rearing (v. 3).[26] God's parental love and nurturing are further described with such phrases as: 'I led them with cords of compassion, with the bands of love'; 'I bent down to them and fed them'; and 'my compassion grows warm and tender' (vv. 4, 8). One final example of divine paternity is from Deut. 32.10: 'He sustained him in a desert land, in a howling wilderness waste; he shielded him, he cared for him, he kept him as the apple of his eye', which follows a reference to God as father and has been interpreted as a father's tender care for his son.[27] Apparently, the biblical writers wanted to portray God as successfully fulfilling the parental stipulation of rearing that is required by adoption agreements.

Providing an Inheritance for the Child
Receiving an inheritance marks the next general stipulation that is associated with an adoption contract. Jer. 3.19 neatly identifies not only the inheritance, but also other integral parts of the adoption process:

> I thought *I would set you among my sons*, and *give you a desirable land*, the fairest heritage of all the nations; and I thought *you would call me, My Father*, and would *not turn from following me*.

26. The image of Yahweh carrying Israel is also prevalent in Isa. 46.3-4, where Yahweh is repeatedly portrayed as sustaining Israel all her life, from embryo to elder, 'Listen to me, house of Jacob, and all the remnant of the house of Israel, you who have been *upheld* from your birth, who have been *carried* from the womb; even to your old age I am he, even when you turn gray I will *sustain* you. I have made, and I will *carry*; I will *sustain* and I will rescue.'
27. P.C. Craigie, *The Book of Deuteronomy* (NICOT; Grand Rapids: Eerdmans, 1976), p. 380.

In this one verse, three elements of the adoption process are evident: (1) Israel is appointed as son by the declaration noted before; (2) an inheritance is promised, as mentioned above; and (3) a condition is stated for the adopted children that they will not rebel (this will be addressed later under adoption recision conditions).

We have seen that the issue of inheritance is a significant and often crucial factor in many adoption texts. The following Nuzi-Akkadian texts specify the inheritance apportionment as a primary stipulation of the adoption agreement:

§1: The tablet of adoption belonging to Kuzu, the son of Karmishe: he adopted Tehip-tilla, the son of Puhi-shenni. *As his share (of the estate) Kuzu gave Tehip-tilla 40 imers* [c. 4.5 acres] *of land in the district of Iphushshi.*

§3: The tablet of adoption belonging to [Zike], the son of Akkuya: he gave his son Shennima in adoption to Shuriha-ilu, with reference to Shennima, *all the land...(and) of his earnings of every sort he gave to Shennima one (portion) of his property.* As long as Shuriha-ilu is alive, Shennima shall revere him. When Shuriha-ilu [dies], Shennima shall become the heir.[28]

In a more general description, §§170-71 of the Laws of Hammurabi identify specific goods and portions of property that belong to adopted children.

§170: If the father during his lifetime says to the sons which the slave-girl bore him: '(You are) my sons,' and reckons them with the children of his first wife, after the father dies the sons of the first wife and the *sons of the slave-girl shall divide the goods of the father's house equally.* The child of the wife shall have the right of choice at the division.

§171: Or if the father in his lifetime does not state to the sons whom the slave-girl bore him '(You are) my sons,' after the father dies, *the sons of the slave-girl shall not share in the goods of the father's house* with the sons of the first wife.[29]

Inheritance is what is at stake in the case brought against Shamash-Nasir mentioned previously, and the status of heir is treated in the

---

28. §§1 and 3; cf. §2. *ANET*, pp. 219-20.

29. Harper, *Code of Hammurabi*, p. 61; cf. p. 71, §191: 'If the man, who has taken the infant in adoption to himself and has brought him up, has built him a house (and) afterwards gets sons and sets his face to expel the adopted child, that son shall not then go destitute; the father who has brought him up shall give him one-third of his inheritance out of his property when he goes; (but) he shall not give him a (portion) of field, garden or house.'

closing summation of the adoption of baby Dannu-ahhe-ibni.[30]

Biblical references regarding inheritance can be categorized in two ways: the heritage from one's father or family and that from God. Human heritage records indicate that inherited land was to remain in the family or *bêt-'āb* to which it had been apportioned. The land was not to be sold permanently to anyone outside the family,[31] since that would erode the economic sufficiency of the *bêt-'āb*. It was an easy thing for Israel's political and religious leaders to apply this principle of inalienability[32] to the divine inheritance of God. Considering how a parent provides an inheritance for a child, God as father naturally allots the gift of land to his 'sons'.[33] The result is a theology that views the land as given by God for all time. The outcome would be the same: the *bêt-'āb* or family of God (i.e., Israel) would be guaranteed land and the ability to be economically self-sufficient forever. The quotation above from Jer. 3.19 takes this identity of inheritance one step further. Not only is a legacy of land given, not only is it a 'desirable land', but it is the 'fairest heritage of all the nations'. This phrase defines the inheritance and classifies it generally as something to be desired and relatively as superior to the inheritances of all others.

Punishment for a Rebellious Child

The significance of the inheritance and the inheritance itself depends on the conditions set forth by the adoption agreement. If it is a large or valuable inheritance, the conditions may specifically mention reverence and honor for the adopter as stipulations in the adoption alliance. This would help to guarantee that the costly heirloom (i.e., fertile land) stays within the family. If the conditions are broken, the inheritance is the first to go. The Nuzi text above (§3) contains just such a loyalty clause: 'As long as Shuriha-ilu is alive, Shennima shall

---

30. Cf. n. 24, the adoption formula *ana mārūti šakānu*; n. 12, the Nuzi law suit; and n. 29 above on the expelled adopted son.

31. The Old Testament provides no examples of an Israelite voluntarily selling his land outside the family. 'Sale adoption was a legal device used in Nuzi whereby a landowner could circumvent the law prohibiting the sale of land outside the family by going through the form of adopting the purchaser', *ANET*, p. 219 n. 47.

32. Cf. the Jubilee tradition of returning land to its original owner every fifty years.

33. Cf. Weinfeld, 'Covenant of Grant', p. 194.

revere him.' In the phrase from Jer. 3.19, 'I thought you...would not turn from following me', the adopter (God) obviously expected the adoptee to be loyal.[34] Turning away from God, the father, implies dishonor and rebellion. Isa. 1.2 declares, 'sons have I reared and brought up, but they have rebelled against me', and in Isa. 1.4 and 30.1, 9, the people are labeled 'rebellious children/people', 'lying sons', and 'sons who deal corruptly'. In addition, Jer. 3.14 refers to 'faithless children',[35] and 3.22 to 'faithless sons'. Most of the vocabulary that describes the rebellious son in the Hebrew Bible is used to portray Israel's rebellion against Yahweh.[36] In return for this rebellion, Israel is punished by devastation of the inherited land,[37] loss of the land,[38] and exile from it.[39] Instead of inheriting a desirable land, a new legacy is decreed: 'I will scatter you like chaff driven by the wind from the desert. This is your lot, the portion I have measured out to you, says the Lord, because you have forgotten me and trusted in lies' (Jer. 13.24-25).

The consequences of rebellion often include more than disinheritance, as indicated above. Subjection to exile and slavery are common ramifications of broken adoption agreements. In a Mari adoption text, if the adoptee becomes rebellious, he may be sold into slavery as a penalty for breaking the adoptive relationship.

> Should Yahatti-el say to Hillalum, his father, and to Alitum, his mother;
> 'You are not my father; you are not my mother,' they shall have him
> shaved, and shall sell him for money.[40]

Similarly, a Nuzi text recommends that Paiteshub bind and mark Kinni as a slave if Kinni fails to obey and respect Paiteshub, since this is how, according to the text, a man disciplines his own son.[41]

---

34. Honor is understood as part of the natural child/parent relationship as expressed by the fifth commandment of the Decalogue, and it maintains a theological understanding as stated from Yahweh's perspective in Mal. 1.6, 'A son honors his father, and a servant his master. If then I am a father, where is my honor?'

35. Cf. Deut. 32.20.

36. See E. Bellefontaine, 'Deuteronomy 21:18-21; Reviewing the Case of the Rebellious Son', *JSOT* 13 (1979), pp. 25-26.

37. Cf. Jer. 4.23, 26, 27; 5.17; 9.10; 12.10, 11.

38. Cf. Jer. 8.10; 9.12; Mic. 2.4.

39. Cf. Jer. 9.16; Hos. 8.13; 9.3, 17; Amos 5.27; 6.7; 7.11; 9.9; Mic. 1.16.

40. ARM, VIII, 1.12-18; translated in *ANET*, p. 545.

41. Braaten, 'Parent-Child Imagery', p. 301.

The accusations against Israel and the threat of slavery in Hosea utilize the same dynamics as the above ancient Near Eastern texts. In 11.2, Yahweh accuses Israel of disobedience. Israel has honored the Baals instead of Yahweh, serving them with sacrifice and incense, and has refused to return to Yahweh (11.7). The punishment is the return to slavery in Egypt and bondage to Assyria (11.5).[42]

A pronouncement of disownment can be both the penalty for breaking the adoptive agreement and the reason for breaking it. In such cases, the adoption declaration is reversed and stated negatively. In the Mari text mentioned above, the declarations made by Yahatti-el, 'You are not my father; you are not my mother', are grounds for punishing Yahatti-el and selling him. In a similar situation, in which the disownment declaration is the cause for chastisement, the Laws of Hammurabi recommend a different punishment: 'If the adopted son of a chamberlain or the adopted son of a votary has said to his father or his mother, "You are not my father", "You are not my mother", they shall cut out his tongue' (§193).[43] This punishment would clearly cure the son of becoming a repeat offender.

The Akkadian phrase, *úl maruni atta* ('You are not our son'), is a parental disownment formulation.[44] Sometimes disownment was the punishment for a child's rebellion, as in the following text:

§§168-69: If a man, having made up his mind to disinherit his son, has said to the judges, 'I wish to disinherit my son', the judges shall investigate his record. . . If he has incurred wrong against his father grave enough to be disinherited, they shall let him off the first time; if he has incurred grave wrong a second time, the father may disinherit his son.[45]

A biblical counterpart of the Akkadian pronouncement of disownment is found in Hos. 1.9, where Yahweh is quoted as saying, 'You are not my people'. This assertion is presumably an adaptation of the proclamation, 'You are not my child(ren)', found in the adoption texts

42. Cf. Hos. 7.15 and 9.1-3. Wolff believes that Hosea 11 is an analogy to a legal complaint made by a father against his stubborn son and cites Deut. 21.18ff. and Isa. 1.2ff. as support. H.W. Wolff, *Hosea* (Hermeneia; Philadelphia: Fortress Press, 1974), p. 194.

43. *ANET*, p. 175; Harper, *Code of Hammurabi*, pp. 71-72.

44. Paul, 'Adoption Formulae', p. 180. Cf. the above Mari text reference, 'You are not my father, you are not my mother.'

45. *ANET*, p. 173; Harper, *Code of Hammurabi*, pp. 59-60.

mentioned above.[46] The reversal of the disownment statement, 'You
are not my people', to 'sons of the living God' in the ensuing verse
supports this identification. It is notable that the author of Hos. 2.1
does not reverse the clause exactly—from 'You are not my people' to
'My people'—although it seems natural to do so. Instead, the reversal
is accomplished by the phrase '*sons* of the living God', which serves to
reinforce the identification of Israel as the child of God the parent.

Conclusion

In sum, the ultimate aim of the present study is to understand the
relationship between God and Israel in light of the ancient Near
Eastern adoptive process. But, penultimately, it is often easier—and
more valid—to relate ancient Near Eastern ideas to biblical theology
by way of biblical anthropology and social context. The preceding
discussion has shown that ancient Near Eastern adoption formulas may
have influenced biblical literature in general and the description of the
relationship between God and Israel in particular. A knowledge of
family customs and the importance of propagation in extrabiblical and
biblical texts have provided a wider context for an examination of this
relationship. The desire for children and heirs was crucial for the life
of a family. If sons were not born, adoptive sons were raised. As
Yahweh proclaimed Israel to be his son and spoke of him as his child
(Exod. 4.22; Hos. 11.1), the biblical parent–child metaphor sounded
to Israel like the technical clauses familiar from ancient Near Eastern
adoption laws. The legal stipulations requiring adoptive parents to
rear, nurture, and provide an inheritance were followed not only by
the letter of the law, but by the spirit of the law as well in the biblical
accounts of Yahweh's parenting abilities. Isa. 1.2, Hos. 11.1, 3, 4,
Jer. 3.19 and 31.9 detail Yahweh's constant care and provision for the
child Israel. Israel was given an inheritance that was better than any
other, and in turn, Israel was required to serve and obey the father-
God and to be faithful to the relationship in word and deed (cf. Exod.
4.23; Deut. 32.5; and Mal. 1.6). As the adoption laws provided
punishment for rebellious children, Yahweh, too, chastised with

46. See Braaten, 'Parent-Child Imagery', p. 244. M.J. Buss recognizes a
similarity between the ancient Near Eastern negation statement and Hos. 1.9, but he
interprets the text as the prophet's denial that the child was his son (*The Prophetic
Word of Hosea* [BZAW, 111; Berlin: Töpelmann, 1969], pp. 88-89, cf. pp. 56-57).

similar punishments of slavery and disinheritance.

The biblical writers were interested in portraying Israel as chosen and adopted by God. One wonders why the parent–child relationship was often portrayed as one of adoption, rather than as one of biological birth. Perhaps because the metaphor of Yahweh as parent is almost exclusively a male image, there must be a mother if Yahweh is to father a nation. Although the land is sometimes given this role, the adoptive process conveniently circumvents the need for a birth-mother, and Yahweh is shown to be capable of every other maternal nurturing. By conceiving the relationship as adoption, God's election of Israel, his beloved son, was emphasized. This, in turn, distinguished Israel as the people chosen by God over all other nations, and as the recipient of a desirable land for all generations of God's *bêt-'āb* to enjoy. By identifying Israel as God's child, the biblical writers wrote Israel into a state of legitimacy, recognition, and inalienable inheritance.

SELECT BIBLIOGRAPHY OF THE WRITINGS OF JOHN H. HAYES[*]

Academic Theses

'Kingship in Ancient Israel and Its Influence on Religious Thought', BD thesis, Princeton Theological Seminary, 1960.

'The Oracles Against the Nations in the Old Testament: Their Usage and Theological Importance', ThD dissertation, Princeton Theological Seminary, 1964.

Books

Biblical Hebrew Vocabulary. Anderson, SC: Independent Publishing, 1962.

The Biblical Heritage. With W.O. Walker, Jr. San Antonio: Trinity University Printers, 1966.

Radical Christianity: The New Theologies in Perspective, with Readings from the Radicals. With L.D. Kliever. Anderson, SC: Droke House; New York: Grosset and Dunlap, 1968.

Introduction to the Bible. Philadelphia: Westminster; London: SPCK, 1973.

Understanding the Psalms. Valley Forge, PA: Judson, 1976.

Son of God to Superstar: Twentieth-century Interpretations of Jesus. Nashville: Abingdon, 1976.

An Introduction to Old Testament Study. Nashville: Abingdon; London: SCM, 1979/1982.

Biblical Exegesis: A Beginner's Handbook. With C.R. Holladay. Atlanta: John Knox; London: SCM, 1982; 2nd edn, 1987.

Preaching the New Common Lectionary, Year B: Advent, Christmas, Epiphany. With F.B. Craddock and C.R. Holladay. Nashville: Abingdon, 1984; rev. and enlarged edn, 1987.

Preaching the New Common Lectionary, Year B: Lent, Holy Week, Easter. With F.B. Craddock, C.R. Holladay, and G.M. Tucker. Nashville: Abingdon, 1984.

Old Testament Theology: Its History and Development. With F.C. Prussner. Atlanta: John Knox; London: SCM, 1985.

Preaching the New Common Lectionary, Year B: After Pentecost. With F.B. Craddock, C.R. Holladay, and G.M. Tucker. Nashville: Abingdon, 1985.

Preaching the New Common Lectionary, Year C: Advent, Christmas, Epiphany. With F.B. Craddock, C.R. Holladay, and G.M. Tucker. Nashville: Abingdon, 1985.

---

[*] Book reviews & popular articles are not included.

Bibliography

261

Preaching the New Common Lectionary, Year C: Lent, Holy Week, Easter. With
   F.B. Craddock, C.R. Holladay, and G.M. Tucker. Nashville: Abingdon, 1985.
A History of Ancient Israel and Judah. With J.M. Miller. Philadelphia: Westminster;
   London: SCM, 1986.
Preaching the New Common Lectionary, Year C: After Pentecost. With F.B. Craddock,
   C.R. Holladay, and G.M. Tucker. Nashville: Abingdon, 1986.
Preaching the New Common Lectionary, Year A: Advent, Christmas, Epiphany. With
   F.B. Craddock, C.R. Holladay, and G.M. Tucker. Nashville: Abingdon, 1986.
Preaching the New Common Lectionary, Year A: Lent, Holy Week, Easter. With
   F.B. Craddock, C.R. Holladay, and G.M. Tucker. Nashville: Abingdon, 1986.
Preaching the New Common Lectionary, Year A: After Pentecost. With F.B. Craddock,
   C.R. Holladay, and G.M. Tucker. Nashville: Abingdon, 1987.
Isaiah, the Eighth-century Prophet: His Times & His Preaching. With S.A. Irvine.
   Nashville: Abingdon, 1987.
Amos, the Eighth-century Prophet: His Times and His Preaching. Nashville: Abingdon,
   1988.
*A New Chronology for the Kings of Israel and Judah and Its Implications for Biblical
   History and Literature.* With P.K. Hooker. Atlanta: John Knox, 1988.

Articles

'Tradition of Zion's Inviolability', *JBL* 82 (1963), pp. 419-26.
'The Hydraulic System', in P.C. Hammond (ed.), *The Excavation of the Main Theater
   at Petra, 1961–62.* London: Bernard Quaritch, 1965, pp. 52-54.
'Prophetism at Mari and Old Testament Parallels', *ATR* 49 (1967), pp. 397-409.
'Ugaritic Studies and the Old Testament', *Trinity University Studies in Religion* 8
   (1967), pp. 1-17.
'Studies in Jonah', *Trinity University Studies in Religion* 8 (1967), pp. 18-29.
'The Resurrection as Enthronement and the Earliest Church Christology', *Int* 22
   (1968), pp. 333-45.
'The Usage of Oracles Against Foreign Nations in Ancient Israel', *JBL* 87 (1968),
   pp. 81-92.
'The History of the Form-Critical Study of Prophecy', *SBL Seminar Papers* 1 (1973),
   pp. 60-99.
'The Patriarchal Age—Middle or Late Bronze?' *Trinity University Studies in Religion*
   10 (1975), pp. 11-21.
'The Twelve-Tribe Israelite Amphictyony—An Appraisal', *Trinity University Studies in
   Religion* 10 (1975), pp. 22-36.
'Saul, the Unsung Hero of Israelite History', *Trinity University Studies in Religion* 10
   (1975), pp. 37-47.
'The History of the Study of Israelite and Judaean History', in J.H. Hayes and
   J.M. Miller (eds.), *Israelite and Judaean History.* OTL. Philadelphia: Westminster;
   London: SCM Press, 1977, pp. 1-69.
'Restitution, Forgiveness, and the Victim in Old Testament Law', *Trinity University
   Studies in Religion* 11 (1982), pp. 1-23.
'Wellhausen as a Historian of Israel', *Semeia* 25 (1982), pp. 37-60.

Articles in W.H. Gentz (ed.), *The Dictionary of Bible and Religion*. Nashville: Abingdon, 1986.
'Abomination', 'Abomination of Desolation', 'Abraham's Bosom', 'Achan', 'Adonai', 'Adultery', 'Affliction', 'Alexandria', 'Altar', 'Angels', 'Anointed', 'Apocrypha', 'Aramaic', 'Aramean', 'Ashurbanipal', 'Asia', 'Assurance', 'Daniel (book)', 'Daniel (man)', 'Documentary Hypothesis', 'Interpretation, History and Principles of', 'Intertestamental', 'Jehovah', 'I and II Kings', 'Psalms, Book of', 'Samuel', 'I and II Samuel', and 'Yahweh'.

Articles in E. Fahlbusch *et al.* (eds.), *Evangelisches Kirchenlexikon*. Göttingen: Vandenhoeck & Ruprecht, 3rd edn., 1986- .
'Literaturgeschichte. AT' and 'Masora'.

'Historical Reconstruction, Textual Emendation, and Biblical Translation: Some Examples from the RSV', *Perspectives* 14 (1987), pp. 5-9.

'Leviticus', in J.L. Mays (ed.), *Harper's Bible Commentary*. San Francisco: Harper & Row, 1988. Pp. 157-81.

Articles in W.E. Mills (ed.), *Mercer Dictionary of the Bible*. Macon, GA: Mercer University Press, 1990.
'Covenant', 'Ephod', 'Israel', 'Judah', 'Old Testament', 'OT Theology', 'Pity', and 'Repentance'.

'The Final Years of Samaria (730–720 BC)', *Bib* 72 (1991), pp. 153-81. With J.K. Kuan.

Edited Volumes

Old Testament Form Criticism. Trinity University Monograph Series in Religion, 2. San Antonio: Trinity University Press, 1974.

Israelite and Judaean History. OTL. With J.M. Miller. Philadelphia: Westminster; London: SCM, 1977.

Journal of Biblical Literature (1977–82).

Trinity University Monograph Series in Religion (1971–83).

Knox Preaching Guides to the Bible.

INDEX OF AUTHORS

JOURNAL FOR THE STUDY OF THE OLD TESTAMENT

Supplement Series